Strategic Planning

Strategic Planning

What Every Manager *Must* Know

GEORGE A. STEINER

THE FREE PRESS
A Division of Macmillan Publishing Co., Inc.
NEW YORK

Collier Macmillan Publishers
LONDON

The Free Press
A Division of Macmillan Publishing Co., Inc.
866 Third Avenue, New York, N. Y. 10022

Collier Macmillan Canada, Ltd.

Library of Congress Catalog Card Number: 78–20647

Printed in the United States of America

Library of Congress Cataloging in Publication Data

Steiner, George Albert
    Strategic planning.

    Includes bibliographical references and index.
    1. Corporate planning. I. Title.
HD30.28.S72 1979   658.4'01   78-20647
ISBN 0-02-931110-1

Contents

Preface

Formal strategic planning with its modern design characteristics was first introduced in business firms in the mid-1950s. At the time, it was essentially the largest companies that developed formal strategic planning systems—they were called long-range planning systems. Since then formal strategic planning has matured until virtually all large companies around the world have some sort of system and an increasing number of smaller companies are following the example of the larger companies.

This experience has produced a vast and important body of knowledge about strategic planning. The purpose of this book is to capture the essence of that experience. More precisely, this book seeks to describe in simple and succinct language the fundamental concepts, facts, ideas, processes, and procedures about strategic planning that every manager—at all levels—should know.

The idea that every manager should have a basic understanding of both the concept and the practice of formal strategic planning rests on a number of observations about management and success in business. One is that strategic planning is inextricably interwoven with the entire process of management. Thus, all managers must understand the nature of strategic planning and how to do it. Also, except in comparatively few companies that will be discussed in the book, every company that does not have some sort of formality in its strategic planning system is courting eventual disaster. Some managers have such distorted conceptions of strategic planning that they are repelled by the thought of trying to do it. Others have such fuzzy concepts of what it is that they see it as being of no help to them. Some are ignorant of the potentialities of the process for them and their companies. Some have a little understanding of strategic planning but not really enough to convince them they should be doing it. This book is designed to provide such managers with a reasonably complete, pragmatic, concrete, and clear understanding of what strategic planning is, how to organize to do it, how to do it, and how to implement it.

The main focus of this book is on experience with formal strategic planning in the business world. It is my belief that most of the lessons of this experience have applicability to strategic planning in the not-for-profit sector. Chapter 21 deals directly with this subject. Some lessons of experience with business planning are also applicable to personal planning, whether it be lifetime planning or career planning. This subject is treated in Chapter 20.

Since this book is a succinct state of the art of strategic planning it cannot cover in detail many aspects of the field. To aid those who read this book and want more information than it contains many references have been noted.

I have tried to make it easy for both the busy executive, as well as the general reader, to get a quick overview of the contents and essence of the book by presenting at the beginning of each chapter a short introductory statement of contents and at the end of each chapter a concluding summary and guidelines for action.

It is my firm conviction that a manager need not be an expert in every discipline touching upon the strategic planning process. I do think, however, that every manager should be able to identify those major elements, methods, and practices of disciplines that affect his or her area of planning and should have at least a conceptual understanding, as compared with a specialist's knowledge, of them. This book is designed to help managers meet this need.

The book does not include a technical discussion of the many advanced methods that may be employed in strategic planning; for example, computer based forecasting models. Ample references are given for those interested in learning more about such subjects. Yet, the book does set forth in Chapter 15 what managers should know about these analytical tools and comments are scattered throughout the book about them.

Rarely have I found a planning system, no matter how successful it has been in helping managers, that is completely satisfactory to all managers in an organization. It is my belief that even managers in companies with mature and developed planning systems may find valuable guidelines in this book to improve their systems.

This book is based heavily on the experience of many companies with formal strategic planning. Throughout the book, however, I have generally avoided identifying a particular company with a particular planning practice. The reason is that companies are constantly changing their planning procedures and what is true of their practice today may not be so tomorrow. Hence, to avoid any misunderstandings I have not made a practice of relating companies to specific planning activities.

GEORGE A. STEINER

I Nature and Importance of Strategic Planning

1 Strategic Management and Strategic Planning

Strategic planning is inextricably interwoven into the entire fabric of management; it is not something separate and distinct from the process of management. This point is underscored in this chapter. Also discussed is the shifting focus of management from operations to strategy. Finally, attention is given to the different fundamental approaches to strategic planning that can support management decisionmaking.

The Managerial Task and Planning

Years ago when my colleagues and I were "selling" what at that time was called long-range planning and what I now call strategic planning, we spoke of it as a valuable new tool for management, a major new technique to help managers. I no longer speak of it this way. Strategic planning is inextricably interwoven into the entire fabric of management.

Several years ago, The Conference Board interviewed intensively fifty chief executives about their roles in planning. The first overarching frame of reference most executives articulated was that "planning cannot be usefully distinguished from the rest of the management process. . . .

The researchers summarized the view of the executives in this way: planning cannot be disentangled from such management functions as organizing, directing, motivating, and controlling.

> Although it is acknowledged that each of these functions or elements can be formally defined and contrasted with one another, in terms of the chief executive's daily, weekly, even annual routine it is not realistic from his point of view to break up his job into parts and examine each as a discrete phenomenon. For his role as planner is meshed with his role as organizer, director, and so on, in a seamless web of management; for instance, the thought he devotes to what might be termed planning questions, and decisions he makes about them, have implications for his exercise of control; and vice versa. It is the whole of his job that must be looked at, the interaction of the elements of the management process rather than the individual elements.[1]

The Conference Board survey was concerned with chief executive officers, but the conclusion is applicable to all managers. I believe that no manager is fully discharging his or her[2] responsibility when strategic planning is neglected. Strategic planning is a function and responsibility of all managers at all levels in an organization. It is obvious, however, that the planning responsibilities of managers will vary significantly among types of organizations and different organizational levels.

Strategic Management, Operational Management, and Strategic Planning

To oversimplify, there are two types of management. That which is done at the top of an organizational structure is strategic management. Everything else is operational management.

Strategic planning is a backbone support to strategic management. It is not, of course, the entirety of strategic management but it is a major process in the conduct of strategic management. Everyone recognizes that strategic and operational management are tightly linked. Strategic management provides guidance, direction, and boundaries for operational management. Just as strategic management is vitally concerned with operational management so is strategic planning concerned with operations. But the focus and emphasis of strategic planning as with strategic management is on strategy more than operations.

Years ago the managerial emphasis in the typical corporation was on operations. A major question for management was how to use efficiently those scarce resources at its disposal in producing goods and services at prices consumers were willing to pay. If this task were done efficiently, it was believed, profits would be maximized. Today, efficient use of scarce resources is still a commanding concern of managements of all organizations, but today, because of a turbulent and rapidly changing environment, the ability of an organization to adapt properly to environment, internal and external, is becoming more critical in survival.

General Robert E. Wood, when chief executive of Sears, Roebuck and Company, succinctly captured this thought when he said: "Business is like a war in one respect, if its grand strategy is correct, any number of tactical errors can be made and yet the enterprise proves successful."[3] A company may overcome inefficient internal resource use if its basic strategy is brilliant, but it is not likely to overcome the wrong strategies even with excellent production and distribution performance. The ideal situation, of course, is for an organization to design brilliant strategies and to implement them efficiently and effectively.[4]

In a growing number of companies, particularly the larger organizations, the framework for formulating and implementing strategies is the formal strategic planning system. Strategy can be formulated without a formal system, however, as will be discussed later. But either way, the processes of strategic planning are intertwined with management.

Tasks of Top Management

This is a book about strategic planning and not about the tasks of top management. It is useful, however, to comment a bit more on a point already made, namely, that strategic planning is a central concern of strategic management but not the entirety of the top management job.

In a recapitulation of his monumental book on management Peter Drucker summarized the tasks of top management as follows:

First is the formulation and implementation of strategy. Drucker explained this prime task as

> the task of thinking through the mission of the business, that is, of asking the question "what is our business and what should it be?" This leads to the setting of objectives, the development of strategies and plans, and the making of today's decisions for tomorrow's results. This clearly can be done only by an organ of the business that can see the entire business; that can make decisions that affect the entire business; that can balance objectives and the needs of today against the needs of tomorrow; and that can allocate resources of men and money to key results.[5]

That, of course, is the strategic planning process.

The other tasks of top management according to this eminent observer of management and managers are as follows: standard setting, for example, for the conscience functions; building and maintaining the human organization; fulfilling responsibilities concerning relationships that only the people at the top of an organization can establish and maintain, such as with major customers, very important suppliers, or bankers; performing ceremonial duties, such as at civic events; and being the "standby" organ for major crises.[6]

There is, of course, no idealized or single way for top managers to discharge their responsibilities. For some managers the strategic planning process is a much larger part of the total job than for others. But for all it is of central importance in performing properly the top management function.

Planning Responsibilities of All Managers

It was said previously that strategic planning is a function of all managers at all levels of an organization. This point has been amplified by Marvin Bower, who for several decades was managing director of McKinsey and Company, a well-known, worldwide management consulting firm. In a superb book that summarized the lessons of experience of effective managers over a long period of time Bower concluded that there are

> fourteen basic and well-known management processes [that] make up the components from which a management system for any

business can be fashioned. . . . Fashioning these fourteen components into a tailor-made management system is the building job of every chief executive and every general executive. To support, follow, and enforce the system is a vital part of every top manager's operating job—and of managers and supervisors at every level.[7]

What are these fourteen processes? They are, Bower says, the following:

1. Setting objectives: Deciding on the business or businesses in which the company or division should engage and on other fundamentals that shall guide and characterize the business, such as continuous growth. An objective is typically enduring and timeless.

2. Planning strategy: Developing concepts, ideas, and plans for achieving objectives successfully, and for meeting and beating competition. Strategic planning is part of the total planning process that includes management and operational planning.

3. Establishing goals: Deciding on achievement targets shorter in time range or narrower in scope than the objectives, but designed as specific sub-objectives in making operational plans for carrying out strategy.

4. Developing a company philosophy; Establishing the beliefs, values, attitudes, and unwritten guidelines that add up to "the way we do things around here."

5. Establishing policies: Deciding on plans of action to guide the performance of all major activities in carrying out strategy in accordance with company philosophy.

6. Planning the organization structure: Developing the plan of organization—the "harness" that helps people pull together in performing activities in accordance with strategy, philosophy, and policies.

7. Providing personnel: Recruiting, selecting, and developing people—including an adequate proportion of high-caliber talent—to fill the positions provided for in the organization plan.

8. Establishing procedures: Determining and prescribing how all important and recurrent activities shall be carried out.

9. Providing facilities: Providing the plant, equipment, and other physical facilities required to carry on the business.

10. Providing capital: Making sure the business has the money and credit needed for physical facilities and working capital.

11. Setting standards: Establishing measures of performance that will best enable the business to achieve its long-term objectives successfully.

12. Establishing management programs and operational plans: Developing programs and plans governing activities and the use of resources which—when carried out in accordance with established strategy, policies, procedures, and standards—will enable people to achieve particular goals. These are phases of the total planning process that includes strategic planning.

13. Providing control information: Supplying facts and figures to help people follow the strategy, policies, procedures, and programs; to keep alert to forces at work inside and outside the business; and to measure their own performance against established plans and standards.

14. Activating people: Commanding and motivating people up and down the line to act in accordance with philosophy, policies, procedures, and standards in carrying out the plans of the company.[8]

All these processes, without exception, are in one way or another embodied in a comprehensive formal strategic planning process. But again, managerial responsibilities and actions for some of the processes extend beyond the planning process. For instance, activating people (item 14) is a requirement that is more pervasive than planning. The point of this discussion is that dominant management processes, according to a management observer whose word commands respect, are elements of or rely heavily upon strategic planning.

Intuitive-Anticipatory versus Formal Strategic Planning

There are two fundamentally different ways for a manager to formulate strategic plans for the future. The first is to meet each day as it arrives and make strategic decisions only on that basis. I assume that managers who prefer this "Mickey Finn" approach will not be reading this book. Those managers who think much about the future and devise strategies to help them meet the future in ways they want may take one of two alternative approaches.

The first, the intuitive-anticipatory approach, has several major characteristics. Generally it is done in the brain of one person. It may or may not, but often does not, result in a written set of plans. It generally has a comparatively short time horizon and reaction time. It is based upon the past experience, the "gut" feel, the judgment, and the reflective thinking of a manager. It is very important and must not be underestimated. Some managers have extraordinary capabilities in intuitively devising brilliant strategies and methods to carry them out.[9] For instance, in speaking of Will Durant (the man who put together the companies upon which General Motors Corporation was built), Alfred Sloan (whose leadership built General Motors Corporation) said: "He was a man who would proceed on a course of action guided solely, as far as I could tell, by some intuitive flash of brilliance. He never felt obliged to make an engineering hunt for the facts. Yet at times he was astoundingly correct in his judgment."[10]

Albert Einstein acknowledged the significance of intuition from a different angle in these words:

> I believe in intuition and inspiration . . . at times I feel certain that I am right while not knowing the reason. . . . Imagination is more important than knowledge. For knowledge is limited, whereas imagination embraces the entire world, stimulating progress, giving birth to evolution. It is, strictly speaking, a real factor in scientific research.[11]

If an organization is managed by intuitive geniuses there is no need for formal strategic planning. But how many organizations are so blessed? And, if they are, how many times are intuitives correct in their judgments?

In contrast, the formal planning system is organized and developed on the basis of a set of procedures. It is explicit in the sense that people know what is going on. Frequently, manuals of instruction are prepared to explain who is going to do what and when and what will happen with the information. It is research based. It involves the participation of many people. Support for the decisionmaking in the process is frequently documented and the result of the entire endeavor is a written set of plans.

It is not at all unusual to find in organizations a clash between these two approaches to strategic decisionmaking. A manager who has been successful with his intuitive judgments is not likely to accept completely or readily the constraints of a formal planning system. Such a manager may be uneasy with some of the new language and methods used by sophisticated staff in a formal planning system. Or, the manager may feel a challenge to his authority as those participating in the system engage in the decisionmaking process. The thought processes of these managers may conflict with the requirements of formal planning.

For such reasons, and because of cognitive differences between intuitive and systematic thinkers, there are some who argue that with the intuitive thinker there can be no formal planning.[12] This either-or conclusion is not correct. Limited empirical observation will show that the two approaches are indeed meshed in many organizations. There is often conflict, to be sure, but each can be and often is adapted to the requirements of the other. They can and should complement one another. A formal system can and should help managers sharpen their intuitive-anticipatory inputs into the planning process. At the very least, a formal system can and should give managers more time for reflective thinking.

In a fundamental sense, formal strategic planning is an effort to duplicate what goes on in the mind of a brilliant intuitive planner. But formal planning cannot be really effective unless managers at all levels inject their judgments and intuition into the planning process. Nor, on the other hand, will formal planning be effective if top managers reject it in favor of their own intuition.

Managers do indeed follow different thought processes in decisionmaking. The design of a formal planning system must understand and reflect these differences if the system is to function successfully. I shall return to this point in several subsequent chapters.

Summary

There are two different types of management. One, which is done at the top of the corporate organization, is called strategic management. Everything else is operational management. Strategic planning is central to helping managers discharge their strategic management responsibilities. The central focus of both is on strategy. But, just as strategic management is concerned with operational management, so strategic planning is interrelated with operational planning. For managers at all levels strategic planning is interrelated with the management process. Strategic planning is not something separate and distinct from management.

Strategic management and strategic planning are vital to the success of corporations today. This is so because the wrong strategy can lead to serious difficulties, no matter how internally efficient a company may be. Conversely, a company may be inefficient internally but successful if it has the right strategies. Good marks in both, of course, is the preferred position.

Although strategic planning is of commanding significance in strategic management it is not the whole of strategic management. Top managers have responsibilities other than planning.

There are two ways to help top managers discharge their strategic planning responsibilities: intuitive-anticipatory planning and formal systematic planning. Both are important and must not be underestimated. In many corporations there are conflicts between the two approaches because different thought processes are involved in them. However, formal planning cannot be done without management intuition. If the formal planning system is correctly tailored to managerial characteristics it can help managers improve their intuition,

2 What Is Strategic Planning?

In this chapter I present my definition of strategic planning and a number of conceptual and operational models of the strategic planning system. At the outset it is important to understand that there is no such thing as *the* strategic planning system, which every organization should adopt. Strategic planning systems must be designed to fit the unique characteristics of each organization. Since each organization differs in some respects from all other organizations, it follows that the planning systems of organizations differ one from another. Nevertheless, there are common characteristics among planning systems of organizations with different characteristics, which will be presented in this and subsequent chapters. Although we have a long way to go before we can prescribe precisely what planning system an organization should have, given its particular characteristics, we do indeed know on the basis of much experience many fundamental planning features that must be employed, or rejected, as the case may be, to assure effective planning. These, too, will be presented.

A Note on Definitions

Confucius is reputed to have said that if he were made ruler of the world the first thing he would do would be to fix the meaning of words because action follows definition. It would be helpful to

12

everyone interested in strategic planning if the nomenclature were accepted by everyone, but that is not the case.

Throughout the book an effort is made to define key terms not as a pedantic exercise but because definitions are critical in understanding and understanding is indispensable to proper action.

Formal Strategic Planning Defined

In the 1960s the words long-range planning were used to describe the system that is the subject of this chapter. Other names have subsequently been coined. Long ago, for reasons that I shall develop later, I abandoned the exclusive use of the term long-range planning to describe the system. So have most other writers in the field. Not all would agree with me, however, when I use synonymously comprehensive corporate planning, comprehensive managerial planning, total overall planning, long-range planning, formal planning, comprehensive integrated planning, corporate planning, strategic planning, and other combinations of these words. More and more, however, formal strategic planning is used to describe what is usually meant when the above phrases are employed.

Most writers in the field have their own pet definitions of the terms listed in the preceding paragraph. They vary greatly in terms of level of abstraction, substance, and general acceptance. Most writers would, I believe, agree that strategic planning should be described from several points of view for deep understanding.[1] I define formal strategic planning from four points of view, each of which is needed in understanding it.

FUTURITY OF CURRENT DECISIONS

First, planning deals with the futurity of current decisions. This means that strategic planning looks at the chain of cause and effect consequences over time of an actual or intended decision that a manager is going to make. If the manager does not like what is seen ahead the decision can readily be changed. Strategic planning looks also at the alternative courses of action that are open in the future, and when choices are made among the alternatives they become the basis for making current decisions. The essence of formal strategic planning is the systematic identification of opportunities and threats that lie in the future, which in combination with other relevant data provide a basis for a company's making better current decisions to exploit the opportunities and to avoid the threats. Planning means designing a desired future and identifying ways to bring it about.

PROCESS

Second, strategic planning is a process. It is a process that begins with the setting of organizational aims, defines strategies and policies to achieve them, and develops detailed plans to make sure that the strategies are implemented so as to achieve the ends sought. It is a process of deciding in advance what kind of planning effort is to be undertaken, when it is to be done, how it is to be done, who is going to do it, and what will be done with the results. Strategic planning is systematic in the sense that it is organized and conducted on the basis of an understood regularity.

Strategic planning for most organizations results in a set of plans produced after a specified period of time set aside for the development of the plans. However, it should also be conceived as a continuous process, especially with respect to strategy formulation, because changes in the business environment are continuous. The idea here is not that plans should be changed every day but that thought about planning must be continuous and supported by appropriate action when necessary.

PHILOSOPHY

Third, strategic planning is an attitude, a way of life. Planning necessitates dedication to acting on the basis of contemplation of the future, a determination to plan constantly and systematically as an integral part of management. Strategic planning is more of a thought process, an intellectual exercise, than a prescribed set of processes, procedures, structures, or techniques. For best results managers and staff in an organization must believe strategic planning is worth doing and must want to do it as well as they can. "Not to do it well is not a sin," says Ackoff, "but to settle for doing it less than well is."[2]

STRUCTURE

Fourth, a formal strategic planning system links three major types of plans: strategic plans, medium-range programs, and short-range budgets and operating plans. In a company with decentralized divisions there may be this type of linkage in each division's plans and a different linkage between strategic plans made at headquarters and divisional plans. It is through the linkages that top management strategies are translated into current decisions. The concept of a structure of plans is expressed also in this definition: Strategic planning is the systematic and more or less formalized effort of a company to establish basic company purposes, objectives, policies, and strategies and to develop detailed plans to implement policies and strategies to achieve objectives and basic company purposes.

There are, of course, a great many other characteristics of formal strategic planning, as will be amply demonstrated in the remainder of this book. These four fundamental characteristics, however, will serve as a basis for the development of the conceptual and operational definitions to be described throughout the book. Before proceeding with these matters, however, it is important to comment briefly about what formal strategic planning is not.

What Strategic Planning Is Not

Strategic planning does not attempt to make future decisions. Decisions can be made only in the present. Forward planning requires that choices be made among possible events in the future, but decisions made in their light can be made only in the present. Once made, of course, these decisions may have long-term, irrevocable consequences.

Strategic planning is not forecasting product sales and then determining what should be done to assure the fulfillment of the forecasts with respect to such things as material purchases, facilities, manpower, and so on. Strategic planning goes beyond present forecasts of current products and markets and asks much more fundamental questions: Are we in the right business? What are our basic objectives? When will our present products become obsolete? Are our markets accelerating or eroding? For most companies there is a wide gap between an objective forecast of present sales and profits and what top management would like sales and profits to be. If so, there is a gap to be filled by strategic planning.

Strategic planning is not an attempt to blueprint the future. It is not the development of a set of plans that are cast in bronze to be used day after day without change into the far distant future. Most companies revise their strategic plans periodically, usually once a year. Strategic planning should be flexible in order to take advantage of knowledge about the changing environment.

Strategic planning is not necessarily the preparation of massive, detailed, and interrelated sets of plans. In some big decentralized companies the system does produce a large volume of detailed plans. But, as will be noted later, the basic conceptual nature of strategic planning discussed in this book will accommodate a wide variety of planning systems from the very simple to the highly complex.

Strategic planning is not an effort to replace managerial intuition and judgment. This point was made before but deserves to be underscored.

Strategic planning is not a simple aggregation of functional plans or an extrapolation of current budgets. It is truly a systems approach to maneuvering an enterprise over time through the uncertain waters of its changing environment to achieve prescribed aims.

Conceptual Strategic Planning Models

A conceptual model is one that presents an idea of what a thing in general should be, or an image of a thing formed by generalizing from particulars. An operational model, in contrast, is one actually being used by an enterprise. An insightful conceptual model is a powerful tool because it provides proper guidance for quality performance in practice.

Exhibit 2–1 shows my conceptual model of the structure and process of systematic corporate planning. It further elaborates the meaning of strategic planning and explains how the process can be carried out. Over a number of years I have examined planning systems of many companies and I conclude that those that do

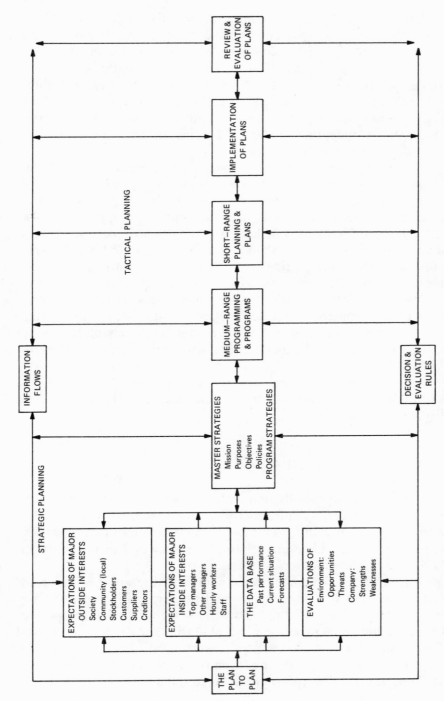

EXHIBIT 2–1: Structure and Process of Business Companywide Planning.

effective comprehensive planning follow this model explicitly or implicitly. Yet, paradoxically, I have never found an operational system diagrammed by a company in precisely the same way as Exhibit 2–1. Operational flow charts vary with the differences among companies but, underneath, the basic elements of Exhibit 2–1 are found in the better systems. If one element of the model is missing, either explicitly or implicitly, the system may not operate effectively. Conceptual models of leading authors in the field are quite comparable to this model.[3]

So long as a manager is interested in undertaking coordinated formal strategic planning, this conceptual model can be made operational and adapted to most business environments. However, although the model is conceptually deceptively simple, it is also deceptively difficult to translate into a first-rate operational strategic planning system. I shall not in this chapter be concerned with the problems of putting the model into operation. That will be the subject of later chapters. My intent here is to present as succinctly as possible the major features of the model and to compare it with other conceptual and some operational models. Since I shall touch upon the main features of the model in later chapters in some detail I can be brief in this chapter with definitions and descriptions.

Exhibit 2–1 is divided into three major sections: premises, formulating plans, and implementation and review. Each will be discussed in turn.

PLANNING PREMISES

Premises mean literally that which goes before, is previously set forth, or is stated as introductory, postulated, or implied. The premises, as shown in Exhibit 2–1, are divided into two types: the plan to plan and substantive information needed in the development and implementation of plans.

Before undertaking a strategic planning program it is important that those involved have a thorough understanding of what top management has in mind and how the system is going to operate. This guidance is incorporated in a plan to plan, which may be oral but is usually written for general distribution.

The substantive planning premises are shown in the four stacked boxes. The information accumulated in these areas is sometimes called the situation audit but other words are also used to classify this part of planning (e.g., corporate appraisal, position audit, assessment of current position, and planning premises).

No organization, no matter how large or profitable, can examine thoroughly all of the elements that conceivably could be included in the situation audit. Each organization therefore must identify those elements—past, present, and future—that are most significant to its growth, prosperity, and well-being and concentrate thought and effort on understanding them. Other elements may be considered in this part of the planning process but they may be estimated without research or taken from published documents.

At the top of the stacked boxes are expectations of major outside interests. For larger corporations it is important, in strategic planning, to have an understanding of what interests major constituents of the enterprise have and how they are expected to change. For a very small corporation the focus can be almost wholly on stockholder interests but for a large corporation other interests must be recognized.

Managers and employees of organizations have interests that also must be appraised and addressed in the planning process. Especially important are those of top executives that derive from their value systems. They are fundamental premises in any strategic planning system.

Included in the data base is information about past performance, the current situation, and the future. This information is essential in helping those doing the planning to identify alternative courses of action and to evaluate them properly. Illustrative of types of past information collected are the following: sales, profits, return on investment, market share, employee productivity, public relations, and product development capability. Information about the current situation, in addition, would include such matters as management capabilities, employee skills, competition, corporate image, social demands on the company, interests of major customers, and product acceptance. Data about the future would, of course, include forecasts of markets, sales, selected economic trends, competition, technology, and other trends of particular concern to the organization (e.g., population, international turbulence, and government regulation).

The last box is sometimes called the WOTS UP analysis, an acronym for weaknesses, opportunities, threats, and strengths underlying planning. Since a cardinal purpose of strategic planning is to discover future opportunities and threats so as to make plans to exploit or avoid them, as the case may be, this is a critical step in the planning process. There is an enormous payoff to the skilled probing of opportunities and threats in a company's future and relating them in an unbiased study of the company's strengths and weaknesses.

FORMULATING PLANS

Conceptually, on the basis of the foregoing premises, the strategic planning process then proceeds to formulate master and program strategies. As shown in Exhibit 2–1 the master strategies are defined as basic missions, purposes, objectives, and policies. Program strategies concern the acquisition, use, and disposition of resources for specific projects, such as building a new plant in a foreign country.[4]

In this part of planning we are concerned with the most fundamental and important ends sought by a company and the major approaches to achieving them. The subject matter includes every type of significant activity of concern to an enterprise—profits, capital expenditures, market share, organization, pricing, production, marketing, finance, public relations, personnel, technological capabilities, product improvement, research and development, legal matters, management selection and training, political activities, and so on.

In contrast to medium-range programming there is no standard approach to planning in this area. What is done depends upon management desires at any particular time. These in turn are stimulated by conditions facing the company at any particular point in time.

Medium-range programming is the process whereby specific functional plans are prepared and interrelated to display the details of how strategies are to be carried out to achieve long-range objectives, company missions, and purposes. The typical planning period is five years. There is a tendency for the more technologically advanced companies to plan ahead for seven to ten years. Companies facing a particularly turbulent environment sometimes reduce the planning horizon to four or three years. In most planning systems medium-range programming follows a standard format that will be discussed later.

The next step, of course, is to develop short-range plans on the basis of the medium-range plans. In some companies the numbers for the first year of the medium-range plans are the same as those in the short-range yearly operational plans, but in others the linkage is loose. Current operating plans will, of course, be in much greater detail than are the medium-range program plans.

IMPLEMENTATION AND REVIEW

Once operating plans are developed they should, of course, be implemented. The implementation process covers the entire range of managerial activities including such matters as motivation, compensation, management appraisal, and control processes.

Plans should be reviewed and evaluated. There is nothing that produces better plans on the part of subordinates than for the top managers to show a keen interest in the plans and the results that they bring.

When comprehensive formal planning was first developed in the 1950s there was a tendency for companies to make written plans and not redo them until they became obviously obsolete. Now, the great majority of companies go through an annual cycle of planning in which plans are reviewed and revised. This process should contribute importantly to the improvement of planning in the next cycle.

INFORMATION FLOWS AND DECISION AND EVALUATION RULES

The box on information flow in Exhibit 2–1 is shown simply to convey the point that information flows throughout the planning process. This flow will, of course, differ significantly depending on the part of the planning process that it serves and the subject of the information.

Throughout the planning process it is necessary to apply decision and evaluation rules. For example, in the development of master and program strategies the values of a chief executive officer stand as important qualitative decision rules. In the development of current operating plans, at the other extreme, decision rules often become more quantitative (e.g., inventory replacement formulas or return on investment standards).

SOME OBSERVATIONS ABOUT THE MODEL

Several observations about the model should be made here. First, the model does not embody one time dimension but many. People often speak of a three-year plan or a five-year plan but generally strategic planning systems do not have fixed time dimensions. In most companies the basic mission and purpose of the company have an unlimited time dimension and are frequently held without change for a long time. At the other end of this spectrum a decision may be made in the process of hammering out program strategies to divest an unprofitable division tomorrow or to hire a chief scientist as quickly as possible.

Second, there is no such thing as *the* objective of an enterprise. Every organization has multiple aims that are addressed differently and have different significance in planning and company operations.

Third, the model moves from left to right as a conceptual process. In practice, however, the process is iterative. For example, there is, typically, considerable iteration between the formulation of long-range concrete planning objectives and strategies to achieve them. If a manager establishes an objective and cannot develop creditable strategies to achieve it the objective ought to be lowered. On the other hand, in seeking alternatives to achieve a particular objective a planner may discover a creditable strategy to do much better. In this event, of course, the objective should be raised.

Fourth, this model is complex. To try to complete it in its entirety the first time an organization introduces a strategic planning process would, for most companies, probably result in failure. As will be shown later, however, the model can be tailored to fit most situations with high probability of success.

Fifth, tactical planning is not identified in Exhibit 2–1. Planning decisions range along a spectrum from strategies at one end to tactics at the other. Tactical planning refers to courses of action used to implement strategic plans. At the extremes there are clear distinctions between the two but as they move closer to one another they may become indistinguishable. Also, it should be noted that what may be a tactic to a chief executive officer may be a strategy to a subordinate.[5]

Finally, the semantic problem in this field may again be noted.

Strategic planning, according to Exhibit 2–1, includes elements in the stacked boxes to the left, plus the box of master and program strategies. To make matters more confusing, I call all that is in Exhibit 2–1 the strategic planning process because it is designed to translate strategies into current actions. Clearly we are in need of new words to define different parts of comprehensive, long-range planning but until we have them we are faced with nomenclature ambiguities.

Conceptual and Operational Steps in Strategic Planning

Exhibit 2–2 presents four steps for creating a strategic plan. These are conceptual models in the sense that they present logical steps in doing planning. They are also, however, operational in the sense that companies can and do follow the steps in practice. Each set of steps emphasizes a little differently some elements in the planning process but fundamentally they all are quite comparable. Like Exhibit 2–1 these steps can be tailored to fit the unique situation of every company. They can result in a comparatively simple planning process or in a very elaborate one, depending upon the detail of the plan to plan.

Strategic Planning Model with Gap and Market Focus

As noted previously it is not necessary for a company to follow the so-called classical planning steps presented previously. In the past most companies focused on the planning gap, shown in Exhibit 2–3. In recent years more companies are focusing on strategy. As shown in Exhibit 2–4 the focal point, in the black bordered box, is a matrix that on its horizontal scale shows market attractiveness and on its vertical scale market strength. (The detailed matrix is shown in Exhibit 11-3.) This approach stands in contrast to setting objectives (filling the planning gap) and then finding strategies to achieve them. Typically the process in setting objectives and formulating strategies is iterative, as noted earlier. It does make a

A

1. Formulate the task
   - Define scope plan
   - Define results sought
   - Determine how plan is to be developed:
     - Who does what
     - Timing
     - Informational requests

2. Develop inputs
   - Past history
   - Major environmental trends
   - Opportunities and threats
   - Internal strengths and weaknesses
   - Present product sales forecasts
   - Values and judgments of managers

3. Evaluate alternative courses of action

4. Define major objectives
   - Sales
   - Profits
   - Product development
   - Manpower
   - Etc.

5. Define major strategies and policies
   - Markets
   - Products
   - Finance
   - Employees
   - Prices
   - Technology
   - Etc.

6. Develop medium-range detailed plans

7. Determine needed current decisions

8. Monitor performance

9. Recycle annually

B

1. Define the kind of company we want

2. Analyze our customers
   - Who are they?
   - How should they be classified?
   - Why do they buy our product/service? Will this change? How?
   - What market segments do we serve? Should this situation be changed?
   - Etc.

3. Analyze our industry
   - Trends
   - Pacesetters
   - Competition
   - Profit potential
   - Etc.

4. Ask: What are the opportunities and threats for us?

5. Ask: What are our strengths and weaknesses?

6. Ask: What strategies are identifiable?

7. Evaluate alternative strategies

8. Develop objectives

9. Prepare detailed plans to implement strategies

10. Develop contingency plans

11. Translate plans into budgets

12. Monitor performance

13. Recycle annually

EXHIBIT 2–2: Four Conceptual Models for Creating a Strategic Plan for Large, Medium, and Small Companies.

EXHIBIT 2–2 *(Cont.)*

C

1. Develop pragmatic understanding of strategic planning in general and for a small company in particular
   - Literature
   - Management consultant
   - Professional seminars
   - Visit other companies doing planning

2. Identification of WOTS UP
   - Weaknesses
   - Opportunities   Underlying
   - Threats   Planning
   - Strengths

3. Identification of strategies to exploit opportunities and avoid threats

4. Evaluation and selection of strategies

5. Implementation plans for priority strategies

6. Formulating major company aims
   - Mission
   - Purposes and philosophy
   - Specific long-range objectives:
     - sales
     - profits
     - market share
     - other

7. Prepare other associated plans
   - Manpower
   - Financing
   - Facilities
   - Etc., as needed

8. Monitor performance

9. Recycle annually

D

1. Where are we?
   - Corporate philosophy, thrust, mission
   - Financial situation
   - Competitive situation
   - Product reliability, acceptability, etc.
   - Market served
   - Etc.

2. Where do we want to go?
   - Preliminary redefinition of aims
   - Strategic alternatives to achieve aims
   - Evaluation of alternatives in light of strengths, weaknesses, constraints, and current momentum

3. Can we get there?
   - Current momentum
   - Organizational requirements
   - People requirements
   - Facility requirements
   - Financial requirements
   - Etc.

4. Which strategies will achieve which aims?
   - Iteration among aims and strategies in light of managerial values and the situation audit
   - Conclusions concerning aims
   - Conclusions concerning strategies to achieve aims

5. What decisions must be made now to get there?
   - Short-term budgets
   - Short-term organizations, personnel, managerial, etc., decisions and actions

6. Monitor performance

7. Recycle annually

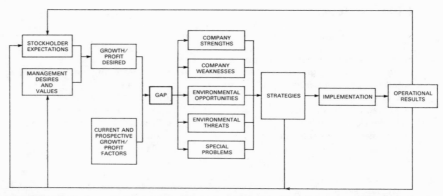

EXHIBIT 2–3:   A Strategic Planning Model Centered on Gap Analysis.

difference, however, which is dealt with first. One emphasizes management by strategy and the other management by objectives. One focuses on what is feasible and the other focuses on what is desired.

In the past many companies followed the model shown in Exhibit 2–3. Objectives were set and the difference between them and prospective growth of present and follow-on products set the size of the planning gap to be filled. In the turbulent environment of recent years managers became less comfortable with forecasts upon which such plans were based. The idea took hold that if a company could achieve strength in attractive markets it would register superior performance. Subsequent statistical analysis, as will be shown later, supported this belief.

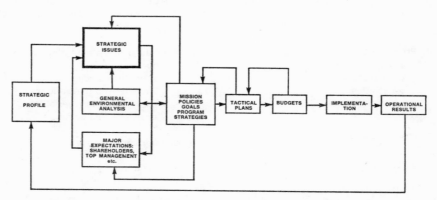

EXHIBIT 2–4:   A Strategic Planning Model with Market Strength and Attractiveness as the Central Focus.

It is not necessary, of course, to begin with the market matrix. Some companies are using the basic approach in Exhibit 2–4 by asking: What are our present strategies? Are they appropriate for the future? What actions are feasible? What can be done to exploit our strengths and to avoid our weaknesses?

There is another modification of Exhibit 2–4 being made by some companies today. For some companies, such as public utilities that recently have begun comprehensive, integrated strategic planning, the problems they face in trying to deal with all the major issues confronting them in the strategic planning process are too many and too complex to be dealt with at one time. One way out is to use the strategic planning process to flush up to top management the strategic issues facing the company. From that list the major items with top priority are chosen for detailed strategic planning.

Two Operational Plans

For illustrative purposes there are presented two operational models. Exhibit 2–5 is the planning system of Rolls-Royce. Exhibit 2–6 presents the planning system of a very small company. Space does not permit a detailed explanation of these systems. They obviously vary considerably in sequence and procedural details.

Types of Business Plans

Exhibit 2–7 identifies a number of different types of strategic planning systems. Posture plans concern the specification of basic company missions, purposes, philosophies, or underlying aims. They are usually formulated by the chief executive officer of a company. A second type of planning done by top management is portfolio planning, which is concerned with resource allocation among major divisions, affiliated companies, or projects. A third type is ad hoc policy/strategy analysis, which is concerned with top management formulation of a major policy or strategy not included in other types of planning. Decentralized planning is done in this company in the sense that the divisions are asked to prepare

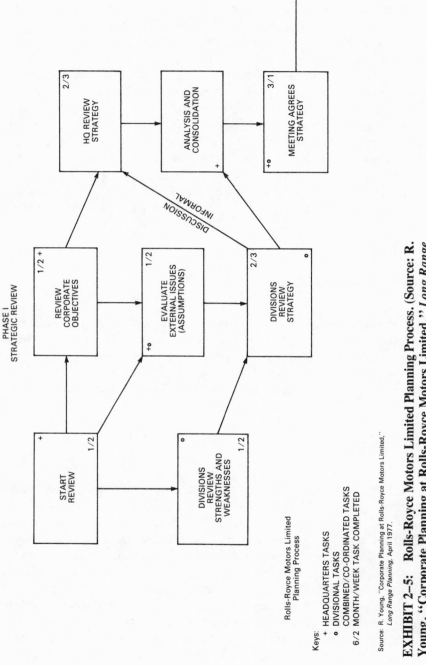

Rolls-Royce Motors Limited
Planning Process

Keys:
+ HEADQUARTERS TASKS
o DIVISIONAL TASKS
  COMBINED/CO-ORDINATED TASKS
6/2 MONTH/WEEK TASK COMPLETED

Source: R. Young, "Corporate Planning at Rolls-Royce Motors Limited,"
Long Range Planning, April 1977.

EXHIBIT 2–5: Rolls-Royce Motors Limited Planning Process. (Source: R. Young, "Corporate Planning at Rolls-Royce Motors Limited," *Long Range Planning*, April 1977, p. 7.)

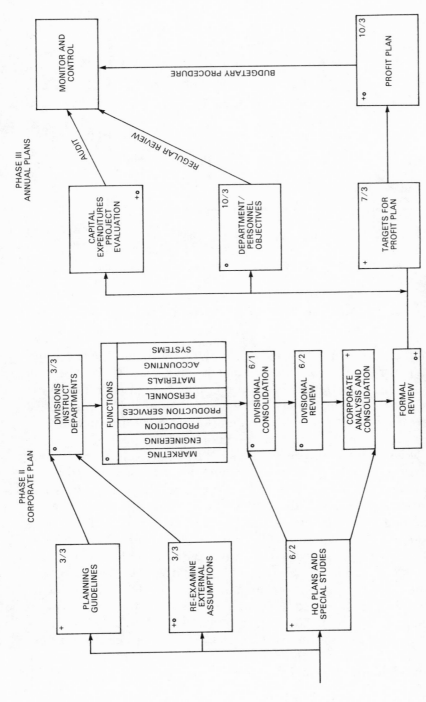

EXHIBIT 2–5: Rolls-Royce Motors Limited Planning Process. (Source: R. Young, "Corporate Planning at Rolls-Royce Motors Limited," *Long Range Planning***, April 1977, p. 7.)**

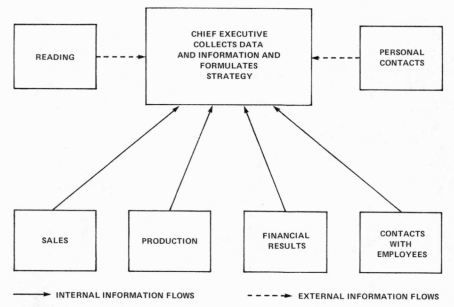

EXHIBIT 2–6:   Strategic Planning in a Small Company.

comprehensive strategic plans covering themselves. The result is a fifth type of plan, the strategic business unit plan. Such plans, of course, can be patterned after the conceptual models presented above. The divisional plans will have, as noted in the conceptual models, functional plans, such as marketing, facilities, manpower, production, research and development, and finance.

When the divisions present plans to top management there may be developed a corporate strategic plan. This plan may set forth the basic policies and strategies of the company, including acquisition of other companies or divestment of present divisions or companies, and a resume, usually financial, of the division plans. Planning done within each of the divisions may be centralized so far as the division is concerned. If the division is a single product producer, for instance, it may act like an individual enterprise and have its planning done by line managers working together as a team with staff. This is called centralized planning. An eighth type of planning is done by headquarters staff offices. Not all staff offices do strategic planning for their own activity but some do, particularly marketing, research and development, and personnel, which here is included in general administration. The degree to which

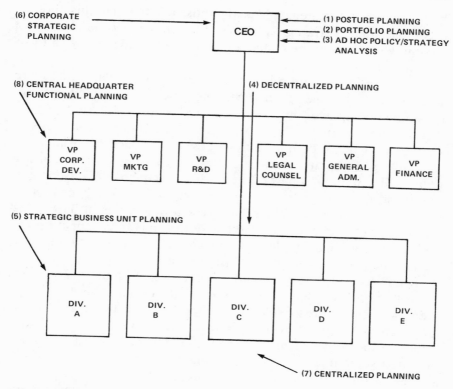

EXHIBIT 2–7: **Types of Business Strategic Planning Systems.**

these plans are meshed in an overall company strategic planning system varies from company to company.

In addition to these plans there are others that should be noted. Here again we face a semantic problem since there is no consensus about the definitions of the plans about to be noted. Profit plans generally are considered to be those that are developed for the next and possibly a second year beyond the current budget and operating plans. These plans are based upon and often are extrapolations of current plans. Such plans commonly are found in companies having no formal strategic plans like those discussed in this book. If a company has a strategic plan like that envisioned here I see no reason why it cannot be called a profit plan if managers wish to so use this phrase.

Project plans are usually included in strategic plans. They are detailed plans for specific undertakings such as new facilities, acquisitions, manpower development, product research, and specific distribution programs. The dimensions, time frame, and details of such plans will, of course, differ considerably one from another.

Contingency plans are associated with strategic plans but are not usually an integral part of them. Strategic plans are based upon the most probable events. Contingency plans are based upon hypothetical situations which have low probabilities of happening but that, if they occur, may have a serious adverse impact on the company. Contingency plans are developed as a precaution to help management meet such crises if and when they occur.

Scenario/exploratory planning (item 12 in Exhibit 2–7) is concerned with possible future combinations of events. Some scenarios and futures explorations overlap with the typical planning period but there is a tendency to develop them for distant future periods of time, such as the year 2000 and beyond. They are prepared sometimes simply to stimulate top management to think about the future. Some of them are prepared as basic premises for strategic planning. As such, of course, they are more elements of the planning process than a planning system. They are included here, however, because the name planning has been attached to them.[6] Scenarios will be discussed at length in Chapter 14.

A final type of planning system in organizations is management by objective. A generic definition is as follows: "Management by objective (MBO) is a process in which members of complex organizations, working in conjunction with one another, identify common goals and coordinate their efforts toward achieving them."[7] The spectrum of MBO systems is wide. At one extreme is the simple setting of a few objectives to be sought by a person, which is essentially associated with the individual and not linked directly to overall corporate goals. At the other end of the spectrum is the type of strategic planning systems discussed in this chapter and called management by objective. This is not, however, common usage of these words.

In a number of companies today MBO as it relates to the objectives of individuals is tightly interlinked with the overall strategic planning process.[8]

Strategic Planning Design Configurations

It should not be thought, of course, that every large company has all the types of plans indicated in Exhibit 2–7. Some companies may have only extended budgeting with major strategies being made intuitively. Some may have both these planning systems plus ad hoc policy analysis of selected issues. Some may have systematic coordinated plans only for key areas such as facilities, manpower, or acquisitions. The variations of strategies for planning are indeed numerous.[9]

Smaller companies tend to have much simpler and less formalized planning systems than larger companies. When a company first starts formal strategic planning the system design should be comparatively simple. For instance, a company can begin formal planning by identifying opportunities and threats in the evolving environment and formulating strategies to exploit and/or avoid them, as the case may be, in light of company strengths and weaknesses. This type of planning may be considered at one end of a spectrum. At the other end would be complex, mature, and complete planning systems of very large companies such as IT&T and GE. In between are many different varieties with characteristics that will be discussed in detail in Chapter 7.

Exhibit 2–8 is designed to picture relative degrees of formality and informality in a planning system. It can be seen that in the

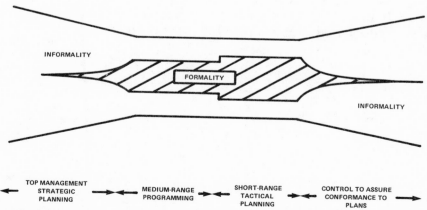

EXHIBIT 2–8: Comparative Formality and Informality in Systematic Strategic Planning.

formulation of basic missions and purposes of an enterprise, at the extreme left, there is no formality and complete informality. At the other extreme, in motivating people to implement plans, managerial processes may be employed that involve no formality. In the process of developing medium-range and short-range plans, however, more formality than informality is involved, yet the process is not completely formal. Configurations of actual planning systems will be different from that of Exhibit 2–8.

Finally, it should be noted that the actual planning process can begin at many different points. It need not follow the conceptual steps noted previously. This point will be discussed more fully in Chapter 7.

Summary

Each writer on planning has his own definitions, and a number were given in a footnote to the chapter. My definition includes the concepts that planning deals with the futurity of current decisions, it is a process, it is a philosophy, and it is a set of interrelated plans. A number of conceptual and operational models of strategic planning were presented.

The point was emphasized that there is no single planning model for all organizations. The formal strategic planning system must be designed to fit the unique characteristics of each company. Formal planning systems can be placed on a spectrum that at one end finds very simple systems and at the other end includes extremely complex and comprehensive systems. These conclusions will be discussed in more detail in later chapters.

3 Why Systematic Strategic Planning Pays Off

It is rare to find a large corporation anywhere in the world that does not have some type of systematic strategic planning system. This approach is also being adopted increasingly by smaller companies. A few of the more important reasons why this is so are discussed in this chapter.

Essential to Discharging Top Management Responsibility

For those top managers who do not feel that the exercise of their own intuition is the only way to make decisions, formal strategic planning must become an integral part of their managerial activities, as noted in Chapter 1. This is especially so for the larger, multiproduct company. Robert C. Gunness, when president of Standard Oil Company (Indiana), validated this point for himself in these words: "There is no doubt whatever in my mind that we simply cannot do without it—particularly in an undertaking as complex and far-flung as ours."[1] Many other top managers have given similar testimony.

Enough has been said on this point, especially in Chapter 1, but it might be added that some companies that have job descriptions for their chief executive officer explicitly identify that official as the leading architect of the firm's future and therefore the principal planner. Whether or not there are job descriptions of the chief executive officer, most chief executives recognize this responsibility. A recent survey of chief executives of the 500 largest industrial and the 50 largest banking, diversified financial, life insurance, retailing, transportation, and utility companies, as ranked by *Fortune*, accumulated 342 replies to different questions. One question asked respondents was what their most important responsibilities were as chief executives. Planning/strategy ranked first in all companies over management selection/development, capital allocation/profits, policy decisions, and maintaining morale, in that order. Among all companies 62 percent ranked planning/strategy first with a range up to 70 percent for companies with sales over $2 billion.[2]

Asks and Answers Questions of Importance to a Company

For top managers as well as for all other managers in a company, formal strategic planning asks and answers some key questions in an orderly way, with a scale of priority and urgency. Such questions as the following come to mind: What is our basic line of business? What are our underlying philosophies and purposes? What are the company's long- and short-range objectives? Are they in balance? What products are going to be obsolete? How and when shall we replace the obsolete products? What will be our cash flow over the next few years? What and where are our markets? What share of the markets do we wish to get? How will we get the shares we desire? Who are our major competitors and what are they likely to do of disadvantage to us? What major changes are taking place in our environment that will affect us? What opportunities or threats exist in the years ahead that we should exploit or avoid?

These questions, especially for a larger company, are becoming increasingly difficult to answer but answers are becoming more urgent as bases for correct decisions. Changing environment is a major factor influencing the introduction of formal strategic planning in many companies. Everyone knows that for most companies the environment is changing rapidly. It offers great threats as well as great opportunities. This point hardly needs elaboration but a few illustrations may serve to reinforce it.

In the product area the typical life cycle is shrinking rapidly but the average research and development time is lengthening and the costs to prototype are increasing. At the same time technological threats to products are growing in numbers and coming from areas other than the industry to which they are related. Government regulations concerning products and their distribution have proliferated and changing social attitudes about products will bring even more regulations in the future. Legal liabilities are expanding for products as well as managerial practices. There is great change taking place in the population mix. Domestic as well as international competition is increasing, and the patterns of competition are changing in ways not easily foreseen. Material shortages, international political and economic problems, domestic inflation, and changing societal attitudes toward business in general create great uncertainty for business. In a sense it can be said, in light of the changing environment, that the times demand systematic strategic planning, especially for the larger corporation, simply to give managers a better understanding of the complex world in which they must operate.

Introduces a New Set of Decision Forces in a Business

Formal strategic planning introduces into an organization a new set of decisionmaking forces and tools. The more important ones are discussed in this section.

SIMULATES THE FUTURE

One of the great advantages of strategic planning is that it simulates the future—on paper. If the simulation does not result in the desired picture the exercise can be erased and started all over again. Simulation choices are reversible; not so brick and mortar decisions made without careful examination of future circumstances.

Simulation has other advantages. It encourages and permits the manager to see, evaluate, and accept or discard a far greater number of alternative courses of action than he might otherwise consider. Although identification of the "right" course of action is far more significant than generating numbers of alternatives, the fact that more alternatives are brought forth for review may produce ideas that a lesser effort would not.

The fact that simulation allows experimentation without actually committing resources encourages managers to try different courses of action—again, on paper. Computers have enormously facilitated such experimentation.

Continuous simulation should make managers better planners. This claim is difficult to substantiate quantitatively, but I agree with Piet Hein's poem "The Road to Wisdom."

The road to wisdom?—well, it's plain and simple to express:

> Err
> and err
> and err again
> but less
> and less
> and less.[3]

APPLIES THE SYSTEMS APPROACH

Strategic planning looks at a company as a system composed of many subsystems. It permits the top management of the company to look at the enterprise as a whole and the interrelationship of parts, rather than deal with each separate part alone and without reference to the others. The sum of the best solutions to individual parts of a problem is never equivalent to the best solution of the whole. The Aswân High Dam in Egypt, for example, is a magnificent engineering triumph, which in truth has harnessed the Nile. But its designers did not consider (or ignored) its impact on other parts of the country. The dam has obstructed the natural flow of silt that enriched the soil of farms along the Nile. It has therefore necessitated the use of much more fertilizer. The organic matter in the silt has deprived sardines and shrimp of an adequate food supply at the river's mouth and these seafoods have virtually disappeared. In addition, the natural flooding of the Nile reduced the rodent population and served as a sewage system for towns bordering the river. To make one final point, the drainage of rich farmland below the dam is now insufficient and the soil is becoming increasingly saline. The result is a drastic decline in agricultural productivity. Try selecting the best components from various automobiles and then try to build with them the "best" automobile. The parts will not fit. The fact is that in large, complex systems the best solutions to each of the parts do not fit together to form a desired whole. Therefore, we must learn to look at the whole.

Strategic planning provides a mechanism for the interrelated parts of an organization to be coordinated, thereby avoiding suboptimization of parts at the expense of the whole. It also permits management, in doing this, to focus attention on the major issues relevant to the survival of the enterprise.

FORCES THE SETTING OF OBJECTIVES

A strategic planning process will not get very far if at some point specific objectives are not set for such things as sales, profits, and market share. There is no doubt that individuals in organizations will generally strive hard to achieve clear objectives that are set for their organizations. They will strive harder if they themselves have had a hand in setting the objectives. Quite obviously, long-range objectives are more likely to be met if plans are carefully prepared to reach them. In this light the objective setting requirement in strategic planning is a powerful force in organizations.

REVEALS AND CLARIFIES FUTURE
OPPORTUNITIES AND THREATS

An important consequence of the situation audit, noted in Chapter 2, is the identification of opportunities and threats. The importance of this result cannot be overestimated. Here is where the intuition of managers and the systematic collection and evaluation of data should mesh to sharpen managerial intuition.

FRAMEWORK FOR DECISIONMAKING
THROUGHOUT A COMPANY

One of the more important attributes of an effective planning program is that it gives guidance to managers throughout a business in making decisions that are in line with the aims and strategies of upper management levels. When a company has developed overall objectives, strategies, and policies, managers down the line have a basis for making both major and minor decisions in conformance with top management wishes. No planning program can or should try to foresee all decisions that managers must make in their day-to-day operations. As a result, there are thousands of decisions managers make that both individually and cumulatively strongly affect the short- and the long-range success of a business. Without an organized planning program it is much more difficult for lower level managers to make decisions in a direction determined by top management.

By participating in and making decisions on the basis of an integrated planning framework, managers are better able to spend their time on activities that pay off. Their efforts are focused on meaningful actions in line with their own and company interests.

BASIS FOR OTHER MANAGEMENT FUNCTIONS

Planning both precedes and is inextricably intermeshed with other management functions. For example, planning is obviously essential to effective control. If the purpose of organized effort is not specified and understood, how can resources be controlled effectively? Resources are used most effectively when the objective of their use is known. Specification of objectives and courses of action designed to achieve them are essential to an adequate measurement of accomplishment. Clearly, measurement of efficiency with which a production program is conducted depends upon volume, cost, and quality objectives that have been set for it.

Planning is closely related to other managerial functions; for example, to coordinating the various elements of an enterprise, to staffing, to leading, and to innovation. This is not to say that planning always is the first in time or always is dominant. There is no doubt that managerial charisma is of outstanding importance in many firms. But other managerial functions are more easily and suitably performed if a planning program of proper scope is conducted.

PERFORMANCE MEASUREMENT

A comprehensive plan provides a basis for measuring performance. Management has available standards of both a quantitative and a qualitative nature in a strategic plan. The performance of a business should not be measured solely in quantitative financial terms, as so many companies try to do. Certainly, financial results are of great importance in gauging success or failure, but nonquantitative characteristics of a business are also of high importance. Creativity, innovation, imagination, motivation, and knowledge, for example, may be reflected in financial results. But if they are not fostered, measured, and appraised by top management, a current financial success can easily disappear. A well-conceived planning program can make it possible for managers at all levels to appraise these attributes in managers under their authority.

FLUSHING UP STRATEGIC ISSUES

It was noted in Chapter 2 that an effective planning system will function to flush up to higher levels of management strategic issues with which they should be concerned. In this way management's attention is focused on key issues and not diverted to lesser concerns. This is, of course, a valuable force for better decisionmaking.

Behavioral Benefits of Strategic Planning

All of the preceding forces may be considered substantive, that is, essential, direct, and important results that should be expected from an effective planning system. Beyond such substantive results are values that are more behavioral in nature. Some of the more important ones are considered on the following pages.

CHANNEL OF COMMUNICATION

A well-organized planning system is an extremely useful communications network. The planning process is a means for communications among all levels of management about objectives, strategies, and detailed operational plans, as noted previously. As plans approach completion, common understanding is generated among all levels of management about opportunities and problems important to individual managers and to the company. The choices made in the planning process are discussed in a common language and the issues are understood (or should be) by all those participating in decisionmaking. Once plans are completed and written there should be a permanent and clear record of decisions made, who is going to implement them, and how they should be carried out. Such a communications system is a valuable asset to any organization.

MANAGERIAL TRAINING

A number of companies have understood that the strategic planning system is a management training process. This is not at all surprising for, as noted earlier, the system forces managers to ask and answer the very types of questions that managers must deal with. Furthermore, as also noted, the planning system establishes a framework within which, presumably, better decisions are made throughout an organization in conformance with top management wishes.

SENSE OF PARTICIPATION

Improved manager motivation and morale should accompany strategic planning. By helping to formulate plans managers should have a sense of satisfaction in at least a partial creation of their own destiny. They know what is expected of them, which when achieved brings a sense of satisfaction. A feeling of personal security may also be enhanced and confidence built. People in organizations today, at all levels, are interested in participating in the decisionmaking process, contributing their knowledge to the organization, and finding opportunities to be creative. A strategic planning process is one in which these desires may be fulfilled. All of the above should make people more adaptable to change, a valuable attribute in organizations.

Formal Strategic Planning Pays Off

A number of quantitative studies have been made in recent years that give concrete evidence that strategic planning pays off in producing good performance in such areas as sales, profit, market share, return on stockholder's equity, operating ratios, and price/earning ratios of stock.[4] It should be noted that superior performance of an organization is not the direct result of formal strategic planning but is the product of the entire range of managerial capabilities in a company. In general terms, however, superior managements know how to develop planning systems to suit their needs. When this is done the entire process of management is strengthened and better results should be achieved than in comparable enterprises without formal planning.

An Assessment

Many of the benefits of planning that I have identified are ideals. Some companies do not achieve these results but it is possible to get them with an appropriately designed and implemented system. Either the substantive or the behavioral values discussed in this chapter should be sufficient to convince management of the value of strategic planning. When both are considered it is easy to see why formal strategic planning has been introduced into so many companies.

Of course, whereas plans are crucial in producing certain types of results, the planning process is important in other ways. Which outweighs the other is not clear but more and more managers agree with the old military saying that "*Plans* sometimes may be useless but the planning *process* is always indispensable."

Plans may indeed be poorly drawn or they may be copied by

competitors. But managerial planning skills are not so easily lost or copied by competitors when they are well developed. This asset is expressed in Kipling's "The 'Mary Gloster'":

> They copied all they could follow,
> But they couldn't copy my mind,
> And I left 'em sweating and stealing
> A year and a half behind.

Success without Formal Planning

There is no question about the fact that many companies have been very successful without formal planning. As was said earlier, if there is an intuitive genius at the helm no formal planning is needed. Even among companies not so blessed, success has been achieved without formal planning. For instance, a company may be lucky. The general run of managers may be of good quality in a nonplanning company and managerial differences may not be dramatic in the short run between such companies and those doing formal planning. In the long run, however, the companies doing planning should, for the reasons noted in this chapter, perform better than those not doing formal planning.

Some Limitations of Formal Strategic Planning

Planning of course has its limitations. It is not the answer to all managerial problems. Some critical shortcomings are reviewed in this section.

ENVIRONMENT MAY PROVE DIFFERENT FROM THAT EXPECTED

Forecasting is not an exact science and plans that are based upon predictions that prove incorrect may fail. Unexpected events in government action such as a contract cancellation, a change in labor union activities, a decline in economic activity, or a sudden price discount by a major competitor—all are uncertainties that make planning difficult.

INTERNAL RESISTANCE

In many companies the introduction of a formal planning system raises antiplanning biases that can prevent effective planning. In larger organizations, old ways of doing things, old rules, and old methods may be so entrenched that it is difficult to change them. The larger companies become, the greater the amount of such debris one finds. Much more will be said about this phenomenon of resistance in Chapter 4.

PLANNING IS EXPENSIVE

In a typical corporate planning effort of even a medium-sized company a significant effort is required to do effective planning. The time of many people is occupied and costs are incurred for special studies and information. Planning is expensive and managers throughout the planning process must continuously apply a cost-benefit gauge. It is not possible to apply this equation quantitatively to corporate planning, but the idea should be kept in mind for it is not difficult to incur costs that exceed potential benefits.

CURRENT CRISES

Formal strategic planning is not designed to get a company out of a sudden current crisis. If a company is on the road to bankruptcy the time that would be spent on strategic planning probably should be devoted to dealing with short-range problems. If, however, a company is in a current crisis and is likely to surmount it, strategic planning should be continued to avoid comparable future crises.

PLANNING IS DIFFICULT

Planning is hard work. It requires a high level of imagination, analytical ability, creativity, and fortitude to choose and become committed to a course of action. Planning involves a different type of mental process from that generally employed in dealing with day-to-day operating problems. The talents required for first-rate planning are not plentiful in most corporations and managements must find ways to improve planning capabilities. One way is to exert pressure on people to meet the intellectual requirements for effective planning. If talents are not available and management does not demand excellence in planning, the introduction of formal strategic planning may wind up as a boondoggle instead of a boon.

PLANS WHEN COMPLETED LIMIT CHOICE

Plans are commitments, or should be, and thus they limit choice. They tend to reduce initiative in a range of alternatives beyond the plans. This should not be a serious limitation but should be noted.

IMPOSED LIMITATIONS

Besides the intrinsic limitations of strategic planning, there are imposed limitations that deserve note. Planning systems will probably not be effective when they are excessively ritualistic and formal, when line managers try to delegate the task to staff, when managers give lip service to planning but make their decisions without reference to plans, or when managers devote all their attention to short-range problems and neglect thinking about the future. There are a great many other pitfalls in planning that will be discussed in later chapters, particularly Chapter 18, that must be avoided if effective planning is to be achieved.

Why Some Companies Do Not Have Formal Strategic Planning Systems

Despite the advantages of planning noted in this chapter there are many companies that do not have formal strategic planning systems.[5] Some have no need but others do have a need that is not recognized. If there are no or only weak competitive pressures on a company whose environment is characterized by low uncertainty, there may well be no formal planning done. Extremely small companies struggling to survive may have no formal planning simply because all the talents of the entrepreneur must be devoted to selling the product or service. Companies with comparatively simple organizations and production arrangements such as selling a patented component to an assembler of a finished product (as in the automobile industry) may have no formal planning because it is so easy to get long-range demands for the product from the assembler.

Some companies have no formal planning because managers have a misconception about what it is and reject it. In the Balkans there is a method of music making called "singing with book" in which the performer puts a volume on his lap, places a hand over it, and proceeds to sing, totally disregarding the book, which he cannot read anyway. This analogy cannot be carried too far, but I frequently have found managers who do no formal planning because they do not know or ignore what is known about making the process operate effectively. Some managers may have a good conceptual understanding of strategic planning but put off this task for many reasons—it is difficult, it may turn out to be a threat to some managers, it may be too difficult to "sell" to other managers, and so on. A company with brilliant intuitive managers, as said repeatedly, needs no formal planning.

Summary

This chapter explained some of the more significant reasons why formal strategic planning is vital to most organizations.

1. Strategic planning is indispensable to top management's effectively discharging its responsibilities.

2. Strategic planning forces managers to ask and answer questions that are of the highest importance to a company and that skilled managers should address.

3. Planning can simulate the future on paper, a practice that not only is comparatively inexpensive but also permits a company to make better decisions about what to do now about future opportunities and threats than waiting until events just happen. Planning itself clarifies the opportunities and threats that lie ahead for a company.

4. Strategic planning is an effective way to look at a business as a system and thereby prevent suboptimization of the parts of the system at the expense of the whole organization.

5. Planning stimulates the development of appropriate company aims, which in turn are powerful motivators of people.

6. Planning provides a framework for decisionmaking throughout the entire company and thereby makes it more likely that lower level managers will make decisions in conformance with top management's desires.

7. Planning is necessary for the better exercise of most other managerial functions.

8. Planning provides a basis for measuring the performance of the entire company and its major parts.

9. Strategic planning flushes up to top management key issues and helps to establish appropriate priorities for dealing with them.

10. Strategic planning systems are superb channels of communication by means of which people throughout an organization converse in a common language about problems of central importance to them and to the organization.

11. Strategic planning helps train managers as managers. It also helps build a managerial and staff capability that facilitates quick and proper response to new events.

12. Strategic planning systems provide an opportunity for people in organizations to contribute their talents to the decisionmaking process, thereby giving employees a sense of participation and satisfaction not otherwise easily achieved.

13. Scholarly surveys show that strategic planning pays off. Those companies that do it have outperformed those that do not.

14. It is quite possible for a company to be successful without formal planning but for most companies success is more likely with formal strategic planning than without it.

15. Strategic planning is not without limitations. Forecasts on which it is based may not occur; internal resistance may thwart its effectiveness; it is expensive and difficult; it requires a certain type of talent that may not exist in a company; it cannot get a company out of a current crisis; and there are many pitfalls that it must avoid.

16. Strategic planning is not for everybody. There are some valid reasons, but not many, why a company may choose not to have a formal planning system.

17. Strategic planning will not guarantee success but, all things considered, managers in most companies will probably be better off with it than without it. To assure this result it will be necessary to tailor the strategic planning system to the unique characteristics of each company introducing it. This is the subject of Chapter 4.

II Organizing for Strategic Planning

4 Organizing the Strategic Planning Process

There is no simple organizational strategic planning pattern that fits all companies, nor is there a single best organization for planning. Factors influencing planning organization vary much among companies, but the experience of the 1960s and 1970s has revealed many characteristics of preferred systems design. This chapter will present the most significant factors influencing systems design; major alternative approaches to systems design; and fundamental lessons of experience governing the design and its development.

Major Factors Influencing Planning Systems Design

In Exhibit 4–1 are listed many factors that influence the extent to which a planning system is more or less formal. These factors also, of course, will influence detailed structural parts of the design, such as the role played by top management as compared with line managers and staff, the complexity of the planning system, and the interrelationships of different types of plans.

Some of the factors in Exhibit 4–1 may lead either to very loose or to rather formal planning systems. It is not so much in point here to be precise about the direction or force of influence of any one factor as to make clear that many factors have a powerful influence

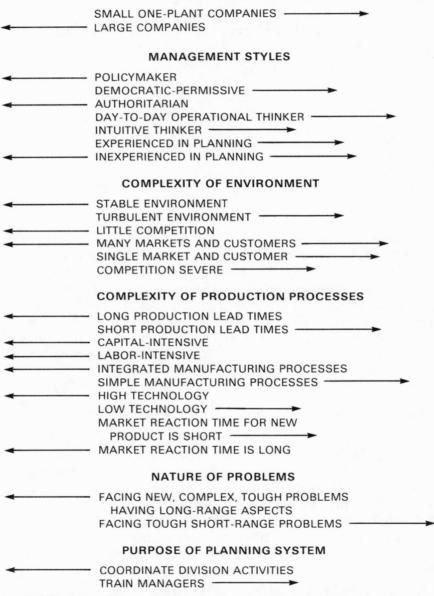

EXHIBIT 4–1: Illustrative Major Forces Influencing Planning Systems Design.

on planning systems design. Although we know a good bit about preparing effective planning systems we do not have a body of knowledge that will tell us exactly what forces will determine what type of planning system for a particular company at a particular period in its history. Developing the planning system is still much of an art. Nevertheless, there are valuable lessons of experience that can be brought to bear on the question. Planning is not all art with no science.

The size of a company is an important dimension in the type of planning system it may adopt. In Exhibit 4–2 are set forth ten

SMALL COMPANY	LARGE COMPANY
1. Chief executive is basically an entreprenuer.	1. Chief executive is a team leader and skilled at conflict resolution.
2. Most important decisions made at top.	2. Exceptional decisions made at top. Many important decisions and routine decisions made at lower levels.
3. Workers and top managers in frequent and close contact.	3. Middle managers stand between top and lower level managers and workers. Middle managers not often bypassed.
4. Lines of authority and responsibility loosely defined. Titles mean little. All top managers participate freely in decisionmaking.	4. Generally, authority flows from title, not personality. Jobs have defined responsibilities and duties.
5. Communications largely face to face, oral, and unspecified.	5. Communications more frequently in writing. Standard procedures are followed.
6. Few explicit policies and rules.	6. Many explicit policies and rules governing subordinate actions and freedom.
7. Staff functions are week and poorly defined.	7. Staff function expanded and expertise respected.
3. Top managers personally check employee performance. Few statistical controls.	8. Formal, impersonal statistical controls established and used.
9. Operations not too complex.	9. Very complex operations.
10. No or little money to hire staff help.	10. Financially able to hire staff experts.

EXHIBIT 4–2: Some Organizational Characteristics of Small and Large Companies That Will Influence Planning. (Source: Adapted from George Strauss, "Adolescence In Organization Growth: Problems, Pains, Possibilities," *Organizational Dynamics,* **Spring 1974, p. 5.)**

comparative characteristics of large and small companies. Only a cursory glance at the exhibit will reveal that the common characteristics of a small company suggest much more looseness, flexibility, and informality than typify a large company. Also, the role in planning of the chief executive obviously is considerably different between the two. Important differences in planning between the large and small companies can also be found in the way goals are established and communicated, how the environment is appraised and used in planning and decision making, how subordinate managers and staff relate to top management, and how operational plans are linked to strategic plans.[1]

In small firms the planning system may be much simpler solely because few people are involved and operations are less complex than in large organizations. Chief executives of small firms also may and often are so hard pressed to deal with current problems that little time is left to engage in strategic thinking. In larger companies the availability of staff makes it possible for chief executives to spend more time and thought on strategic questions.

The ways in which large companies are organized will influence planning systems. A company that is centrally organized and deals with a single business, such as an insurance company or a public utility, will have a comparatively simpler system than a company with decentralized profit centers dealing in multiple, unrelated businesses.

Complexity of environment importantly influences systems design. Companies faced with a comparatively stable environment in which competition is weak will tend to do little planning and if they do it will tend to be formal and ritualistic. On the other hand, an organization faced with a turbulent environment in which competition is severe will tend to have strategic planning but will design it to be flexible and more informal.

Companies having complex production processes with long lead times, capital- or labor-intensive production processes, and highly technical products will tend to have comprehensive, formal planning systems covering a comparatively long period of time, e.g., from seven to ten years. Companies having the opposite characteristics will tend to have much simpler and more flexible planning systems.

Styles of top managers will have an important bearing on planning systems. Styles of management refer to the way executives think, their philosophy, their problemsolving and decisionmaking processes, the way they manage and how they relate to people. (The role of the chief executive officer is so vital in the design and implementation of a planning system that Chapter 5 is devoted to the topic.)

The nature of the problems facing a company will influence design. As indicated in Exhibit 4-1 a company facing new, complex, and tough problems such as growing competition for markets, declining market share, and constraints on raising capital will tend to be more concerned with strategic planning and organize the process to contribute to the making of difficult decisions. A small company trying to survive, on the other hand, will do little formal strategic planning.

Although not shown in Exhibit 4-1 there are other forces affecting planning design. The purposes sought from a strategic planning system are an important influence that will be discussed shortly. Other factors are interpersonal relationships, authority processes, conflict resolution processes, ability to change organizational structures, readiness of managers and staff to engage in planning, relative emphasis in the company on strategy versus operations, availability of information needed for effective planning, and antiplanning biases.

It is not difficult to hypothesize about the design of a system under different circumstances.[2] For instance, as noted previously, a small company will have a much looser planning system than a large one; the system will be either top-down or team approach (discussed later in this chapter); the system will not likely be complete even after a number of cycles; and there will likely be close linkage between the strategic plans and operating budgets and plans. However, the influence of any of the many different forces discussed here varies from situation to situation. At any time one may govern. Nevertheless, as discussed in this book, there are guides growing out of experience that can help managers and staff design a system appropriate to their unique situation at a given point in time.

The Purposes of Strategic Planning

Before a planning system is introduced into an organization the top managers especially, but others also, should have a clear understanding of what strategic planning is and is not. This book tries to provide this perspective. Then, top managers should know what strategic planning can do for them and their organization. Top managers must also decide precisely what it is that they want from the strategic planning system. Only then is management ready to design the process.

There are many purposes that a strategic planning system may address. Exhibit 4–3 identifies twenty that managers may set for their planning system. They are not, of course, mutually exclusive. Some are subsets of others. Many closely interrelate. Some will be recognized as dealing only with parts of a complete strategic planning system. They are not arrayed in any particular order of importance.

One planning system may try to achieve many of these purposes. A company at a particular period may have need for achieving certain goals more than others. For example, a large, diversified

1. Change direction of the company.
2. Accelerate growth and improve profitability.
3. Weed out poor performers among divisions.
4. Flush up strategic issues for top management consideration.
5. Concentrate resources on important things. Guide divisions and research personnel in developing new products. Allocate assets to areas of best potential.
6. Develop better information for top managers to make better decisions.
7. Develop a frame of reference for budgets and short-range operating plans.
8. Develop situation analyses of opportunities and threats to provide better awareness of company's potential in light of its strengths and weaknesses.
9. Develop better internal coordination of activities.
10. Develop better communications.
11. Gain control of operations.
12. Develop a sense of security among managers coming from a better understanding of changing environment and company's ability to adapt to it.
13. Mind stretching exercise.
14. Train managers.
15. Provide a road map to show where the company is going and how to get there.
16. Setting more realistic, demanding yet attainable objectives.
17. Review and audit present activities so as to make proper adjustments and modifications in light of changing environment and company aims.
18. Provide awareness of changing environment in order to adapt better to it.
19. Pick up the pace of a "tired" company.
20. Because others are doing it.

EXHIBIT 4–3:   Some Purposes of Formal Strategic Planning.

firm may find that the need to coordinate plans among divisions is particularly urgent (item 9). A company that has not been performing well may find item 2 to be an urgent objective. I believe the purposes as stated in Exhibit 4–3 are for the most part understandable without further comment here. The importance of some of them has been discussed in previous chapters and others will be examined later.

The Plan to Plan

Once managers have decided what they wish to get from their planning system it is crucial that the details be carefully thought through. This is the plan to plan, or the planning guide, often called the planning manual. For a very small company the plan to plan may be conveyed to managers verbally but in a larger company it is wise to put the plan in writing.

Parenthetically, it may be noted that the issuance of the first planning manual is really the end of a sequence of steps in the plan to plan. Planning to plan may begin with an assessment of planning presently being done in an organization and a determination of whether more or different planning is needed. If the answer is affirmative, then a decision about purpose must be made. Preliminary systems designs then may be devised and tested among managers and staff. When there is reasonable agreement and understanding among all managers and staff the manual may be written.

Planning manuals provide the basic guides for the planning to be done in an organization. To do so they should contain a strong statement of the chief executive officer's commitment to effective formal planning as an essential managerial need, especially for the first planning cycle; a glossary of key terms; a specification of data required from the planning system; a specification of who is to supply what data; a schedule of data flow; and any special planning rules, such as whether pricing used in the planning process will be on a constant or a current basis.

Data requirements, noted previously, cover a wide territory, which will be made clearer in later chapters. Typically, however, plans call for data about such matters as objectives, strategies, and tactical programs, which means information on sales, profits, share of market, finance, marketing, products, capital requirements, manpower, research and development, and so on, as appropriate and as desired by top management.[3]

Planning manuals may also contain information such as the way in which top management sees strategic planning fitting into the managerial task; company missions and philosophies; major issues of concern to top management; an evaluation of the environment to be used as a premise in planning; strategies and policies that top management wishes to include in the thinking of all those involved in the planning process; standard capital allocation procedures; a critique of past results; an explanation of forecasting techniques of interest to the divisions; and illustrations of various elements of the planning process, such as strategies, objectives, contingency plans, and scenarios.

A manual containing this type of information will of course clarify what is expected of those involved in planning. It can perform more functions than that of outlining data requirements. It can, of course, provide a frame of reference, a common language for everyone involved in planning. It can set standards for judging the quality of plans. It can make the consolidation of plans easier. Of considerable importance, a well-conceived planning manual may stimulate creative thinking. It is not easy to divert managers from their day-to-day problems. Planning manuals that provide clear guidelines, permit innovative responses to data requirements, show clearly top management commitment and involvement, and demand creativity, however, are likely to stimulate innovative thinking. Finally, manuals can help to educate managers and staff about all important aspects of the planning process. Not only can these manuals educate managers about planning and help train them to do it well but they can also serve as vehicles for explaining top management philosophies, major policies, and aspirations.[4]

Planning manuals vary much in size and content. In the same industry one may find a company with a planning manual 200 or more printed pages in length, another with a short, succinct set of instructions contained in a half dozen mimeographed pages, and another with no printed manual because "our company is very informal and each division understands what we want and is given 'carte blanche' to prepare plans any way they see fit."

The thrust of the plans also varies. Some may have a strong pedagogical orientation because they are used as training manuals in company seminars and management development programs. Some bark out orders like a drill sergeant. Some explain the nature of data to be reported but give divisions great flexibility in responding. Some contain information needed by divisions, such as detailed environmental forecasts.

Generally speaking, financial data requirements are requested in a standard fashion, a useful practice that facilitates comparisons and consolidations. There is a tendency, however, for nonfinancial materials to be reported in ways considered best by those preparing the plans.[5] The movement toward less structure in planning guides is undoubtedly a result of experience with planning—a recognition that divisions have different problems, different management and staff capabilities, different requirements, and different approaches to planning and reporting. As a company matures in planning capability it is likely that managers and staff will pay less attention to the written plan to plan. Nevertheless, for companies of any size, irrespective of planning sophistication, there should be a written set of guidelines to serve as a basic reference, if nothing else.

It was stated previously that the first plan to plan should carry a strong statement of commitment of the chief executive. This is needed because the planning system introduces some new elements into the organization and unless people understand what is required and that top management is fully behind the new system they will understandably take a "wait and see" attitude. Not only is the chief executive officer's commitment to be stated but the real depth of that commitment should be conveyed. A shallow statement will not do the job.

Also noted was the inclusion of the meaning of key words used in planning, an important task because planning terminology is not standardized. The clarification of important words such as strategy, goals, objectives, and plans will avoid interminable arguments over nomenclature. Such discussions can be anticipated because it is easier to argue nomenclature than to develop creditable plans. Since there is no consensus on definitions each company can define its own terms as it sees fit. The definitions used in this book may be adopted but that is not necessary for effective planning so long as definitions do not go too far beyond generally accepted usage.

Space does not permit the inclusion of detailed tables of contents of different planning manuals, but for illustrative purposes one table of contents is presented in Exhibit 4–4 without comment.

Considerably more will be said in the remainder of this book

Introductory statement by the chief executive officer about the importance of
  planning and the main purposes of the present cycle.
Background information
  The company's philosophy about strategic planning
  History of strategic planning in the company
  Function and role of the corporate planning department
  A succinct diagram of the planning process
Strategic planning instructions to divisions
  Changes from last year
  Planning assumptions
  Structure of narrative description
    Summary of total plan
    Current strategic position
    Strengths and weaknesses
    Principal objectives
    Description of strategies
    Financial schedules
    Major decisions requested of top management to implement plans
The strategic planning environment
Strategic planning assumptions
Glossary of terms
Bibliography

EXHIBIT 4–4:   Table of Contents of a Corporate Planning Manual.

about details that may be included in a company's plan to plan.
These details will differ from company to company. In a cross-
sectional study (industry, size, type, location, and ownership) of
over 200 companies the conclusion was reached that neither size
nor type of business was strongly correlated with the dimension
and details of the final plan.[6]

Finally, a word of warning should be given about dangers in
preparing the plan to plan. One danger is that the plan to plan may
be drafted too hastily or take too long. When a planning system is
introduced into a company great care should be taken to make sure
that everyone involved has an understanding of what is going on
and expresses reasonably complete acceptance of it. Conflicts must
be erased or seriously reduced and individual interests should be
considered. This process takes time. On the other hand, it is easier
to discuss how the organization is going to do planning than actually to get down to doing it for the first time. Furthermore, managers and staff get involved in urgent daily problems and naturally

spend time dealing with them. The result is that the plan to plan is delayed and the initial momentum to get moving becomes lost. Managers must seek a proper balance between a too quickly prepared planning manual and one that consumes too much managerial and staff time to complete.

It obviously is a serious mistake to think that form is substance. The best procedures and forms will not necessarily produce acceptable plans. A first-rate plan to plan may stimulate the development of quality plans but not make them.

Four Approaches to Systems Design

There are four fundamentally different approaches to doing formal planning. The first is the top-down approach. In this approach, in a centralized company, planning is done at the top of the corporation and the departments and outlying activities develop plans, if any, within specific constraints. In a decentralized company the chief executive gives guidelines to the divisions and asks for plans. The plans are reviewed at headquarters and are either sent back to the divisions for modification or accepted. If the division plans altogether do not achieve objectives sought by top management, additional plans are made at the corporate level for acquisitions, divestment, or refinancing.

An obvious advantage of this approach is that top management determines where it wants the company to go and gives the departments and divisions specific guides about their planning to get there. In this approach top management is forced to think ahead and devise aims it seeks to achieve and strategies to implement them. Unfortunately, top management may not be ready to give specific directions; it may grow frustrated with current planning and give directions not thought through. Another disadvantage may occur if managements in divisions feel constrained under top-down direction.

With the bottom-up approach top management gives the divisions no guidelines and asks them to submit plans. Information such as the following may be requested: major opportunities and threats; major objectives; strategies to achieve the objectives; and data on sales, profits, market share sought, capital requirements, and number of employees for a specified number of years. This material is reviewed at top management levels and the same process as noted in the top-down approach is followed.

An advantage of bottom-up is that top management may not be ready to give specific directions to the divisions. Top management may believe that the divisions will feel less constraint with no top-down direction and prepare better plans. Top management may wish to use bottom-up as a learning process to force divisions to plan. A disadvantage may be that some division managers are uncomfortable without top-down direction.

A third approach is a combination of top-down and bottom-up. Accordingly, not only do line managers at headquarters and in the divisions continuously engage in dialogue during the planning process but so also do the staffers at headquarters and in the divisions. Exhibit 4–5 portrays this approach, which is used in most large decentralized companies having had experience in planning. There are many ways the process can work. Generally, top management gives guidelines to the divisions. They usually are broad enough to permit the divisions considerable flexibility in developing their own plans. Sometimes top management may hammer out a basic objective or strategy by dialogue with division managers. Such objectives as return on investment may be derived in this way, especially if the performance of the division manager is measured upon the basis of this standard. Frequently, staffs at headquarters and in divisions get together to discuss changes in the planning manual, the development of data to use in the planning process, and recommendations of strategies to managers. A great advantage of this approach is that much better coordination of effort can be effected. As a result, more creative plans can be prepared, requiring less time and effort.

A fourth basic approach is team planning. In smaller centralized companies the favored approach to planning is for the chief executive to use main line managers as staff in developing formal plans. This approach is also used in some large centralized companies. The chief executive in this setup is the first among peers of a team. In many companies the president meets with a group of executives on a regular basis to deal with the problems facing the company. Part of the time of this group may be spent on strategic planning. Over time the group may develop written plans. Sometimes the planning is done by a formal planning committee chaired by the chief executive or perhaps his designee. The committee may set aside specific times to plan or it may go to a retreat for a few days to do the planning.

This approach can be very fruitful if there is a proper interpersonal relationship between the chief executive and the committee and among the committee members. If, on the other hand, the chief executive has an authoritarian manner and threatens line and staff, the result is not likely to be effective.

There are, of course, many modifications of these four basic approaches. For instance, in the team approach, some companies ask one executive to prepare a preliminary plan for the other committee members to use as a base for planning. The combined top-down/bottom-up approach may be used differently from the arrangement discussed in this section. For instance, a chief executive may work directly with a division manager on a one-on-one basis to develop plans for that division.

Major Design Alternatives

Within each of these four systems there are many alternatives, which illustrates that there is great flexibility in designing systems to fit particular organizational characteristics. Nine classes of alternatives are considered here.

COMPLETENESS OF THE SYSTEM

To follow the complete model shown in Exhibit 2–1 would be very demanding for a company beginning formal strategic planning and it is not advisable. When first starting formal planning a company might simply develop a list of major opportunities and threats and identify strategies to exploit the opportunities and to avoid the threats. It might go a bit further and, skipping over medium-range planning, specify current budgets in light of these strategies. Another alternative in beginning the process is to select one or two major strategies appropriate to the company and to work out detailed tactical plans to implement them. The central point here is that the name of the game for most companies is the identification

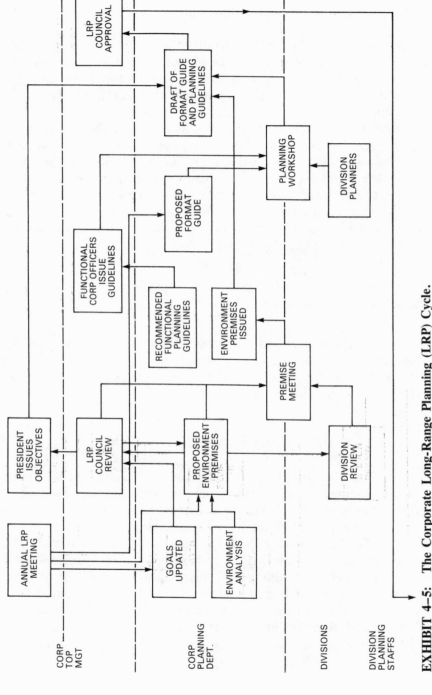

EXHIBIT 4–5: The Corporate Long-Range Planning (LRP) Cycle.

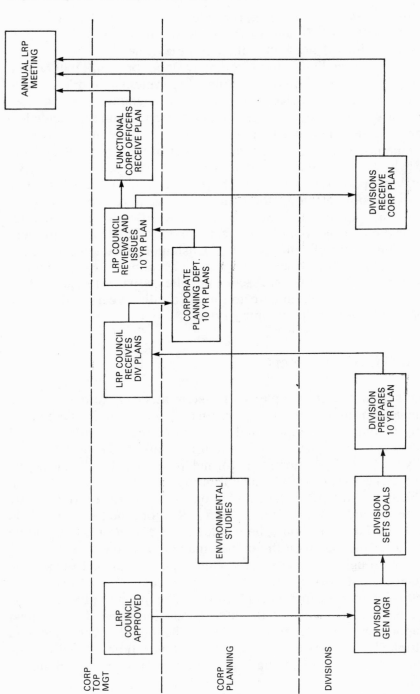

EXHIBIT 4-5 *(Cont.)*

and implementation of the appropriate strategies to adapt to changing environments. Simple systems can often accomplish this purpose as well as if not better than complex ones.[7]

It is highly unlikely that a company, large or small, will be in a position to introduce in the first planning system a comprehensive design that demands rigorous analysis throughout. For example, the Norton Company, a large abrasives manufacturer, decided to adopt a comprehensive planning system. Coincidentally, Robert Cushman, who had been general manager of the abrasives division and who had an effective long-range planning system in that division, was appointed executive vice-president. While he was managing his division, Norton's top management acquired companies in a wide range of products other than abrasives. Believing that neither he nor the managers of Norton were ready to tackle a comprehensive, long-range planning system, Cushman junked the program and asked product managers to prepare accounts of opportunities, threats, strengths, weaknesses, and alternative strategies. This process worked well and Norton in succeeding years added more scope and rigor to the planning system.[8]

DEPTH OF ANALYSIS

When first starting a planning system it is easy to overload the management and staff with overdemanding data analysis. Yet for many planning data inputs and evaluations the best judgments of managers may be acceptable without rigorous staff research, especially for the first attempt at formal planning. To illustrate the point, Ernest Dale, who studied thoroughly the history of Du Pont de Nemours, told the story of a famous document prepared shortly before the end of World War I. John J. Raskob, the treasurer of Du Pont, and Pierre du Pont, the president, discussed what should be done after the war with the money made during the war. One day Raskob brought to Du Pont a recommendation to invest $42 million in General Motors on the following persuasive grounds: "The greatest economy after World War II will be the United States. The greatest industry will be the automobile industry. The greatest company can be General Motors." The initial investment had multiplied over forty times when Du Pont was directed to divest its General Motors stock by the Supreme Court of the United States.[9]

DEGREE OF FORMALITY

Systems can be highly formalized and ritualistic or they can be very informal. The larger a company becomes, the more diversified it is, the greater the research and development lead time, the higher the technology, and the more complex are its production processes, to name but a few parameters, the more formal the planning system tends to be. Managers should constantly evaluate their systems to determine whether formality is eroding originality.

LINKAGE

As noted earlier, the current budget numbers and those in other operating plans can be the same as the numbers in the first year of a medium-range detailed plan. Or, they can simply "reflect" the five-year plan. There are pros and cons for tight or loose linkage, which will be discussed in detail in a later chapter.

TIME HORIZONS

The choices here are rather obvious. The worldwide planning period for many years has been five years. In years past the more technologically advanced firms like the aerospace companies and IBM have stretched their planning periods to ten and seven years, respectively. In recent years, under pressures from a more turbulent environment the planning period in many companies has been reduced to three years. Some companies like utilities may plan for a twenty-year period of time. Timber company plans often cover an even longer time frame.

There are time choices to be made about the planning cycle. Will it be annual, semiannual, or quarterly? Most companies use the annual cycle. Also, scheduling the flow of events obviously requires choices. Exhibit 4–6 is a reasonably typical, simplified flow chart of planning activities.

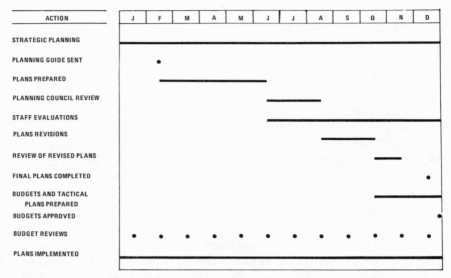

ACTION	J	F	M	A	M	J	J	A	S	O	N	D
STRATEGIC PLANNING												
PLANNING GUIDE SENT		•										
PLANS PREPARED												
PLANNING COUNCIL REVIEW												
STAFF EVALUATIONS												
PLANS REVISIONS												
REVIEW OF REVISED PLANS												
FINAL PLANS COMPLETED											•	
BUDGETS AND TACTICAL PLANS PREPARED												
BUDGETS APPROVED												•
BUDGET REVIEWS	•	•	•	•	•	•	•	•	•	•	•	•
PLANS IMPLEMENTED												

EXHIBIT 4–6:   A Planning Time Schedule.

THE CORPORATE PLANNER

The role of the corporate planner has been examined at length in many books and articles.[10] My purpose here is not to subject the corporate planner to intensive analysis but rather to note some of the significant choices a company has with respect to this person and role.

To begin with, a company has the choice of whether or not to appoint a corporate staff planner. In some companies, as noted earlier, a chief executive uses line managers as staff to do the planning and needs no other staff help. As companies become larger and more complex, top executives will find a need for staff help in discharging their planning responsibilities.

When a corporate planner is to be appointed a great many choices must be faced. What will be the functions of the corporate planner? To whom shall the planner report? Will the planner have responsibilities other than planning? What personal and intellectual characteristics should the planner have?

Space does not permit detailed examination of these questions but a few observations based on experience about them may be in order. Exhibit 4–7 sets forth roles of a corporate planner. I have never found a corporation which charged its corporate planner

	Number of
A. Responsibilities for Ongoing Businesses	Mentions*
Proposing, or participating in the formulation of corporate objectives	106
Proposing, or participating in the formulation of corporate strategy	102
Developing, revising and monitoring the proper functioning of the planning system	101
Serving as an "idea" man for the chief executive and other members of top management as they think about the future	100
Counseling operating management about planning issues and problems	100
Educating top and operating management about planning techniques	91
Investigating the socio-economic-technological environment and formulating assumptions or making forecasts about it	84
Evaluating operating management's plans	82
Identifying new opportunities for internal development	80
Monitoring performance against plans	75
Consolidating and editing written plans prepared by operating management for top management	71
Serving on a management planning committee	71
Proposing, or participating in the formulation of operating-unit (divisions, subsidiaries, etc.) and/or functional-unit (marketing, production, etc.) objectives	64
Proposing, or participating in the formulation of strategy of operating units and/or functional units	64
Developing and maintaining computer-based models of the company, industry, etc.	54
Sales or market forecasting	38
Other (including guidance of related research: catalyst to line management; implementing new ideas for internal development; problem-solving; organization planning)	18

B. Responsibilities for Mergers, Acquisitions, Joint Ventures	
Identifying needs or opportunities that a merger, acquisition or joint venture would fill or exploit	83
Setting criteria for mergers, acquisitions and joint ventures (e.g., types of industry; size of company; financial strength; etc.)	79
Recommending specific firms for additions to, or association with, the company	75
Conducting negotiations with acquisition, merger or joint venture candidates	54
Other (including critical analysis of the acquisition candidate; broker contacts; structuring the package)	21

C. Responsibilities for Divestitures	
Recommending specific businesses for the company to spin off	65
Locating buyers	32
Conducting negotiations with buyers	29

EXHIBIT 4–7: Typical Responsibilities of Corporate Planners. (Source James K. Brown and Rochelle O'Connor, *Planning and the Corporate Planning Director* (New York: Conference Board, 1974), p. 2, 3.)

and/or planning department with all the tasks enumerated. However, different corporate planners and their staffs do perform these functions. Basically, the corporate planner is responsible for helping the chief executive officer (CEO) discharge the strategic planning responsibilities of that office. This means first of all that the corporate planner helps the CEO to the extent to which the latter wishes to formulate objectives and strategies for the corporation and to review divisional plans. Second, the corporate planner may coordinate divisional plans. Usually this means consolidating financial results and appraising strategic and tactical coordination among divisional plans. Third, the planner helps top management to devise the planning system. The corporate planner usually prepares the planning manual, if there is one. Fourth, the planner may prepare environmental analyses for divisions and in other ways give them guidance in doing their planning. Fifth, the planner may develop overall corporate plans for top management for such matters as acquisitions or division and product divestment. Sixth, the planner may prepare in-depth studies of issues of concern to top management. In sum the corporate planner and staff, if any, is fundamentally a coordinator, a top executive advisor, and a strategic evaluator. The planner also helps to design the planning system, stimulates creativity and innovation, consults with line and staff throughout the company, and aids managers and staff in doing more effective planning.

Corporate planners must of course have the intellectual equipment to meet the responsibilities placed on their shoulders. Also, and of great importance, the corporate planner must be acceptable personally and intellectually to the chief executive and other principal line managers. The relationship between the corporate planner and the chief executive is a complex, delicate, and sensitive one. The planner simply must be compatible with the chief executive and complement his interests and abilities. If the fit is not good, the planner will be ineffective.[11]

A question of concern is the location in the managerial hierarchy of the corporate planner. In the 1960s and 1970s the typical corporate planner tended to rise in the hierarchy and in most companies has come very close, if not reporting directly, to the chief executive officer. The closer the two can become in the organizational hierarchy,[12] the better. In a study of sixty companies Lorange found that the closer planners were to line managers the better were the communications between the two and the more management oriented were the planners.[13]

Great care must be taken, in sum, to appoint a well-qualified corporate planner and to locate the job in the proper position in the company. The corporate planning task, particularly in a large company, is difficult and important. The planner must manage complex relationships among many managers and staff, often where there is sharp conflict, and retain the respect, good will, and trust of those involved. The ideal choice for a corporate planner, according to one observer of the job, is "a man who is both philosopher and realist, theoretician and practical politician, soothsayer and salesman and . . . he probably should be able to walk on water."[14]

GETTING THE SYSTEM STARTED

As noted a number of times it is not necessary to start the planning process as described in Exhibits 2–1, 2–2, or 2–3. It can proceed from many different points. Nevertheless, sooner or later all the blocks in Exhibit 2–1 should be explicitly or implicitly covered in an effective planning system. Exhibit 4–8 identifies various legitimate starting points for strategic planning.

PARTICIPATION OF PEOPLE

One of the outstanding characteristics of formal strategic planning is that many people, line and staff, in an organization participate in the process. Choices must be made with respect to who participates with whom and about what, the composition of groups, the interrelationships among groups, accessibility to sensitive information, and delegation of planning authority to staff, to mention a few areas of choice. To illustrate the range of personnel and group interrelationships Exhibit 4–9 is presented.

Generally speaking the greater the degree of participation of people in planning the easier will be the task of top management in developing and implementing plans for the company. But it is not easy to decide precisely what type of participation must be related to the values, expectations, and skills of people involved. If groups are formed they must be composed in a manner fitting respon-

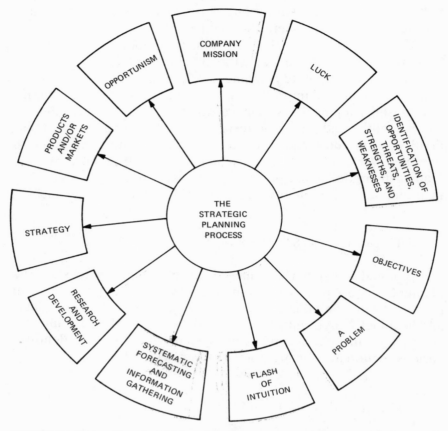

EXHIBIT 4–8:   Starting Points for Formal Strategic Planning.

sibilities. So important is this subject that a chapter will be devoted
later to people in planning.

A number of dilemmas arise in determining participation. For
example, some strategic decisions may be very sensitive and
should not be the subject of widespread participation in a company.
How much can a line manager delegate to a planner without becoming captive to the planner's thinking? How much planning can a
staff planner do without having line managers attribute the plans to
the staff planner? How can committee deliberations be made creative? Staff should not make plans for line managers but there are
degrees to which management may and must rely on staff help in
making the plans. Where is the line? Depending upon leadership of

| | FUNCTIONAL RESPONSIBILITY | | | | |
| | Corporate | | Divisional | | Other |
Planning Activities Phase	Top Management	Corporate Planning Department	Divisional General Management	Divisional Staff Groups	Intermediary Planning Groups
Establish corporate goals and objectives	▲				
Establish corporate goals and objectives	●	●			
Set planning horizon	●		●		
Organize and co-ordinate planning effort		●			●
Make environmental assumptions					
Make environmental assumptions	▲	●	▲	●	
Collect information and forecast					
Forecast sales	▲		▲	●	
Assess firm's strengths and weaknesses			▲	●	
Evaluate competitive environment			▲	●	
Establish divisional goals and objectives					
Establish divisional goals and objectives	▲		▲	●	▲
Develop divisional plans	▲	O	▲	●	▲
Formulate alternative strategies		O		●	
Select alternative strategies		O	●	●	
Evaluate and select projects			▲	●	
Develop tactics			▲	●	
Revise objectives and plans if objectives are not met	▲				
Integrate plans		●			
Allocate resources	▲				
Review progress against the plan	●		●		
Evaluate plan's effectiveness		●			

Key: ▲ Approves
      O Reviews, evaluates and counsels
      ● Does the work

EXHIBIT 4–9: Functional Responsibility Relationship in Strategic Planning. (Source: Ronald J. Kudla, "Elements of Effective Corporate Planning," *Long Range Planning*, August 1976, p. 89.)

committees and committee composition the results can be imaginative or pedestrian. There are no easy answers to such questions.

THE ROLE OF THE CHIEF EXECUTIVE OFFICER

As every chief executive officer who has thought seriously about his role in strategic planning knows, there are many complexities and sensitive relationships involved. So important is this matter that the next chapter is devoted to it.

Planning Design and Company Life Cycles

Corporations go through life cycles and, other things being equal, the planning system will vary depending upon which stage a company is in. To oversimplify, at first there will be very little if any formal planning as the entrepreneur of a small new business strives desperately to find customers so that the company can remain solvent. Then, as sales increase, it will be necessary to watch cash flows carefully, especially the changes taking place in current assets and liabilities. Later, with more growth, it may be necessary to integrate major functions more carefully to insure efficient production. Then, additional products may be added to the line and divisions established. This will require a different management style and planning system. A company subsequently may become very large and mature and a different system will evolve. If it becomes complacent and gets into difficulty a new system may be developed to reinvigorate it.

Antiplanning Biases

Every planning system faces antiplanning biases. The most effective planning system recognizes them and takes pains to counteract them with a system and climate that is congenial to effective planning. These matters will be discussed at length in Chapters 5 and 6 and are only noted here as being important in designing and organizing the process.

Make Haste Slowly

The introduction and development of a formal strategic planning system is not easy to accomplish without serious problems. As a result wise managers make haste slowly.

Line Manager Responsibilities

Planning is the responsibility of line managers but, as was said before, much or little of the planning work can be done by staff. The general proposition should be that line managers should get as deeply involved in planning as possible. As organizations develop their planning systems over many cycles, however, it is understandable that more of the planning activity be done by staff.

Cost-Benefit Analysis

It is recommended that managers continuously apply a cost-benefit analysis to the planning system. Both cost and benefit are used here in the broadest sense of those words. It has been my experience that when managers watch this equation carefully they make certain that the benefits of planning are greater than the costs.

Avoid Major Pitfalls

Finally, the introduction and development of an effective planning system must avoid pitfalls that have been identified by experience as important to avoid. Since these will be discussed at length in Chapter 18 the matter need only be mentioned at this point.

Summary

1. There is no such thing as an ideal planning system for all companies. Each company is unique. This chapter began with a list of many key factors that influence the design. A company can learn much by studying the planning systems of other companies but it is a serious mistake to think that any system, no matter how success-

ful and effective it appears to be, can be transferred overnight without change to another company.

2. Smaller companies will tend to have simpler, looser, and less routinized planning systems than large companies.

3. Styles of chief executives are very important in designing the planning system for the system must be designed to meet the needs of the chief executive.

4. An effective planning system can be designed and introduced only after top management has a clear understanding of strategic planning, what strategic planning can do for the top management and the company, and what the top management wants the planning system to do. There are many different purposes of a strategic planning system.

5. When this requirement is met the company is in a position to prepare the plan to plan. In small companies it may be transmitted orally but in most larger companies it is printed in a planning manual. The planning manual should be prepared after much discussion with those who will be involved. People doing the planning must know what is expected of them, who is going to do what, and what will happen to the results.

6. Planning will fail if adequate time and resources are not devoted to the development of the plan to plan and the doing of planning. It is a danger, however, to spend too much time on the plan to plan and too little on the planning.

7. There are four fundamentally different approaches to strategic planning: top-down, bottom-up, combination of the two, and the team approach. The latter is used mostly in small companies and in a number of large centralized firms.

8. A company has many important choices in designing the planning system irrespective of the approach used; for example, completeness of the system, depth of analysis, degree of formality, linkage, time horizons, whether there should be a staff planner and his role if one is employed, getting the system started, the degree of participation of people, and the role of the chief executive officer.

9. Companies go through life cycles and the planning system will vary depending upon the stage in the life cycle.

10. There are many antiplanning biases in an ordinary company and measures must be taken to reduce or eliminate them.

11. Designing an appropriate planning system and implementing it for effective results is not easy. The advice on the basis of experience is to make haste slowly.

12. Line managers, the doers, must be dominant in strategic planning. Planning is a line, not a staff, function but staff obviously can help in the process. An often quoted axiom attributed to Peter Drucker is: "Planning and doing are separate parts of the same job; they are not separate jobs."

13. Managers should constantly keep an eye on the cost-benefit equation for planning to make sure that benefits outweigh costs.

14. The systems design should of course provide adequate machinery for implementing plans, for reviewing progress, and for evaluating results.

5 The Chief Executive Officer and Strategic Planning

There can and will be no effective formal strategic planning in an organization in which the chief executive does not give it firm support and make sure that others in the organization understand his depth of commitment. This principle should be obvious but often it is not. Even when it is accepted, the proper role of the chief executive officer in strategic planning is far from clear. Each situation is different and requires different relationships. But as noted in Chapter 4 there are lessons of experience that provide useful guidelines as to what the fundamental role of the chief executive officer should be for best results. This chapter will illustrate the more important roles of the CEO in planning and how they vary from one CEO to another.

Meaning of the Term Chief Executive

The term chief executive officer is used in this book in its generic sense, that is, the authority to manage a business. This authority may rest in only one individual, say, the president, or it may be shared by a president and an executive vice-president. In a divisionalized company this authority may be exercised by the general manager of the division at least as far as the division is concerned.

The CEO's Need for Planning Help

In Chapter 1 a brief description of some of the major responsibilities of the chief executive was presented. It was pointed out that planning is of the highest importance in the effective discharge of many of these duties. One further step should be taken here to show why it is that the chief executives of all but the smallest companies need both line and staff help in doing planning.

A CEO's duties are spread over a wide range of substance and, in the larger company, ceremony. The CEO must be a leader of people; a skilled judge of human character, motivation, and capability; a business statesman in dealing with government and community leaders; a thoughtful person who can look ahead and know how to get there; a person of action who can make decisions; an architect of the company management system; an innovator; and a vigilant seeker of opportunities who is willing to come to grips with and take risks.

Except in the smallest of companies, it is obvious that such a job cannot be done properly by one person working alone. As companies grow, therefore, means are devised to reduce the burdens of CEOs. These include splitting tasks at the top, delegating authority, wider use of committees, creation of staff groups, and reliance on individual staff assistants.

As a company grows in size and the complexity of the management task increases, the CEO's managerial problems and functioning change. From a one-person executive, the job changes to that of an executive presiding over other executives. Although the CEO is the final arbiter, only certain types of decisions come to him. There is no rule about this but in most companies the types of decisions that go to the top become developed and generally recognized. The larger the organization the less is the tendency for a CEO to get involved in details. The CEO must rely more and more on others.

The planning role of the CEO tends to change as the organization grows in size. As it expands, planning tends to be done more in terms of fundamental strategies, such as the missions and purposes of the enterprise, long-range substantive aims (sales, profits, market share, return on investment, etc.), and program strategies to achieve these ends. As the organization grows in size there is a

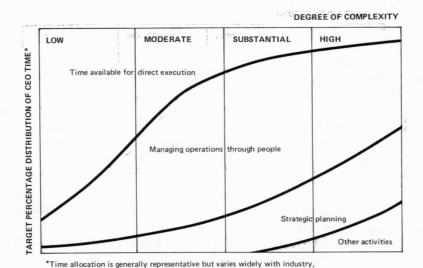

*Time allocation is generally representative but varies widely with industry, economic conditions, and CEO style.

EXHIBIT 5–1:   The Changing Role of the CEO as the Organization Becomes More Complex. (Source: Donald K. Clifford, Jr., *Managing the Threshold Company* (New York: McKinsey, 1973), p. 21.

tendency for the chief executive to spend more time on planning. Exhibit 5–1 pictures these changing CEO roles.

To illustrate better the key position of the CEO in planning, I next present seven fundamental conceptual roles of the CEO in formal strategic planning. How the CEO will discharge them, however, will depend upon many forces in an actual operational setting, such as the managerial style of the CEO. Some of the more important dimensions in practice will follow the conceptual roles.

Conceptual Roles of the CEO in Formal Strategic Planning

STRATEGIC PLANNING IS THE CEO'S JOB

First, the CEO must understand that strategic planning is his responsibility and also a major one. William May, when chairman and president of American Can Company, acknowledged:

As we look at corporate planning at American Can, we agree that it is indeed one of the most important functions of top management; but go even beyond that, and consider the direction of corporate planning to be a specific responsibility of the top manager—the Chief Executive of the corporation.

As we see it, he's got to be the chief planner! Not the only planner, of course, but the leader of his company's planning operations. If the practical objective or purpose of corporate planning is to be better prepared to seize tomorrow's business opportunities, while effectively dealing with today's urgent business, who is better enabled to lead it—and with the most expeditious effect possible—than the chief executive? He possesses the broadest perspective of the company's operations and potential. He has the power of decision that can draw all the elements of planning into one concerted and logical whole.[1]

It should not be necessary to dwell on the CEO's responsibility in strategic planning, but apparently there are still some CEO's who have for one reason or another misjudged their obligations. As Myles Mace commented:

Probably the single most important problem in corporation planning derives from the belief of some chief operating executives that corporate planning is not a function with which they should be directly concerned. They regard planning as something to be delegated, which subordinates can do without responsible participation by chief executives.[2]

Although there are no available current surveys on this point, my observation is that most of today's CEOs, particularly of larger companies, understand this responsibility.

A CEO of any but the smallest company must delegate part of the planning task to others. As S. C. Beise put it when he was president of Bank of America:

I think it is demonstrably clear that this job of planning and keeping the organization moving toward its goal is the task of the chief executive. He alone can serve as "ringmaster" in keeping all the diverse efforts and operations of his company headed in the same direction. He may share the task in some measure and delegate operational problems, but his hands must be on the reins at all times to ensure optimum coordination and continuity.[3]

One of the reasons why the point was underscored in Chapter 4 that before trying to do planning top management must have a clear understanding of what strategic planning is all about is that proper delegation is not likely without it. Proper delegation can be based only on a clear perception of the purposes and methods of strategic planning, a well-balanced assignment of roles among managers and staff, a careful identification of the procedures appropriate to the company, and a thorough grasp of the types of skills needed to do effective planning.

THE CLIMATE FOR PLANNING

Second, the CEO must make sure that the climate for effective strategic planning is established and maintained in the organization. The planning climate, or culture, refers to the environment within the organization in which planning takes place. If nothing is done about developing a proper climate it is altogether likely that in most corporations the climate will be hostile, for reasons discussed in Chapter 6. So, CEOs have a responsibility to insure that the proper climate exists.

Some of the more significant characteristics of a congenial planning climate are as follows, not in any particular order of importance:

Managers and staff maintain an open mind concerning alternatives available to the company. This means, among other things, there is receptivity to new ideas: There is nothing as fragile as a new idea, so they must be encouraged and protected. A proper planning climate is one in which there is a perception that new ideas will be entertained even though hard work may be needed to get them adopted. (Reception does not mean automatic acceptance.)

There is an acceptable level of mutual respect and confidence between staff planners, if any, and line managers.

Managers are willing to face up to unpleasant facts. Many managers resist dealing with unpleasant facts if they are concerned with events in the future. They are even less inclined to look at them if the probability of their occurrence is low. In strategic planning, however, such unpleasantries must be faced and analyzed.

Managers and staff honestly and as objectively as possible appraise the weaknesses as well as the strengths of the company.

Managers and staff are willing to accept critical evaluations of their judgments in the decisionmaking process. In strategic planning, values and ideas of both managers and staff should be subject to question in an open atmosphere.

Managers and staff are able to lift their eyes above their narrow disciplines and see the overall corporate position.

The planning system is introduced only after careful discussion of it with all managers and staff involved in the process and general acceptance of the scheme. If the system has been in existence for some time it should not be radically changed without thorough and broad discussion.

The planning system is properly designed in light of company characteristics. It is flexible. There is an appropriate amount of participation. It seeks to achieve the "right" purposes for the CEO and the company. The cost-benefit equation is balanced correctly. And so on.

The reward system provides some incentive for managers to prepare effective strategic plans. If the reward system is based solely on the short-range bottom line, the CEO cannot expect top quality strategic planning.

Strategic planning is considered to be an integral part of the total management job, not something separate from it.

Antiplanning biases are nonexistent, muted, or well controlled.

The climate in the company fosters creativity, imagination, and innovation. The routine and the mediocre are rejected.

CEOs can and should demand creative excellence and develop a climate that fosters it. The father of England's great prime minister Disraeli made the case for this position in these words: "It is wretched taste to be gratified with mediocrity when the excellent lies before us." Louis Lundborg, former CEO of Bank of America, spelled out this view in more detail in these words:

I believe that an exciting, creative environment is the greenhouse in which growth and vitality flourish. With this as my basic thesis I further hope to show that: (1) while business has long acknowledged the need for such an environment at the top management level, the tempo and technology of our times and the composition of our population make it imperative today that the creative environment be cultivated at every level of our companies; and (2) the deadly enemy of this type of environment is mediocrity. By mediocrity I don't mean simply the innate talent or intelligence of people—although obviously people are the key element. Rather I refer to the lazy habit of mind that tolerates mediocre performance, mediocre standards, and mediocre leadership—the willingness to settle for second-best.[4]

Some people believe that there is a contradiction between formal planning systems and the stimulation of creativity. I do not share that view nor do many other observers of planning systems.[5] What is needed, of course, is the development and nourishment of the proper climate for creative strategic planning.

Two skilled observers and practitioners of strategic planning have concluded: "The success of long-range planning in an organization is less sensitive to the parameters of the planning techniques than it is to the overall *culture* within which the planning is accomplished."[6]

INSURING THE PROPER SYSTEMS DESIGN

A third fundamental conceptual role of the CEO is to make sure that the system designed for the organization is the proper one. Others in the organization must help the CEO to design the system but it is the CEO's responsibility to see that the proper approaches are taken in designing the system and that the final design is the most suitable one from the CEO's and the organization's point of view. The many alternatives were discussed in Chapter 4.

DESIGNATION AND ROLE OF THE CORPORATE PLANNER

Fourth, with few exceptions the CEO's responsibility is to determine whether a corporate planner should be appointed and, if so, what the responsibilities of the job will be. The CEO ought to make sure also that on the organization chart the corporate planner is as close to the CEO's office as practical. The basic reason for this conceptual role of the CEO is that the corporate planner is helping the CEO do his job and should therefore be as close to that office as practicable.

THE CEO MUST GET INVOLVED IN THE PROCESS

This fifth conceptual role was articulated by Robert Haigh when group vice-president and director of the Xerox Corporation:

> Often, we hear that the key to an effective planning experience is the need for *direct involvement* on the part of the president or other key people in the process. I believe this is true, but I do not think the word "involvement" is a strong enough one to describe what needs to be done. In a very real sense, I believe the key executive must do the job. He must make all of the key decisions, with appropriate staff and organizational support, of course. Only when he does the planning job and has his long-range objectives firmly in mind, will he make each short-range decision that comes along appropriately in light of his longer-term goals. He will recognize short-term tradeoffs for what they are, and he will know that he is doing the things today that he should be doing in order to prepare for the long-term future.[7]

Conceptually, the CEO tends to be much more involved in the planning process when it is first introduced into the organization than in later cycles, when the process has been perfected. In the early stages of planning the CEO often will personally write out the basic planning objectives for the company. In later stages staff assistants may prepare the statement of objectives for the CEO's approval.

A major purpose of involvement is to make the CEO visible to others so as to display his interest, concern, and commitment. As one CEO put it: "Planning to be done effectively in my organization demands more pressure from me than any other function of the business." Such pressure cannot be exerted without involvement.

There is of course a vast range of other meanings to the word involvement, a few of which will be discussed shortly.

FACE TO FACE: EVALUATION AND FEEDBACK

Sixth, the CEO should meet face to face with managers to discuss the plans they have prepared. There are many advantages to such a meeting. The CEO will be much better informed of the plans and will have a better basis for accepting, rejecting, or modifying them. Also, the manager involved will understand clearly the interest and commitment of the CEO. Contrast this with a situation in which decentralized divisions submit plans to central headquarters and receive no return communications! In such a system the second planning effort is not likely to be undertaken with enthusiasm.

In very large organizations the CEO may not be able to find the time to review personally, one at a time, the plans of each division. In such a case the CEO may designate another top manager to discuss plans individually with managers and report to the CEO. A popular timesaving method is to hold an annual conference at which all division heads and major functional officers make presentations. Whatever is done, however, it is the CEO's responsibility to see that there is provision for evaluation of plans and appropriate feedback to those who prepared them.

REPORTING TO THE BOARD OF DIRECTORS

Seventh, it is a basic conceptual role of the CEO to report to, or discuss strategic planning decisions with, the board of directors of the company. There are many alternatives available in performing this function. In some companies the CEO reports only the highlights of the strategic planning process. In others this is not done on the ground that the CEO brings to the board for its approval all major policy and strategy decisions when they are about to be made.

Alternative Operational Roles of the CEO

Even when a CEO accepts fully these conceptual responsibilities it is not always easy to determine precisely what ought to be done in the many activities involved and with the many individuals and groups concerned with planning. There is no single way to discharge properly the CEO's responsibilities. The issues are subtle and complex and vary much from one company to another, from one CEO to another, and over time. Space does not permit a comprehensive discussion of the many alternatives facing the CEO so in what follows I shall simply illustrate how CEOs have in practice assumed their roles and how operational realities have influenced their roles.

MANAGERIAL STYLES

Probably the most important influence on operational roles of CEOs is their managerial style. By managerial style is meant a person's way of thinking, way of managing, management philosophy, and demeanor. There is no generally accepted classification of managerial styles, especially as they relate to strategic planning. In this section I review a few CEO managerial styles that influence how the CEO chooses to discharge the conceptual roles noted earlier.

First is the entrepreneur of a very small company just getting started. This executive, who holds a majority of the stock of the company, tends to make all the decisions. Even when the business flourishes such a CEO generally finds difficulty in changing this managerial style.

Second is the team leader mentioned in Chapter 4. This style can foster group discussion and decisionmaking. The CEO with this style becomes much more involved with others in planning activities. However, the distance from group leader to group autocrat if the CEO owns the company is often short. In a company apparently managed by a five-man group, the leader of the team, who was also the chairman of the board and controlled a majority of the stock, invited a friend to visit the company to watch the team in action. Before the team was a proposal to build a new plant. After full discussion the chairman asked for a vote and found that four members of the team voted no. The chairman was in favor of the construction and crisply said, "The ayes have it. The plant will be built," and adjourned the meeting. The friend was surprised at this conclusion of the discussion and said so. "Well," responded the chairman, "some days we count the votes around here, and other days we weigh them. Today we weighed them."[8] Managers who participate in the team approach to planning are likely to contribute more if the CEO adopts a more democratic and less authoritarian style in decisionmaking.

A different type of style is that of the CEO who makes the main decisions but solicits help from others in gathering information to do so. The following description of how the CEO of Ralston Purina Company operates came from the executive vice-president:

> At the corporate level, the chief executive is his own planner. He specifically requires certain corporate officers to provide inputs to him. The controller and the treasurer combine on financial inputs. Our vice chairman must provide strategic opportunity thinking often in a time range 5 to 10 years ahead, along with his evaluations. Several of the rest of us also contribute in specific areas. Together, our internal executive council meets and engages in frank give-and-take talks in critiquing plans and objectives. Ultimately, the chief executive zeroes in on all of this, and our objectives are defined and redefined. Then each of us begins to work out the procedures, etc. The actual mechanics are handled by a section in the corporate controller's department.[9]

Very permissive CEOs give their line and staffs great flexibility in planning. One CEO with this style requires that divisions and affiliated companies prepare five-year plans. He listens to the presentation of the plans of each of the divisions and affiliated companies and will make one of two comments: Either he will say "That's fine. I like it. Go ahead"; or, "Well, I think you can do better than that but if that is what you want to do go ahead." This approach for this executive has proven to be a powerful stimulant.

Some CEOs are negotiators. They will ask headquarters staff to prepare a study on what each of the main divisions or affiliated companies should be achieving over the next five years in terms of sales, market share, profit, and return on investment. The general managers of the divisions or presidents of the affiliated companies will then be asked to bring their staffs and meet with the CEO to discuss the conclusions of the report. Numbers will be negotiated and then the managers will prepare their detailed five-year plans.

CEOs should become personally involved in planning but how much? Generally speaking, the higher the level of strategic planning the more the CEO will become involved. The lower the level of planning, e.g., divisional operational planning in a large company, the less will the CEO be involved. But this is a matter of personal choice of the CEO unless other demands prevent the type of personal involvement desired.

Some CEOs like to meet informally with their top executives, both line and staff, to review company affairs and make decisions. Others introduce formalities in these meetings. Organized agenda may be prepared, meetings take place at specified times and places, and minutes are kept. Similarly, some executives prefer to hold informal discussions with divisional line and staff; others like to make these meetings formal.

The larger companies become the greater is the tendency to build up formal mechanisms and procedures in the planning process. However, even in the larger companies planning is more informal at the higher levels than at the lower levels. Lower level operational planning is usually much more formalized than, say, planning to change a company's mission or to decide upon new acquisitions or divisional divestments.

There are trade-offs between formality and informality. As one executive put it: "Planning must be formalized to provide adequate communication and to promote a sense of accountability and responsibility; but the formal system must be continuously scrutinized to keep the planning process from becoming burdensome beyond the value it brings the business."[10]

One final style to be noted here is that of the office of the president. This is a system in which several top managers share the duties of the top executive. Each office is unique and functions differently but surveys of the practice conclude that "the case for the multiple-executive office as an aid for better planning was cited by virtually all the executives interviewed."[11] This is so because more talent is made available at the top of the corporate pyramid. Furthermore, one person in the office of the president can be made responsible for the strategic planning process. When there is only one CEO this process may not get the attention it requires.

Managerial styles of other managers will also influence what the CEO does. If a CEO has general managers of divisions who resist strategic planning largely because they are not used to thinking in strategic conceptual terms the CEO has an educational job to perform. On the other hand, if a CEO of a centralized company is surrounded by line managers and staff who are thoroughly skilled in the requirements for effective strategic planning the system may be very loose; in it the CEO is essentially a coordinator and an arbiter.

COMPANY SIZE AND COMPLEXITY

This parameter has been noted before but it is important in determining the CEO's role in planning. The tendency is for the

CEO to become much more involved in doing the planning in a small company than in a large one. In a large company the CEO tends to be more of a coordinator and a final policy setter in strategic planning. But, as noted previously, there are instances in which the CEO even in large companies makes all the major decisions.

TYPE OF PLANNING AND CEO DECISIONMAKING

Late one evening in May 1975 Reginald Jones, chairman of General Electric, and Edmund Littlefield, chairman of Utah International, sat talking in the GE suite at the Waldorf Towers in New York. Littlefield was in town to attend a meeting of the GE board, of which he was a member. The two men discussed a possible merger of their companies, which appeared to answer major problems that each company had. Jones wanted a new source of growth for GE and Littlefield wanted access to more capital and resources to support the high risks of Utah International. Both men worked diligently on the merger for the next six months, with great secrecy. Jones confided in only one person at GE. He did not use his skilled strategic planning staff except indirectly and without its knowledge of the uses to which Jones's information requests were to be put. Jones personally led GE into the largest merger in United States history and changed significantly the basic mission of GE.[12]

This illustrates well the fact that CEOs may make strategic decisions without involving other managers in the decision. In most companies that have formal planning a good bit of planning and strategic decisionmaking is done outside the context of the formal planning system.[13] This all does not mean that CEOs ignore formal plans. Rather, it means that there are decisions that should be made by the CEO alone. They may be suggested by the formal planning system but the formal planning system does not make them without CEO authority or approval.

OTHER FACTORS INFLUENCING THE CEO PLANNING ROLE

Enough has been said in this and previous chapters to illustrate the wide range of operational alternatives open to a CEO in the development and implementation of a strategic planning system. A few other factors influencing the role played may be noted in passing. The time a CEO can devote to planning is important. The experience of the CEO and others in the organization in doing successful strategic planning is a significant factor. How the CEO sees the need for dealing with antiplanning biases, discussed in Chapter 6, is a major dimension. Finally, as suggested elsewhere, there is a broad range of approaches to the CEO's evaluation of plans that have been prepared.

Summary

The CEO is the linchpin in the development and operation of the strategic planning system. No other person has anywhere near the influence of the CEO in what is done. The term CEO does not necessarily refer to a single person but is used to identify the officer or officers who are accountable for the company's total efforts and total results. The CEO is the person(s) with the authority to manage the business. Thus, the CEO can be the chief of a major divisionalized corporation as well as a general manager of a division.

CEOs of larger companies simply cannot by themselves discharge their planning responsibility. They need help. In this chapter were presented fundamental conceptual roles and illustrative alternative operational roles of CEOs in discharging their planning function. The conceptual roles of the CEO were presented as follows:

1. The understanding by the CEO that strategic planning is his responsibility. Parts of this task can be delegated but certainly not all of it.
2. The CEO is responsible for establishing a climate in the organization that is congenial to strategic planning.
3. It is the CEO's responsibility to insure that the design of the planning system is appropriate to the unique characteristics of the company.
4. The CEO is responsible for determining whether there should be a corporate planner. If so, the CEO generally should appoint this person and see that the office is located as close to that of the CEO as practical.

5. The CEO must get involved in doing the planning.
6. The CEO should have face-to-face meetings with executives making plans and insure that there is a proper evaluation of the plans and feedback to those making them.
7. The CEO has a responsibility to report the results of planning to the board of directors.

The practical alternatives in performing these conceptual roles are numerous. The issues involved in choosing are complex, and subtle, varying considerably from one executive to another and from one company to another. The discussion in the chapter merely tried to illustrate the range and complexity of the alternatives.

The most significant determinant of operational choice is CEO managerial style. A number of managerial styles were noted, along with how choices of role were influenced by them.

Company size and complexity also influences choice in practice.

Different types of planning will have different types of CEO involvement. In nearly all companies with formal planning systems the CEOs make strategic decisions outside of or beyond the formal planning process. Some CEOs do more of this than others.

These are major influences on operational roles of CEOs in planning but, as noted in the chapter, there are also others. In short, how a company is managed is determined by the CEO's managerial style. The way a company is managed will have more to do with the success of a strategic planning system than the extent to which the system compares with a textbook ideal.

6 Overcoming Antiplanning Biases

There is no doubt that in most organizations the introduction and development of a strategic planning system raises all types of antiplanning biases that must be understood and overcome if the system is to operate effectively. In this chapter the underlying causes of antiplanning biases and how they may be overcome will be examined. The intent is not to cover the subject thoroughly but rather to alert managers to the nature of antiplanning biases so that they can be addressed properly in the development and/or major modification of planning systems.

Surface Reasons for Resisting Planning

Managers who resist formal strategic planning give various reasons for their antipathy:

"I do not have enough time to do my day-to-day work so how can I spend time making future plans?"
"I don't understand what I am asked to do."
"Long-range planning is too complicated."
"We can't forecast accurately six months ahead let alone five years, so how can we plan that far?"
"Why should I do it? My division is doing fine."
"It's too much paperwork."

"What I need more than long-range planning to assure my future profits is better cost control and worker productivity."

Many managers who voice such objections probably believe what they are saying. For most of them, however, these are surface objections that rest on much deeper antiplanning feelings.

Underlying Sources of Antiplanning Biases

The following underlying causes of antiplanning biases are not mutually exclusive. They interrelate and overlap but are grouped as they are for easier exposition.

PLANNING ALTERS INTERPERSONNEL RELATIONSHIPS

The introduction of a new planning system into an organization, or a substantial change in an old system, will cause the breakup of old groups and the creation of new groups. Individual relationships in groups will therefore change. New face-to-face encounters of individuals may bring new challenges to individual values, the necessity for facing new facts and ideas, and the need to interact with new personalities. Individuals with set ways of doing things must face the prospect of changing them.

With planning, people will have new visions of the future and their role in it. Their perceptions of reality, priorities, goals, roles, and organizational relationships will alter. They will see things in a different light.

These changes may create considerable uncertainty and that is not something people like. Life will likely get a little more complicated and frustrating since planning may bring to the fore ambiguities with which people must deal. For instance, the meaning of objectives in planning may cause puzzlement about the relationship of personal to company goals.

In sum, planning changes so many things in organizations that it raises all sorts of doubts, misunderstandings, frustrations, and insecurities—and that adds up to antiplanning barriers in the organization.

PLANNING CHANGES INFORMATION FLOWS, DECISIONMAKING, AND POWER RELATIONSHIPS

New channels of information are generally developed in the planning system. New flows of information bring new patterns of decisionmaking. New patterns of decisionmaking embody changes in power relationships. Managers quite naturally are concerned with their powers and become apprehensive when they are changing. Their apprehension is intensified when it is not clear precisely how the power relationships will ultimately be determined.

Formal strategic planning, especially in a large company, brings staff more into the decisionmaking process. This becomes at one and the same time an aid to managerial decisionmaking and a potential threat to some managers. For example, managers of decentralized profit centers that heretofore had a free hand may now find their plans evaluated more closely by central headquarters staff. Middle managers may view this new source of authority as a threat.

A coordinated formal planning system may also bring managers and staff at all levels into more immediate contact with top management. Middle managers may find their subordinates involved in intimate contacts with other managers in a way not practiced before. They may believe this will loosen their authority over them.

PLANNING MAY HIGHLIGHT CONFLICTS IN ORGANIZATIONS

There are many potential points of conflict in the typical medium to large organization caused by struggles for power and/or capital allocations. Strategic planning systems can sometimes amplify these conflicts. For instance, there is a natural conflict between the demands for capital in an aggressive division and the ability of central headquarters to meet these demands fully. Within divisions, conflicts arise among functional groups—production, manufacturing, sales, finance, and so on. Conflicts can arise between staff groups at different levels in an organization. Such potential sources of conflict nourish reluctance of managers to embrace strategic planning because they may feel the inevitable result of the conflicts will be of some disadvantage to them.

Incidentally, sometimes such conflicts are at the root of problems that erroneously are charged as failures of planning. For instance, a division manager eager to acquire capital for a pet project may overestimate income and underestimate cost so as to reveal a favorable return on investment. When the capital is allocated and the investment return is not achieved, it is easier to blame the planning system than to explain how the numbers became biased in the first place.

OPERATING PROBLEMS TEND TO DRIVE OUT PLANNING EFFORTS

The typical division manager has achieved success precisely because of capability in resolving current operating problems. These managers not only are highly skilled in dealing with short-range problems but also get satisfaction from having resolved them successfully. In many companies their performance ratings and bonuses are based upon this skill. Furthermore, middle managers quickly learn that success in dealing with current problems leads to promotion and more challenging jobs. These managers find much less attractive decisionmaking in strategic planning, which will not produce results for years and which of course is tinged with uncertainty. They are used to quicker results, quicker satisfactions, and quicker rewards.

RISKS AND FEARS OF FAILURE

Strategic planning involves flirting with possible error. Managers know of other managers who were heavily penalized, including loss of jobs, because they made wrong strategic choices. Managers may perceive that it is less risky for them to avoid strategic planning. In our society failure is associated with incompetence, stupidity, laziness, and ineptness; for the manager, it is to be avoided like the plague. If one must plan, the problem becomes how to avoid error or, if there is error, how to attribute it to someone or something else. The easiest way out is not to get involved in long-range planning.

NEW DEMANDS PLACED ON MANAGERS

A major source of resistance to planning arises from the fact that it demands new ways of thinking, the mastery of new concepts, the meeting of new challenges, and the necessity for devising new ways to do things. It deserves to be emphasized that in strategic planning managers must adopt a much different point of view from that acceptable in short-range operational planning. The focus must shift from day-to-day specifics to perception of trends and patterns. The manager must become a conceptual thinker. Managers must think beyond the narrow confines of their areas of immediate authority to other parts of the company and to the company as a whole. They must look more carefully at future environmental forces than they are in the habit of doing. For many managers this will involve greater dependence on formal planning procedures in decisionmaking than reliance on their own intuition. These are difficult transitions to make and managers who must make them naturally are reluctant to do so—especially when the transition must be made with no release from the demanding requirements of day-to-day managerial responsibilities, which is usually the case.

Someone has observed that the better an operating manager the poorer a planner. In light of what has just been said there may be some truth to this observation.

DESIRE TO AVOID UNCERTAINTY

People do not feel comfortable where there is great uncertainty and will resist procedures that seem to increase it. In strategic planning people face all sorts of potential uncertainties. They face uncertainty about how planning will be done. They face uncertainty about how their goals may mesh with organizational goals. They face uncertainty about how decisions will be made. They face uncertainty about how their success in the new system will be achieved.

Such uncertainties provoke different types of anxiety. For instance, people may feel they face situations in which they will lose control. They may believe they will be held responsible for errors or mistakes of judgment. They may perceive planning to be a process that orders their lives too rigorously. Altogether, they see planning as a threat.

AUTHORITY CONFLICT

Reichman and Levy identify authority conflicts that extend back into childhood as an underlying cause of antipathy toward planning. As we grow up, they say, we assimilate and identify with the norms and values of our parents. We remember, for example, parental admonitions to plan ahead. Many executives attribute their current success to early learned habits of doing their school homework before playing and not leaving chores until the last minute. On the other hand, most adults had early failures in thinking ahead. Parents have a habit of pointing out to their children the need for studying during the Christmas holiday to prepare for final examinations given immediately following the vacation. Those who do not heed parental advice, and many do not, have pangs of conscience about not obeying. These early experiences leave the adult torn between rebelling against authority and feeling guilty about this urge. The adult may perceive planning to be the imposition of a directed and ordered life. They oppose this perceived exercise of authority but feel uncomfortable about it. Such ambivalence leads to a reluctance-resistance syndrome, which in turn leads managers simply to "go through the motions of planning."[1]

> There is a powerful tendency to attribute to superiors at work some of the same qualities that people experience in their relationships to their parents. Some people therefore act in a meek and submissive way, expecting to be criticized and attacked by the superior, some in an arrogant and demanding way, as if a good offense is the best defense, and some in a recalcitrant way, as if recapitulating the stubbornness of childhood. Thus, employees unconsciously will tend to bring into work situations some of the same expectations of power figures—superiors—that they had of their own parents. This means that the superior-subordinate relationships take on even more significant psychological proportions than most people assume.[2]

In a different vein, the responsibility for planning felt by the adult may conflict with the concern of the child only for the desires of the moment. This conflict, according to Reichman and Levy, is settled "either by putting off planning or by forcing ourselves to create plans that are ponderous projections, unrelated to reality, and therefore useless."[3]

OTHER UNDERLYING CAUSES OF RESISTANCE TO PLANNING

There are many other sources of antipathy of people in organizations toward planning. For instance, some managers have a proclivity for low-risk actions and resist planning into the uncertain future. A manager's personal cost-benefit assessment of planning may be tipped too far on the cost side. Many managers prefer oral communications to written ones. In strategic planning, of course, much communication is in writing. People in organizations generally resist anything that increases paperwork and planning tends to do that. Most people cling to old ways of doing things and resist changing them, but planning necessitates doing just that, so they resist planning. Managers may feel that the introduction of a planning system to help make better decisions is a criticism of their past decisionmaking, and it probably is. There is generally present the "not invented here" factor. If managers did not initiate planning, this barrier to ready acceptance may exist.

Planning Can Advance the Interests of People

The point should not be neglected that a strategic planning system helps not only to avoid many of these antiplanning biases but also to fulfill personal desires and interests. For instance, it is well known that people in organizations today wish to participate in decisionmaking processes. They want to use their skills to contribute to the organization. They want challenges to their talents. They want to be creative. A strategic planning system is a mechanism to help individuals achieve these ends.

Most middle managers wish to become better managers. As noted in a previous chapter a planning system is an excellent mechanism to train managers. Furthermore, the system should help these managers produce better decisions, which should improve their performance, increase their salary and bonus, and give them greater self-satisfaction.

Top and middle managers may find security in a planning system. Robert Haigh, for example, onetime group vice-president and director of the Xerox Corporation, warmly embraced formal planning because the answers it gave to major questions he had constituted for him "a cure for presidential insomnia."[4] Top executives should feel more secure the more thorough and systematic analysis they can acquire of the future environment, the better is their identification of major opportunities and threats, and the more certain are they that their strategies are credible. If the great benefits of planning as outlined in Chapter 3 are realized, top management should believe that its interests, those of others in the organization, and the company's are being well served by the planning system.

The problem in this chapter, of course, is that of reducing the causes of antiplanning biases and advancing the attributes of a planning system that will achieve the desirable substantive and personal results possible in a good system.

Offsetting Antiplanning Biases

Obviously, management can do more about overcoming some antiplanning biases than others. Here again, however, space does not permit extensive coverage of what might be done; thus, what follows must be considered essentially illustrative.

TOP MANAGEMENT MUST RECOGNIZE THE PROBLEM

The first step in solving a problem is to recognize it. Antiplanning biases do exist in organizations and if not understood and countered can easily bring about the failure of planning. From what was said earlier it would seem desirable for top managers systematically to examine antiplanning biases that may exist in the organization. Casual observation of the phenomenon is not likely to help management get a handle on it.

EXCELLENCE IN PLANNING CORRELATES
WITH EXCELLENCE IN MANAGEMENT

The best planning is most likely to take place in organizations with the best management. Antiplanning biases accordingly are more likely to be overcome or at least muted in organizations that exhibit certain features:

Excellence in overall management is sought continuously.

The organization seeks out, stimulates, develops, and rewards good management.

The organization is vibrant and not stagnant.

There is a continuing central concern for individuals.

A good system of internal communications exists.

The organization is not burdened by voluminous procedures and archaic policies.

The organization seeks and is capable of continuous renewal in John Gardner's sense of having found the means to combat vested interests that grow up to sustain the status quo.[5]

LEADERSHIP IN PLANNING

Within this type of organization top managers must fulfill carefully all their conceptual roles and make sure that the operational relationships they choose reflect the needs of the people involved in planning. The system should be designed only after a good bit of discussion with people. The first system probably should not be too complex or too ambitious. The climate in the company must be designed to be congenial to planning and the top managers must be appropriately involved in the process.

INTRODUCE NEW OR SIGNIFICANTLY REVISED
SYSTEMS CAREFULLY

Efforts must be made to determine precisely what may produce resistance to planning in the minds of people. This is a slow process that should continue until antiplanning biases seem to be well under control. Once the biases are understood, various efforts to deal with them obviously should be made: educational or training programs of different types, personal interviews with key managers, and ongoing dialogue among managers and staff.

As part of this educational process, guides and rules of thumb may be developed to fit the needs of the company. To illustrate, top management of one company concluded that the generally accepted idea that people do not like change was only partly true: People in their company liked some types of change especially if they had a hand in it. The managers developed a set of guidelines that they believed were helpful in making people more agreeable to changes required in a planning process:

Change is more acceptable when it is understood than when it is not.

Change is more acceptable when it does not threaten security than when it does.

Change is more acceptable when those affected have helped to create it than when it has been externally imposed.

Change is more acceptable when it results from an application of previously established impersonal principles than it is when it is dictated by personal order.

Change is more acceptable when it follows a series of successful changes than it is when it follows a series of failures.

Change is more acceptable when it is inaugurated after prior change has been assimilated than when it is inaugurated during the confusion of other major change.

Change is more acceptable if it has been planned than it is if it is experimental.

Change is more acceptable to people new on a job than to people old on the job.

Change is more acceptable to people who share in the benefits of change than to those who do not.

Change is more acceptable if the organization has been trained to plan for improvement than it is if the organization is accustomed to static procedures.[6]

DO NOT ASK PEOPLE TO DO THE IMPOSSIBLE

As noted previously, a new planning system generally requires that people think in new ways and do things differently. Part of the educational process in introducing the new planning system should be to ease this transition. The demands of the new system can and probably should be a bit ahead of the educational program but not too far ahead.

COMMITTEES SHOULD BE COMPOSED WITH CARE

Formal strategic planning systems generally involve group decisionmaking. It cannot be assumed that such decisions will be correct even with group participation. Group decisionmaking can be better than that of individuals because more diverse views can be expressed and weighed. On the other hand, group decision-making can be much worse than that of one individual because of the special problems that may be associated with it. For example, a number of studies show that there is a tendency for individuals in groups to be willing to accept high-risk decisions they would not have made singly.[7] There is nothing wrong with risky decisions per se, but one must view with caution situations in which individuals accept higher risks after talking with others in a group than they would have before.

Other studies of group efforts reveal other problems. Van de Ven and Delbecq, for instance, have concluded that a number of reasons may inhibit a group from realizing the full idea producing potential of all the people participating. They note, for example:

1. Interacting groups often become focused on one train of thought for long periods of time, to the exclusion of alternatives.
2. Individuals tend actually to participate in the discussion only to the extent they view themselves as equally competent with others.
3. Even though more expert group members may not express criticism, others tend to expect that they will and thus hold back their ideas.

4. Lower level managers often are inhibited and go along with the ideas of their superiors even though in their own minds they have better solutions.
5. Group pressures for conformity with the implied threat of some kind of punishment are almost inevitable.
6. More dominant individuals tend to monopolize and control the group with the result that the ideas of others are lost.
7. Groups as such tend to devote time to their own maintenance and survival and to the members' getting along with each other; this takes away from decision effectiveness.
8. Groups have a tendency to move to quick decisions, short-circuiting the search for relevant information.[8]

To conclude, committee and group participation in planning can be extremely helpful in dealing with antiplanning biases and in producing better decisions than individuals acting alone. However, much care and wisdom needs to be applied to the nature of participation, the composition of groups, the leadership of groups, and the use of groups.

These deficiencies of committee efforts can be corrected when they are recognized. Janis, for example, specified a number of ways to avoid "groupthink":[9]

The leader of the group should give high priority to airing objections and doubts.
At the outset the leader should be impartial and not advocate a specific course of action.
More than one group should work on a complex problem. Each should have its own leader.
Members of the group should discuss the proceedings of the group with trusted associates and report their views to the group.
Experts from outside the group but within the organization ought to be asked to present their views to the group.
At each meeting where policy and strategy alternatives are discussed one member of the group should be asked to take the role of devil's advocate.
When policy issues concern rivals, great care should be given to examining all pertinent information about their intentions.
Once a decision is reached it should be reconfirmed again at a later meeting.[10]

Although these guidelines have particular reference to top level government policymaking groups, they also can be applied to corporate decisionmaking bodies.

REWARD EFFECTIVE STRATEGIC PLANNING

Incentives ought to exist for those doing effective strategic planning. If rewards to managers are made solely on the basis of short-term economic measures of performance there is no incentive for them to do effective strategic planning. Also, sanctions should be applied for poor planning.

Summary

Antiplanning biases must be understood and countered if planning systems are to be successful. A list of the more significant psychological causes of antiplanning biases follows.

Planning alters personal and work relationships, which in turn generates ambiguities, uncertainties, fears, and doubts.

Planning changes information flows, decisionmaking, and power relationships, which also generates uncertainties, apprehension, and resistance to change.

Planning highlights conflicts in organizations such as those between divisions and headquarters and among divisions.

The typical operating manager is highly skilled in solving current problems and resists getting involved in the more risky task of strategic planning, whose outcomes must remain uncertain for some years into the future.

Planning introduces new risks and fears of failure into the lives of managers, which they resist.

Planning places new intellectual demands on managers that they may find difficult to meet.

People feel uncomfortable with uncertainty. Although planning is supposed to reduce uncertainty it also can increase it.

Planning stimulates authority conflicts that have roots in child-parent relationships.

Attention was drawn to the great potential benefits of strategic planning in contributing to individual's aims. The system is exceptionally able to meet many of the new aspirations of people in organizations. A critical problem for managers is how to reduce antiplanning biases and increase the benefits of strategic planning.

Some of the principal methods to overcome antiplanning biases were presented:

Top management must recognize the problem of biases.

The better the total management of the company the less likely there will be antiplanning biases.

Top management must strive to meet all of its major conceptual responsibilities in developing an effective planning system and must insure that its operational roles reflect fully the needs of the people who are to do the planning.

The planning system ought to be introduced into an organization only after considerable discussion among people about who is to do what, where, when, and how.

People should not be asked to do something they cannot do.

Committees should be composed with care so as to avoid the unique problems that can arise from poorly chosen committees.

The reward system should be related to effective and/or poor strategic planning.

One dimension of doing planning that was not mentioned in this chapter is the way people think in collecting and using information. If not understood, this aspect of human thinking can create serious blocks to planning, as will be discussed at some length in Chapter 7.

III Key Considerations in Planning

7 Alternative Planning Postures, Cognitive Styles, and Values

In this part of the book each of the major elements in the strategic planning process will be examined. The elements treated and the sequence of analysis are shown in the chapter headings. For each there will be presented the nature of the element and major considerations the practitioner should have in mind in completing that stage. In contrast to the discussion on alternative designs for strategic planning presented in Chapter 4, the focus in this part of the book is on doing planning.

The following analysis of doing planning should be considered in light of previous discussions. To this perspective this chapter adds three important additional background considerations: alternative planning postures, differing cognitive styles, and personal values, that managers bring to the planning process. All have an underlying and significant impact on how planning is done.

Alternative Planning Postures

Three fundamentally different planning postures were discussed in Chapter 1, namely, intuitive-anticipatory planning, formal strategic planning, and informal, day-to-day problem resolution. Other planning postures should now be added to this list.

ENTREPRENEURIAL OPPORTUNISTIC PLANNING

In this approach the central focus is on finding and exploiting opportunities. The manager using this approach is constantly searching the environment for new opportunities in both old and new markets, new products, and/or new business ventures. Managers adopting this planning mode are said to thrive on environmental uncertainty and are willing to make high-risk decisions.[1]

This planning pattern is usually found among managers of very small organizations. But, as Robert McNamara pointed out in the following statement,

> I think that the role of public manager is very similar to the role of a private manager; in each case he has the option of following one of two major alternative courses of action. He can either act as a judge or a leader. In the former case, he sits and waits until subordinates bring to him problems for solution, or alternatives for choice. In the latter case, he immerses himself in the operations of the business or the governmental activity, examines the problems, the objectives, the alternative courses of action, chooses among them, and leads the organization to their accomplishment. In the one case, it's a passive role; in the other case, an active role. . . . I have always believed in and endeavored to follow the active leadership role as opposed to the passive judicial role.[2]

INCREMENTAL MUDDLING THROUGH

Lindblom was the first person to articulate this planning posture.[3] Managers adopting this planning pattern do not have distinct long-range objectives but develop them in the process of evaluating policy alternatives. Only those policy alternatives that differ incrementally from existing policies are considered, only a small number of policy alternatives are considered, and only a restricted number of consequences for each policy alternative are analyzed. The problem is continuously analyzed and redefined and decisions to deal with it are made in small, incremental steps never too far from the status quo. A "good" policy decision is not one that meets the test of rigorous analysis but rather is one that analysts of the policy agree on. The approach is remedial and geared more to correcting present imperfections than to formulating strategies to meet specific objectives of a challenging nature. This is a reactive in contrast to a proactive stance. Managers following this planning pattern adopt a wait and see attitude. They constantly churn the evaluation process until agreement is reached that a prospective move is acceptable.

THE ADAPTIVE APPROACH

In this approach managers make a strategic decision and then modify it through successive decisions. This procedure involves a successive narrowing and redefining of the basic decision.[4] To illustrate, a manager may decide that to achieve a desired sales level the firm must expand beyond current products and markets. Once the decision to expand is made the next task may be to answer the question: Shall we expand through acquisition or in-house new product development? If the answer is to expand through acquisition the next question may be: Shall we acquire a large company or several small companies? If the answer is a large company: What products must the company produce? The analysis thus proceeds with a cascade of decisions and appropriate feed-back between the stages.

VARIATIONS AMONG AND MIXING OF PLANNING POSTURES

This list does not exhaust the types of planning postures that exist in both theory and practice but it does show clearly that there are a number of fundamentally different possible approaches to planning. Why discuss such alternative planning patterns here? The answer to this question is that very few organizations, especially the larger ones, rely on any one of these planning patterns, including the formal strategic planning model. In practice there is a mixture of these planning models in organizations. For example, in the infancy of most organizations the entrepreneurial opportunistic model is likely to be dominant, aided by the intuitive-anticipatory posture. In the more mature stages of a large company the formal strategic planning model is likely to be predominant although one

may find the entrepreneurial opportunistic approach to be dominant in one or more divisions. The incremental muddling through
posture may be adopted in the development of basic company
missions and purposes. The adaptive approach is often followed
along with formal systematic planning, especially with respect to a
major strategic decision. So, these different modes can be found in
the same company at the same time. One or another may be used
by top management in contrast to the divisions; different divisions
may use different approaches; and different planning issues may be
addressed with different planning models.

Cognitive Styles

Managers differ significantly in the way they gather and
evaluate information. This factor in turn will naturally have a major
bearing on how they do planning. McKenney and Keen developed
a model of cognitive styles, shown in Exhibit 7–1, that is very
helpful in explaining different managerial approaches to planning.

There are two broad types of thought processes used in information gathering, according to McKenney and Keen. One is preceptive and the other receptive. By information gathering is meant
"the processes by which the mind organizes the diffuse verbal and
visual stimuli it encounters."[5] The result is information.

Preceptive information gatherers begin with a set of patterns,
systems, or concepts about how to relate data. They look for
patterns and relationships in the data and for facts that fit their
mental concepts. They jump about from one set of data to another
looking for patterns. Their eyes are more on the forest than the
trees in it.

Receptive information gatherers, on the other hand, are very
attentive to details. They focus on and ponder individual facts and
clues without trying to fit them into conceptual patterns. They are
more concerned with individual facts per se than their relationships
with one another. They suspend judgment, avoid preconceptions.
and insist on a complete examination of all the data available before
coming to a conclusion.

As Exhibit 7–1 shows, individuals differ not only in the way in
which they gather information but also in the way in which they
evaluate it. At one extreme are intuitive thinkers. They avoid

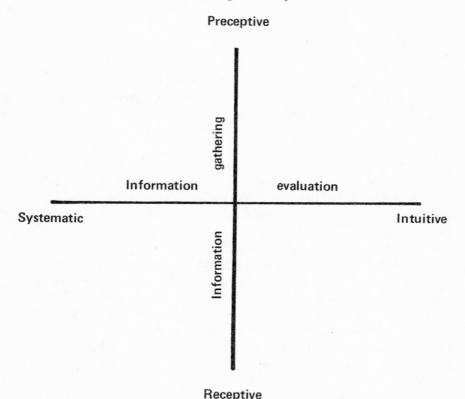

Preceptive

gathering

Information | evaluation

Systematic | Intuitive

Information

Receptive

EXHIBIT 7–1: A Model of Cognitive Styles Used in Gathering and Evaluating Information. (Source: James L. McKenny and Peter G. W. Keen, "How Managers' Minds Work," *Harvard Business Beview,* **May– June 1974, p. 81.)**

committing themselves until the last moment of decision. They continuously search for new information, keep redefining the problem, jump around from one set of data to another, constantly examine alternative solutions, and in effect keep reinventing the wheel. In evaluating the data they depend on hunches and cues in reaching conclusions.

Systematic thinkers have different characteristics. They examine the available information about a problem in a structured fashion. Their solution to a problem proceeds logically, step by step. Alternatives are examined in each step and discarded quickly as the analysis moves toward resolution. They search for a rational method to solve a problem and defend the final solution on the basis of the rationality of the method used.

Cognitive Styles and Planning

The significance of Exhibit 7–1 for this chapter is that different people approach planning problems in fundamentally different ways. Also, certain planning problems that are encountered in an organization will respond more readily to one or another of the cognitive styles.

For example, intuitive-preceptive thinkers are more likely to excel in problems that are elusive or difficult to define, such as specifying basic company missions and purposes. Systematic-receptive thinkers, on the other hand, excel in dealing with problems responding best to quantitative models, such as inventory control or production scheduling.

McKenney and Keen gave a problem of decoding a ciphered message to both systematic and intuitive thinkers. The intuitive subjects solved the problem—"sometimes in a dazzling fashion." None of the systematic thinkers solved the problem. In this particular case, "there seemed to be a pattern among the intuitives: a random testing of ideas, followed by a necessary incubation period in which the implications of these tests were assimilated, and then a sudden jump to the answer."[6]

An important, but not unexpected, finding of the research reported here is that most people apply their preferred style to all problems. They fit facts and problems to their particular mental processes rather than changing cognitive styles to fit facts and problems.[7] Only a minority of people in the research of McKenney and Keen appeared to change cognitive styles. This finding partly explains some of the reasons for antiplanning biases in formal planning. It also underscores the point that different levels of strategic planning, and different problems, need the application of different cognitive styles.

Each of the styles discussed here is superior for a particular type of problem. The systematic thinking style has definite strengths in specialized tasks. So, too, does the intuitive style. McKenney and Keen stress the point that "the intuitive mode is not sloppy or loose; it seems to have an underlying discipline at least as coherent as the systematic mode, but is less apparent because it is largely unverbalized."[8]

Recent brain research has concluded that systematic, so-called logical thinking takes place in the left hemisphere of the brain. Here is where information is processed sequentially in an orderly way. The right side of the brain, in sharp contrast, is specialized for dealing with emotions, processing information simultaneously, and evaluating information in a relational, holistic fashion. These two brain hemispheres correspond, of course, with the systematic thinker (left side of the brain) and the intuitive thinker (right side of the brain).[9]

Mintzberg has concluded that managers think on the right side of the brain and planners on the left side,[10] an oversimplification, to be sure. Right hemisphere thinking probably is more important at the top of the organization than at the bottom. One major reason for this is that the higher one goes in an organization and the more difficult the problem is, the fewer are the available quantitative facts that bear upon it. The more important is the intuitive element in the final solution. Harlan Mills expressed this point well:

> There is a curious natural law in business that places a premium on managerial imagination—The Bigger the Problem the Fewer the Facts. This law manifests itself in the necessary paradox of the "scientific foreman and intuitive president." Many problems at the supervisor's level can be quantified, analyzed and optimized down to the last few percent-problems in production scheduling, make-or-buy, even allocating salemen's time to customers. But most problems at the president's level involve such intangibles that any decision at all takes courage. For instance, the problems of whether or not to build a plant, or how to build the plant, are of completely different orders of magnitude.
>
> Thus, this simple law places increasing emphasis on the art of sensing essentials early, of drawing inferences from barely sufficient information. For example, a major decision, by the time it is supported by a solid factual basis, in all likelihood should have been made several years ago! Such an art places an increasing burden on the managerial imagination—not in imagining nonexistent facts, but in erecting, demolishing and re-erecting conceptual structures to organize and use the few facts available as intelligently as possible.[11]

The reader now knows that formal strategic planning is a process with very wide variations. Both systematic and intuitive thinking is involved in doing it. Each is superior in parts of it and in certain planning modes; each is inferior in parts of it and in certain planning patterns. The problem for managers is to see that the appropriate application and mixture of system and intuition be made at the appropriate steps and for the right issues in the planning process.

For the most significant decisions the ideal is to be sure that the result is based upon rigorous and painstaking analysis guided and reinforced by intuition based upon experience. Intuition is needed to determine the method of rigorous analysis to be employed, the data collected, and the method of analysis. The final decision is intuitive. If this were not so, all managerial problems would be solved by mathematicians.[12]

Types of Intuition and Planning

There are different types of intuition and they have different impacts on planning. Elsewhere I defined intuition as "the power of knowing, or the knowledge obtained, without going through a process of formal reasoning or recourse to conscious inference. It is reason in a hurry. It is innate, instinctive knowledge."[13] Intuition is strongly based on experience but it also involves "sensing" a situation where experience may not be present.[14]

Three types of intuition affect planning. The first is intuition that is applied solely as a reaction to immediate phenomena. In the face of a takeover bid an executive may make an immediate decision to counter by announcing a broad expansion program that would create problems for the acquiring company. The second is the intuitive-anticipatory mode. In this case a manager will set long-range objectives and intuitively make decisions from day to day and over time to achieve the objectives. A third mode is undirected mulling over. This takes place when a manager senses the need to do something but is not sure precisely what should be done. The mental process is one of pondering events and possible responses.

These types of intuitive response can of course be used by the same manager in different situations for different parts of the planning process. Obviously, doing planning will be influenced by which type is employed.

Managerial Values and Value Systems

Throughout this book managerial aims, aspirations, interests, expectations, attitudes, and personal philosophies are mentioned as being important in planning. They all rest on an individual's value system but are not the same as values. For example, values are similar to attitudes but are more stable and ingrained than attitudes.[15] At any rate, values and beliefs derived from them can and often do determine managerial choices throughout a planning system.[16]

A value establishes for a person a standard upon which basis important decisions are made. Values concern not only the ends a person considers to be preferable to another state but also the preferred means to achieve them. Values are settled habits of regarding, and attitudes toward, events or phenomena. They are fundamental beliefs and ideas held by an individual. They serve as criteria for choosing among alternatives. A person's basic values are enduring and change slowly. Specific values are integrated and ordered in priority in a person, and that is a person's value system.

Value systems of managers differ and, as a consequence, managers faced with the same set of facts may make different decisions. To illustrate, one manager may attribute more importance to economic values and stress growth while another may be more concerned about social values and sacrifice growth to improve conditions for employees. One CEO may have a strong prejudice against long-term indebtedness as a means to growth while another may embrace borrowing to expand operations. An executive with deep religious convictions will likely insist on stricter moral codes for employee behavior than one not so devout. One chief executive in the aerospace industry with whom I worked many years ago decided to diversify. It soon became clear that he was interested in diversifying only into high technology products, especially those that were airborne. Some chief executives will sacrifice profits for growth while others prefer profits to growth. Some seek worldwide organizations while others, because of their values, prefer to do business only at home. The values of some CEO's lead them to seek to build large organizations while others prefer smaller ones. The relationships between values and decisions will be amplified further in remaining parts of this book.[17]

Managers throughout an organization should, of course, have an understanding of their value systems and the ways in which they influence their decisions. It is also important that they try to understand the value systems of other managers, especially those at the top of the organization.

Other Background Considerations

Throughout the planning process, choices are made upon the basis of different types of decision processes and tools. Space does not permit detailed examination of these processes and tools. Chapter 15, however, seeks to pull together what is important for managers to know about this subject.

Finally, attention should be drawn to the various alternatives in doing planning that were presented in Chapter 4. The chapters following this one are sequenced in conceptual steps but, as pointed out in Exhibit 4–8, the planning process can proceed from any one of many different points in the planning process and upon the basis of a number of different steps.

Summary

This chapter examined three important background considerations that, together with what has been said in previous chapters, will make the following chapters on actually doing planning more valuable to the reader.

The first overarching consideration is that there are a number of fundamentally different planning patterns. The important insight is that in many corporations, especially the larger ones, all of the major planning postures are used in one form or another— intuitive-anticipatory planning, formal strategic planning, day-to-day reactive planning, entrepreneurial opportunistic planning, incremental muddling through, and the adaptive approach.

The second major background consideration treated in the chapter is that managers have preferred cognitive styles for collecting and evaluating data. They are not easily changed and have varying degrees of effectiveness in doing planning. I discussed systematic preceptive, systematic receptive, intuitive-preceptive, and intuitive-receptive modes. Certain types of problems in planning, and different levels of an organization at which planning is done, will be more or less amenable to these styles.

I also pointed out that there are three types of intuition— immediate reaction to phenomena, intuitive-anticipatory approach, and intuitive undirected mulling over—all of which may be used by the same manager at different times with respect to different problems.

The third background consideration, and the most fundamental of the three, are the values and value systems of managers. They influence all actions and decisionmaking of managers. Those held by top managers have a significant influence on planning in an organization.

8 The Situation Audit

At precisely 0513 on the morning of April 18, 1906, a cow was standing somewhere between the main barn and the milking shed on the old Shafter Ranch, on the outskirts of San Francisco. Suddenly the earth shook and the cow disappeared; a few feet of tail sticking up in the air was all that remained.

The Shafter cow story symbolizes the dangers of the turbulent organizational environments of our times. Suddenly, and without warning, the forces struck, changing the configuration of the earth, destroying a city, and swallowing the cow.

Few managers today are unaware of the great changes taking place in the environments of their businesses. Most managers understand that success in business depends significantly on the ways in which they adapt to their changing environments. The central question for most managers is how to appraise properly the environment within which their business operates. The process by which this evaluation is done is called the situation audit and is the subject of this chapter.

What Is the Situation Audit?

The situation audit refers to an analysis of data, past, present, and future, that provides a base for pursuing the strategic planning process. The activity covered is sometimes called the current appraisal, or the planning premises, or the market/business audit. There is no consensus about the content of a situation audit but generally the concept includes information in boxes A through F in

Exhibit 8–1. This conceptual model is comparable to Exhibit 2–1 but highlights in a different fashion the situation audit.

There are several dimensions of the situation audit that should be understood at the very beginning. First, there is no one way to make a situation audit. In some companies the situation audit is rather complete and comprehensive; in other companies with strategic planning systems the process is loose and unstructured.

Second, the potential range of a situation audit is wide—covering anything of importance in the internal and external environments. For the most part, however, the situation audit covers the conventional dominant areas of a business: production, markets, finance, competition, and management.

Third, the situation audit will differ depending upon the organizational entity involved in planning. In decentralized strategic business units the situation audit may cover that unit. In a centralized company it may cover the entire company. In some instances the audit may be for a part of a business unit, such as a

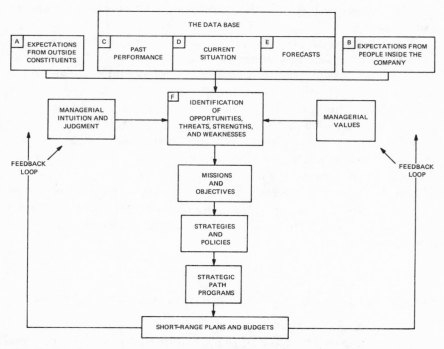

EXHIBIT 8–1: A Conceptual Development and Implementation Model.

marketing audit in a division.[1] The situation audit may be made for special products or groups of products.

Fourth, the situation audit is not something that can or should be completed in the planning process solely on a formal basis. A very important part, if not the most important part, of the situation audit is done continuously in the personal surveillance of environments by individual managers. This type of environmental scanning is performed in a variety of ways from methodically reading business journals to casually conversing with fellow managers at lunch.

Managers will of course rely in varying degrees on different informational sources for different types of information about specific aspects of their environments. For example, Aguilar in his early research on environmental scanning found that managers relied comparatively little for external environmental information on internal reports, memoranda, and scheduled company meetings. Their most important source of such information was subordinates![2] In a more recent study Stevenson surveyed fifty managers in six companies and concluded that they relied less on formal than on informal procedures for their assessment of company strengths and weaknesses.[3]

The situation audit as described here covers much more territory than that studied by either Aguilar or Stevenson. It is obvious from a sampling of corporate planning manuals that more and more companies are tending systematically to conduct the situation audit. Much of this job, and an important part of it, however, will always be done by individual managers in their own ways. I strongly believe that a proper blending of the two approaches will strengthen each. For this reason the remainder of the chapter will be devoted to approaches in systematizing the development of the situation audit. The reader who is interested in exploring further individual environmental scanning methods is referred to Aguilar's study, which is still the best and most comprehensive analysis of this subject.

Fundamental Purpose of the Situation Audit

First, a major objective of the situation audit is to identify and analyze the key trends, forces, and phenomena having a potential impact on the formulation and implementation of strategies. This is a critical planning step for two reasons. First, there are changes in the environments of a business that will have a profound impact on the affairs of the enterprise. Best results will be achieved if these forces are identified before their impact can be felt, in contrast to what happened to the hapless Shafter cow. Second, the environmental changes must be given appropriate examination and evaluation. It is quite obvious that the total volume of environmental data included in boxes A through F in Exhibit 8–1 is immense. No company can track every piece of information that directly or indirectly may have some influence on the planning process. As a consequence, each company must identify what it is in the changing environment that is of the greatest potential significance to the affairs of the company. Next, decisions must be reached about the depth and rigor of the analysis to be made. Research into changing environmental phenomena can be expensive and each company, no matter how profitable, is obliged to determine how thoroughly environmental changes should be analyzed.

The problem becomes complicated because within the same company different managers at different levels will require different analyses of the same information or different types of information. The sources relied upon will differ among these managers even for the same types of information. For example, a chief executive may feel the need for a reliable estimate of future short-term interest rates. He may feel quite comfortable in relying for this information on the estimates of a local banking officer. The manager of a division, however, may rather rely on staff analysis for such an estimate. In short, each manager must determine the information need, where to get data, and how best to get it.

Second, the situation audit emphasizes the importance of systematic assessment of environmental impacts. The search for and evaluation of environmental forces should be continuous and more or less systematic. Experience teaches that the more systematically one attempts to perceive changing forces in environments the more likely one is to avoid being surprised. Experience also teaches that the more systematically one assesses changing environmental forces the more accurate one is likely to become in gauging properly the impacts of the changes.

Third, the situation audit is a forum for sharing and debating divergent views about relevant environmental changes. There is usually a good bit of room for argument about the current situation in which a company finds itself, not to mention uncertainties about potential environmental changes.

Fourth, and closely associated with the preceding, vague opinions about different parts of the situation audit can be made more explicit in the process. Systematic attempts to appraise the environment can help individuals sharpen vague amorphous attitudes about forces operating in the environment.

Fifth, the intellectual exercise associated with the situation audit should serve to stimulate creative thinking.

Finally, all of the information collected in the situation audit should, as shown in Exhibit 8–1, provide a basis for completing the strategic planning process in all of its phases, from reevaluating missions to making short-range plans and budgets. Abraham Lincoln expressed this idea shrewdly in observing: "If we could first know where we are, and whither we are tending, we could then better judge what to do, and how to do it."

With these purposes in mind, approaches to content and methods of evaluation in different parts of the situation audit may now be discussed.

Expectations of Outside Constituents

Constituents are those individuals and groups having such an important interest in the affairs of an enterprise that their views should be taken into account in the strategic planning process. For the typical small business the dominant constituent interest is of course that of the common stockholders. Generally in a very small business the chief executive is also the major common stockholder. At any rate, for such businesses the analysis of box A in Exhibit 8–1 is that of stockholder interest.

For very large corporations there are many constituent interests, aside from those of stockholders, that management considers in strategic planning, such as customers, employees, suppliers, self-appointed consumer and environmentalist advocates, inhabitants of communities in which the company does business, government, and the general public. Larger companies are systematically examining these interests as a prelude to strategic planning. General Electric, for example, examined the demands of fourteen groups of constituents and derived a list of ninety-seven—such as federal chartering of corporations; more stringent effluents/

emissions standards; provision of day-care centers for working mothers; broader representation of interests other than those of the stockholders on boards of directors; disclosure of more information about products; and an end to tax deferrals for offshore profits.[4] These ninety-seven demands were then ranked in terms of their convergence with major domestic trends perceived over the next decade. Some of the trends used in the ranking were increasing affluence, rising level of education, proliferating technology, increasing emphasis on individualism, and growing emphasis on quality of life. A second score was developed from a subjective measure of how much pressure each of fourteen constituent groups might exert for each demand. On this basis the leading potential demands on General Electric over the next decade were determined.[5]

The results of this analysis were summarized into six areas of challenge to companies like General Electric, as follows, in descending order of importance:

1. Constraints on corporate growth—a spectrum of issues ranging from national growth policy through economic controls and environmental protection to questions of antitrust policy and industrial structure.
2. Corporate governance—including matters of accountability, personal liability of managers and directors, board representation, and disclosure of information.
3. Managing the "new work force"—dealing with the growing demands for job enlargement, more flexible scheduling, more equality of opportunity, greater participation, and individualization.
4. External constraints on employee relations—the new pressures from government (employment opportunities, health and safety, "federalization" of benefits), unions (coalition bargaining), and other groups (class action suits, "whistle-blowing").
5. Problems and opportunities of business-government partnership—including a redefinition of the role of the private sector in public problem solving.
6. "Politicizing" of economic decisionmaking—the growing government involvement in corporate decisions through consumerism, environmentalism, industrial reorganization, inflation control, etc.[6]

These conclusions were then injected into the strategic planning process at the very top of General Electric.[7]

Not many large companies have gone about appraising their constituent interests as systematically and continuously as General Electric. Increasingly, however, they are looking at such environmental forces in a more than offhand manner. The assumption here is that the strategic planning process of a large company rests on the fulfilling of its basic socioeconomic responsibilities. Today, those responsibilities include meeting past economic obligations plus some not clearly identified social concerns.

Expectations of People Inside the Company

In very small companies the expectations of people inside the company are dominated by the interests of the owner-manager. As companies grow larger, managements become more sensitive to the interests and values of people in the organization. So far as the planning process is concerned the values and aspirations of the chief executive are of high importance. A chief executive's views with respect to such matters as company mission, ethical standards in business arrangements, geographic location of plants, and company aims are, when articulated, basic premises in the strategic planning process. These are not usually determined by systematic analysis but are decided by the chief executive acting alone or in discussion with others.

Values of other top managers of a company also frequently are significant in planning. In many corporations the top management acts as a team and in such cases the views of these managers are considered carefully in the development of company objectives and strategy. The emergence of such values is generally a gradual development resulting from dialogue, accommodation of diverse views, and compromise.

More and more the interests of others in organizations are being taken into consideration in the planning process. Middle and lower level managers, for example, when asked to define success responded in the following terms, in descending order of importance: achievement of goals (meaning a general reaching of all major aims); self-actualization; harmony among personal, professional, family, and social objectives; making a contribution to a great good; happiness or peace of mind; greater job satisfaction; self-respect and the respect of others; enjoyment in doing or in being; and job and financial security.[8]

Many studies have concluded that the great mass of blue-collar workers are dissatisfied with their jobs and want a variety of things, including more control over their immediate work environment, more prestige, more interaction with co-workers, opportunities to develop their special talents, and job security.[9]

Aside from the details of these managerial and worker interests the fact is that they are changing and companies are considering them in the planning process. They certainly are, when strongly felt, basic premises in planning. General Motors, for example, might well have avoided the disastrous impacts of worker dissatisfaction at its new Lordstown plant several years ago if worker interests had been carefully appraised. This is not to say, of course, that all worker demands should be addressed in the planning process, but the more important ones should be considered as a basic planning premise.

The Data Base: Past Performance

Data about past performance are useful as a base for assessing the present situation and possible developments in the future. If, for example, market share of product A has been declining over the past five years, an appraisal of current performance as being satisfactory is hardly justified should the trend continue. Furthermore, any projected rise in share must be thoroughly justified in light of this trend. Past data also are very useful to those who are not intimately familiar with a product or division in understanding the unit's operations, history, strong points, weak points, and so on.

What is included in the past performance data base should be that which can be gathered without too much cost and which can be helpful in evaluating the present situation and prospects. Generally, relevant performance information of a product division would include:

Sales (dollar and volume)
Operating profit (before taxes)
Cash flow
Depreciation
Capital expenditures
Investment base
Return on investment
Market share

Other types of information that might be included are strengths and weaknesses in marketing, product development, and labor relations; productivity per worker; research and development expenditures; sales volume from new products; short-term debt; and long-term debt in relation to stockholder equity.

The Data Base: Current Situation

The volume of data in this part of the data base is understandably much greater than that concerned with past performance. Included should be anything that management wishes to measure as being important in appraising the present situation of the company. Basically, the data about the current situation should include:

Analysis of customers and markets
Resources of the company
Competition
Environmental setting
Other measures of performance or areas of interest

What is included in these groupings is a matter of individual company and managerial choice. The approach of most companies is, first, to identify that which appears to be of significance in a current appraisal and then try to hold the volume of work involved in getting it to a reasonable level. Some companies provide forms for divisions and planning units to report this information. Others ask pertinent questions and allow the divisions to report the information as they see fit. Both these approaches will be illustrated here. Before illustrating different approaches, however, some discussion of the content of the categories of data noted in the preceding list may be useful.

ANALYSIS OF CUSTOMERS AND MARKETS

Most managers would agree with Peter Drucker: "The customer defines the business. A business is not defined by the company's name, statutes, or articles of incorporation. It is defined by the want the customer satisfies when he buys a product or a service."[10] In this light it is appropriate to begin the analysis of the current situation in the data base with customers. Such questions as the following about customers would seem to deserve answers:

Who are our customers?
In what markets do we find our customers?
How are customers geographically distributed?
How are customers classified in terms of volume?
How many are repeat sales?
How do we compare with the industry average with respect to repeat sales, customer volume concentration, geographic distribution, and so on?
How do our customers perceive us in terms of product quality, service, price, and so on?
May any of our customers decide to produce our product for their own use?
Is our market start-up, growth, mature, or declining?
Is technology in the market dynamic or static?
What is the market potential for our products?
What share of the market do we now have?
Is the market highly seasonal? Cyclical?

Of course, key questions about customers and markets will depend on many considerations, such as whether a producer makes components or end products, frequency of customer purchase, whether the product price is high or low, whether customer behavior is stable or changeable, and whether the market is growing or declining.

RESOURCES OF THE COMPANY

Major resources that might be studied in the current situation appraisal would include:

Financial resources
   Profits
   Sales
   Debt
   Cash flow

Resource use efficiencies
   Sales per employee
   Profits per employee

    Investment per employee
    Plant utilization
    Use of employee skills

Employee evaluation
    Skills
    Productivity
    Turnover
    Ethnic and racial composition

Facilities
    Major production units
    Rated capacity
    Modernization rating

Inventories
    Raw materials
    Finished products
    Percent obsolete

Environmental situation
    Conformance with pollution laws
    Conformance with safety regulations
    Public image

Marketing and distribution system
    Number of salespersons
    Sales per salesperson
    Independent distributors
    Exclusive distributors

New product development
    Research and development expenditures
    New products to be introduced

Managerial performance
    Leadership capabilities
    Planning
    Development of personnel
    Delegation

In the accompanying exhibits are some approaches used in developing information about the current situation. In Exhibit 8–2 is a series of questions suggested for a small firm. Exhibit 8–3 is another set of questions. Exhibit 8–4 is a form that may be used to evaluate the current situation with respect to categories of information considered important by the company. The general profile produced when evaluations are made will give a quick picture of how well things are going. Exhibit 8–5 is a more traditional reporting form. The unique feature of the form is that it asks for stage of product life cycle and requires information about products that makes evaluation of past performance and cross-product comparison easy.

COMPETITION

The better understanding a company has about its competition the more likely it will avoid surprises and keep ahead of the competition. The focus should be on competition in the industry in general and specific competitors in particular. The following list presents questions that might be raised about competition in an industry:

Is the market dominated by one, two, or three competitors?

Is competition in the industry predominantly from many small competitors?

Who are our most important competitors?

Is entrance into the market easy or difficult for new competitors?

Is competition in the industry predominantly price? service? quality? performance? technological innovation? image?

So far as individual competitors are concerned, questions such as those given in Exhibit 8–6 might be raised. This list could easily be expanded. For instance, how much capital does our major competitor have for new product development? How "hungry" is our competition? What are new product potentialities of our competitors? If a simple form like Exhibit 8–6 is completed by knowledgeable managers and staff it is surprising what one may learn about the competition.

ENVIRONMENTAL SETTING

There are, of course, many environmental forces that can have an important influence on the operations of a company. The more significant categories of such environmental forces are:

Economic
   Gross national product, interest rates, inflation, employment, factory output, electric production

Demographic
   Fertility rates, infant mortality, population growth at home
   and abroad, population by age distribution, population
   growth by region

Social
   Consumer demands, environmentalist pressures (in this category the types of analysis mentioned in connection with
   constituent demands can be included)

Political
   Hostile or favorable local, state, or federal political climate
   Relative power of company in the political arena
   Government regulatory pressures

Technological
   Trends in new technologies, impact of new technology on
   market structures and production techniques

Legal
   Legal liabilities past, present, and future

Products-Services (P-S)
   What are the P-S for which customers come to us?
   What are the most distinctive P-S we offer?
   What are the new P-S? The fading P-S?
   What are our plans for developing new P-S?
   How do we compare with competitors?
   What economic (value added) factor do we provide?
   What are the most profitable P-S we offer? The least profitable?

Customers
   What business do we do with what customers at what profitability and
      investment?
   What markets do we now serve?
   What new markets should we serve?
   How do our customers see us?
   What do they think we do well or poorly?

Prices
   How are our prices set?
   When were they last reviewed?
   How do they compare competitively?

Facilities (Plant and Equipment)
Do we have the facilities we need?
Do we know what is available in the industry?
Do we have controls over productivity? Over obsolescence?

Finance
What is our flexibility for growth? For recession?
What sources of funds do we use? What sources should we use?
What risks are we exposed to?
What controls do we have over cash, receivables, inventories, debt?
What controls should we have?

Information
What are our sources of information as to what's going on in the outside world?
What action do we take with the information we have?
What action would we take with additional information?
Do we know its cost-effectiveness ratio?
Where do we stand in relation to computerization?
Do we have adequate input from external sources?

Decision Making
What decisions are critical to our business?
Who makes what decisions on what bases? (a key question)

Profitability
How do we compare with the industry? With our own best period?

Are our decisions based on adequate information?
How can our decision making be improved?

People
What do we know about our present management and technical staff in terms
   of age, skills, potential, turnover, and retirement?
How does our fringe benefit program compare with that of other firms? With
   the expectations of our staff?
How do our people feel about the company? About its prospects? About their
   own future?

Dangers
What would we do if substantial changes took place in our products-services;
   customers; competitors; key staff; location-environment; sources of supply?

EXHIBIT 8–2: The Situation Audit: Questions for a Small Firm's Planning Activity (Each question should be answered in light of the firm's strengths and weaknesses). (Source: Theodore Cohn and Roy A. Lindberg, *Survival and Growth: Management Strategies for the Small Firm*, (New York: AMACOM, 1974), pp. 52–53.)

To evoke more substantial contributions to the planning process from the heads of the nine groups making up an industrial and consumer products company, a few years ago the firm's director of planning and market research prepared for the president a *list of 18 questions that group heads were to answer. The president pared the list to the nine set forth below.*

1. What steps can be taken to minimize effects of annual business cycles upon your profitability?

2. If you were to ignore the cost of entry, what new venture, new market or new product line would you recommend entering, and why?

When you fully consider entry price, how does your answer change?

3. Are there competitive patents expiring which enable you to take action previously denied to your group?

Are there new competitive patents issuing or likely to issue which appear to offer you problems? If so, are you considering requesting a license?

Are there company patents expiring in the five-year plan period which open doors for competitive action previously limited by our patent position?

4. As you ponder your competition and what action from each important competition you might anticipate, what actions do you believe might occur in the next three years which would either hurt you or help you?
- New technology or new product introductions?
- Marketing programs or policies?
- Pricing policies or practices?

5. Put yourself in your competitor's shoes. What market or product area in your group would you attack as the most vulnerable, and why? If you conclude that more than one warrants mention, do so.

6. What additional information or "intelligence" about your industry, competition, customers, trends, etc., would help your group be more effective in strategic or tactical planning?

If it might be possible to obtain any such information or intelligence from an outside source (Arthur D. Little, Stanford Research Institute, etc.), how much would you be willing to pay for it?

7. Consider the product life cycle as it applies to your key products.

Which do you identify as on the downgrade toward phasing out? Will any go out in the next three years?

Which do you identify as mature but still strong? Do they appear to be likely to remain for at least three more years?

Which do you identify as successfully introduced and on the upgrade toward a strong position in your industry? Are they enough to replace those in the first group?

Which you have recently introduced or are about to introduce which offer yet unproved promise?

8. In your opinion, are there unexploited opportunities for us to make more effective use of total division or total corporate strengths? If so, please describe.

9. Given freedom of action, would you increase your R&D budget beyond present levels? If so, how much and for what?

How about marketing?

If you did either of the above, how long would it take for results to show in increased profit and R.O.A.? One year? Two?

EXHIBIT 8–3: The Situation Audit: An Excercise in Strategic Thinking. (Source: James K. Brown and Rochelle O'Connor, *Planning and the Corporate Planning Director*, Report No. 627 (New York, 1974), p. 10.)

Instructions:

Evaluate for each item, as appropriate, on the basis of the following criteria:

I   Superior. Better than anyone else. Beyond present need.
II Better than average. Suitable performance. No problems.
III Average. Acceptable. Equal to competition. Not good, not bad.
IV Problems here. Not as good as it should be. Deteriorating. Must be improved.
V   Real cause for concern. Situation bad. Crisis. Must take action to improve.

Category	I	II	III	IV	V
Finance					
Acid test					
Current ratio					
Debt-equity ratio					
Inventory turnover					
Margin					
Sales per employee					
Etc.					
Production					
Capacity					
Labor productivity					
Plant location					
Degree of obsolescence					
Quality control					
Etc.					
Organization & Administration					
Ratio staff to line managers					
Quality of staff					
Quality of middle managers					
Management turnover					
Communications					
Etc.					
Marketing					
Share of market					
Product reputation					
Product line					
Advertising efficiency					
Consumer complaints					
Etc.					
Manpower					
Management succession					
Quality of skilled workers					
Quality of salesmen					
Etc.					
Technology					
Product					
R&D capabilities					
Etc.					

EXHIBIT 8–4:   The Situation Audit. (Source: Adapted from Meritt L. Kastens, *Long-Range Planning for Your Business* (New York, AMACOM, 1976), pp. 52–53.)

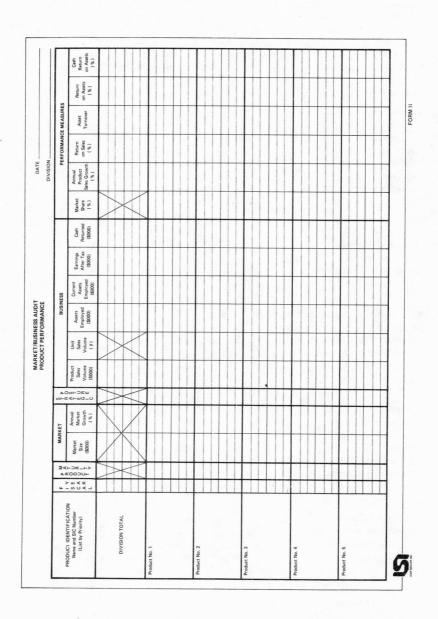

EXHIBIT 8-5: Market/Business Audit; Product Performance. (Used with permission of Lear Siegler, Inc.)

ITEM	COMPETITORS			
	A	B	C	D
Name				
Estimated Sales ($000)				
Estimated Share of Market				
Price Advantage*				
Quality Advantage*				
Technology Base*				
Sales Force Base*				
Distribution Advantage*				
Cost Advantage*				
Overall:				
Standing in industry (today)*				
Standing in industry (next year)*				
Seriousness of competition (today)*				
Seriousness of competition (next year)*				
Seriousness of competition (two years ahead)*				
Anything special to which we must react?				
Soon				
Next year				
Longer range threat				

*Evaluate on the following scale: 1 = great, highest, best; 2 = above average; 3 = average; 4 = below average; 5 = worst, no threat, very poor.

EXHIBIT 8–6. Evaluation of Competitors.

OTHER MEASURES OF PERFORMANCE OR
AREAS OF INTEREST

Additional factors to consider are union relationships, creative climate in the organization, relationships of company executives and employees to the communities in which plants are located, the strategic planning process, and control mechanisms.

The Data Base: Forecasts

Not many years ago all of the forecasts that were made to facilitate strategic planning were economic. They generally focused on environmental-economic factors directly related to the company such as consumer disposable income, wage rates, productivity of employees, general economic conditions, and changes in the consumer price index. They also were concerned with company economic trends, primarily forecasts of sales, market share, available manpower, and so on.

Today, many companies make additional forecasts. Technology is a source of great opportunity as well as significant potential threat to many companies. To such companies technological forecasts are essential. Already mentioned are forecasts of changing social attitudes of people, which may have an impact on a company. Some companies are now making forecasts of potential changes in federal, state, and local regulations. These are in the realm of political forecasts. Forecasts of what competitors are likely to do would seem quite appropriate in a situation audit. Depending upon the special interests of a company there are other types of forecasts that may be made, such as changes in the socioeconomic-political conditions of foreign countries in which the company does or is interested in doing business, demographic forecasts, forecasts of a changing legal environment, forecasts of military procurement, and forecasts of special markets such as medicine.

There are three key issues in forecasting. The first concerns the identification of factors to forecast. Here we can discern three categories. The core is composed of those factors of clear and immediate concern to the company, such as a forecast of product sales. Next are forces (such as changing social values) that may not be recognizable as having a direct impact on the company but that may indeed be doing so. The outer layer of forces are those whose future impact is difficult to foretell. They should be monitored, but how much? The second issue is whether or not the forecast can readily be acquired from a source available to the company. Third is what forecasting methodology should be used to make the forecast if the company decides to take on this task.

Many forecasts are useful to a company in making a situation audit but great accuracy may not be required. In such instances forecasts made by reputable individuals and agencies may be used at little or no cost. In this category, for example, are gross national product, wage rates, price inflation, and demographic changes. In some cases there may be no ready-made forecast, or the company may wish to make its own rigorous analysis; for example, in determining the future demands for energy of a local utility, the future demands for military products of interest to an aerospace industry, or the changes in consumer tastes affecting purchases of automobiles, which would be of direct concern to an automobile manufacturer. Most companies prefer to make their own forecasts of their own products. A company's sales forecasts should be made in light of general economic and industry conditions, but some companies (larger ones excepted) that forecast their own sales do not follow this rule.

When a company decides to make its own forecasts the question of methodology immediately arises. Space does not permit even a listing of different forecasting techniques let alone examination of them. There are, however, a few guidelines that managers might consider in deciding on forecasting methodology.

First, there is a good bit of easily read, nontechnical literature about different forecasting methods for managers who may be interested.[11]

Second, managers should not take forecasts from staff or other managers on faith. They should expect a clear, brief statement of assumptions underlying a forecast and the methods used to make it. When a manager knows the assumptions used in a forecast it will be easier to develop mentally a modified forecast if the assumptions are not acceptable. Furthermore, the basic methodology used in developing a forecast should be understood by the manager. Fore-

casts should not be loaded with excessive details about methodology, especially if the details involve a language foreign to the
manager.

Third, managers should demand forecasts that are not too qual-
ified. If a forecast is to be used to make decisions upon which basis
internal resource allocations are to be made, managers must have
forecasts that are precise in time and quantity. On the other hand,
long-range forecasts of, say, evolving social attitudes or population
shifts or political conditions in a particular country do not need to
be precise. Trends are much more important than precise numbers.

Fourth, the system of forecasting and any particular forecast
should be economical. Forecasting can be very costly and the
cost-benefit equation requires constant attention.

Fifth, managers must understand that a forecasting method that
has produced accurate results in the past may suddenly fail. Furthermore, an expert forecaster who has had high marks in accurate
forecasting may suddenly produce a very inaccurate forecast.
There are few if any coming events that are important to a company, whether internal or external, that can be predicted precisely.
Generally speaking, however, the more managers and their staffs
work on forecasting the more accurate they will likely be in their
projections.

The WOTS UP Analysis

As noted previously WOTS UP is an acronym for the weaknesses, opportunities, threats and strengths underlying planning
(see the F block of Exhibit 8–1).

USE OF THE RESULTS OF THE ANALYSIS

The situation audit, if done with reasonable attention, should
produce an accurate list of weaknesses, opportunities, threats, and
strengths. As noted in Exhibit 8–1 this information is very useful in
revising missions and purposes, setting tentative long-range objectives, and devising program strategies. As shown in Exhibit 8–7 a
WOTS UP analysis suggests strategies. Once strategies are iden-

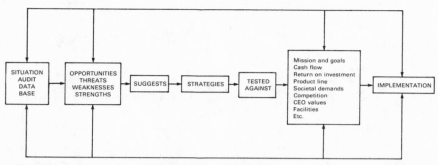

EXHIBIT 8–7: The WOTS UP Analysis Suggest and Evaluates Strategies. (Source: Adapted from George A. Steiner and John B. Miner, *Management Policy and Strategy: Text, Reading, and Cases* (New York: Macmillan, 1977, p. 189.)

tified they must be evaluated on the basis of various criteria; a considerable body of the evaluation data will have been developed in the WOTS UP analysis.

So significant is this step in the planning process that some companies begin strategic planning with a WOTS UP analysis. One company for a number of years has used the form shown in Exhibit 8–8 as a first step in the planning process. Each manager is asked to complete as many forms as desired. The forms are then collected and sorted into groups, such as product related, marketing related, and finance related. Then managers are organized into teams to evaluate the forms. From the results of these deliberations the company identifies the most outstanding opportunities and the most serious threats that it appears to be facing and develops alternative courses of action to deal with them, depending upon its own strengths and weaknesses. This type of procedure does not need to rest on a systematic situation audit, as discussed earlier.

There are variations of this approach. I have seen companies get started with strategic planning by having a meeting of top executives who spend several days identifying what they perceive to be weaknesses, strengths, opportunities, and threats, after which a few strategies are selected for implementation. In the better developed systems formality in staff preparation of data should parallel and strengthen this type of managerial assessment.

The results of the WOTS UP analysis can be presented very simply, as shown in Exhibit 8–9.

```
┌─────────────────────────────────────────────────────────────┐
│                 WOTS UP PLANNING ISSUES                       │
│                                         ISSUE NO.____         │
│                                                               │
│       OPPORTUNITY  [   ]          STRENGTH  [   ]             │
│                                                               │
│         THREAT  [   ]             WEAKNESS  [   ]             │
├─────────────────────────────────────────────────────────────┤
│  STATEMENT OF ISSUE                                           │
│                                                               │
│                                                               │
│                                                               │
│                                                               │
│                                                               │
├─────────────────────────────────────────────────────────────┤
│  OBSERVATION BASED ON                                         │
│                                                               │
│                                                               │
│                                                               │
│                                                               │
├─────────────────────────────────────────────────────────────┤
│  WE SHOULD                                                    │
│                                                               │
│                                                               │
│                                                               │
│                                                               │
└─────────────────────────────────────────────────────────────┘
```

EXHIBIT 8–8: (Source: George A. Steiner and John B. Miner, *Management Policy and Strategy: Text, Readings, and Cases* (New York: Macmillan, 1977, p. 386–388.)

PROBLEMS WITH THE ANALYSIS

The WOTS UP analysis appears to be a simple and straightforward process but it may encounter problems, for example, in the measure used to determine whether or not there is a strength, a

I. WEAKNESSES

Factor	Strategic Implication
(1) Managerial	(1) Managerial
(a) We have six different products and continue with a centralized organization that is not working well.	(a) Decentralize
(b) Too many middle managers have a poor performance rating.	(b) i. In acquiring companies insist on strong management.
	ii. Begin management development program.
(2) Markets and Products	(2) Markets and Products
(a) Product A is losing market share because it is becoming obsolete.	(a) Redesign product A.
(b) One customer buys 50% of product B.	(b) Find new markets for product B to reduce reliance on one customer.

II. STRENGTHS

(1) Managerial	(1) Managerial
(a) Strong research and development group.	(a) Rely on in-house product development as well as acquisition for expansion.
(2) Markets and Products	(2) Markets and Products
(a) Product C has a growing share in a growing market.	(a) Invest to expand market share and increase return on investment.

III. THREATS

Factor	Strategic Implication
(1) Competition	(1) Competition
(a) New government safety standards are likely at plant B and cannot be met easily.	(a) Begin now to devise methods to meet the standards to avoid a shutdown.
(2) Facilities	(2) Facilities
(a) Chile threatens to nationalize and expropriate our plants.	(a) Begin negotiations with the U.S. State Department and the government of Chile.

IV. OPPORTUNITIES

(1) Markets and Products	(1) Markets and Products
(a) Strong growth is forecast for product D in South America.	(a) Prepare studies as to whether we should build plants, export, or license in South America.
(2) Finance	(2) Finance
(a) We have a strong cash position, low debt/equity ratio, and a high price/earnings ratio.	(a) Search for new acquisitions.

EXHIBIT 8–9. One Way to Summarize a WOTS UP Analysis.

weakness, an opportunity, or a threat. In Exhibit 8–4, for instance, several measures are used in the ratings. Measurement against competition stands out but some of the evaluations are purely subjective with the measure not clear. To illustrate the problem: One measure of a weakness or a strength can be past performance of the company. Performance compared with that of competitors is an important measure, but there are others, such as consultants' opinions, normative judgments based on management's understanding of the standard criteria in the literature, personal opinions, or special targets of accomplishment (e.g., budgets).[12]

In appraising opportunities other standards may be applied such as value in achievement of some purposes of the company, potential profit impact, possible cost reduction, or fit with top management's interests.

Threats can be evaluated in these terms plus others; for instance, managerial problems growing out of government regulations or consumer attitudes, technological developments that have an impact on the company's products and research and development programs, managerial problems arising from the possibility that a few key managers may leave, or production difficulties arising from potential raw material shortages.

To achieve a consensus in light of such different measures is not easy. Agreement is made more difficult by the fact that managers at different levels inevitably come to different conclusions even if the same measure is used. For example, a division manager may see a significant profit opportunity in producing product A. A group vice-president may see an even greater opportunity in putting the same capital in product B in a different division and, as a result, denying capital for product A.

Another problem exists in mental barriers of people searching for weaknesses that may be associated with them or their departments. In watching planning processes I have seen many times a myopia grip managers when their own shortcomings were at issue.

Finally, irrespective of the measure used the degree of strength or weakness or opportunity or threat may vary much among managers and staff. For instance, there may be agreement that increasing difficulties will arise in acquiring raw materials but there may be great disagreement about the probability of the threat and the availability of alternatives to counter it. Or, an opportunity to increase business in a foreign country may be seen as real by all managers but there may be much disagreement about just how attractive the opportunity really is.

Summary

The assessment of past performance and current and future environmental factors (internal and external) is an important step in the planning process. This step can be performed by managers making their own individual assessments without any formal process. Their observations are likely to be strengthened, however, with some formalization of the situation audit.

There is no standard format for a situation audit. It will vary from company to company.

The situation audit has a number of purposes; for example, to help management identify and analyze the more significant forces in the environment for the company, to systematize the environmental evaluation process for better results, to provide a forum for sharing divergent views about the changing environment, to firm up vague opinions about the evolving environment, to stimulate creative thinking, and to provide a base for continuing the strategic planning process.

In line with planning models discussed previously, the first step in the situation audit is an examination of expectations or interests of constituents outside the company. The second is to understand the interests of managers and employees within the company. As companies grow larger the more important are these constituent interests in the planning process. For both large and small companies, however, the interests of the chief executive officer are of paramount significance in planning.

Next is the data base, which is composed of information about past performance, the current situation, and the future. The range of data that might be collected in this area is very wide. Managers must choose what is to be studied and how deeply each factor is to be analyzed. The types of information included in this section and approaches to developing them are illustrated in the chapter.

From this information the situation audit proceeds to the WOTS UP analysis, or the identification of weaknesses, opportunities, threats, and strengths underlying planning. Illustrations were given of how the WOTS UP analysis is used in planning and the forms in which the results are prepared.

The chapter concluded with some observations about difficulties in conducting a situation audit. Although the basic concept is simple, a number of problems appear when doing such an audit. Thus, how does management determine what measure is to be used in the evaluation of weaknesses, strengths, opportunities, and threats? Also, managers at different levels may consider the same factor and use the same measurement but come to different conclusions. Finally, managers may accept the reality of an opportunity or a threat but give them different probabilities or appraise their importance very differently.

9 Developing Basic Business Purposes and Missions

One of the most important responsibilities of top management is to formulate the basic purposes and missions of the company. As Peter Drucker put it, management must decide: "What is our business and what should it be?"[1] It must not only identify lines of business and markets served but also determine how the business will operate. This task requires nothing short of thinking through and spelling out, as Drucker has said, the "theory of the business."

This might sound a bit abstract but it is one of the most pragmatic tasks a top executive can perform. It is only upon the foundation of the basic purposes and missions of the company that more detailed objectives, strategies, and tactical plans can be worked out.

The Network of Business Aims

Basic business purposes and missions are the foundation for a network of aims in a business. There is no uniformity in the structure of the network of aims found in business. What is included or excluded, how the aims are ordered, and how they relate vary from company to company and from time to time in the same company.

It is convenient to view the network of business aims as a

pyramid, as shown in Exhibit 9–1. The number of statements associated with each segment tends to increase as the pyramid is descended.[2] Thus, statements about basic purposes and missions are normally short. Specification of short-term goals, at the other extreme, tends to be lengthy. At the top of the pyramid, statements tend to be general, broad, and fairly abstract. The lower in the pyramid, the greater the concreteness and specificity of aims. For small companies statements of aims frequently do not exist in written form, especially for missions and purposes; when written they tend to be only for short-range goals and then for but a few such as cash, production, and employment. As companies grow in size, the list of aims tends to grow and to be written.

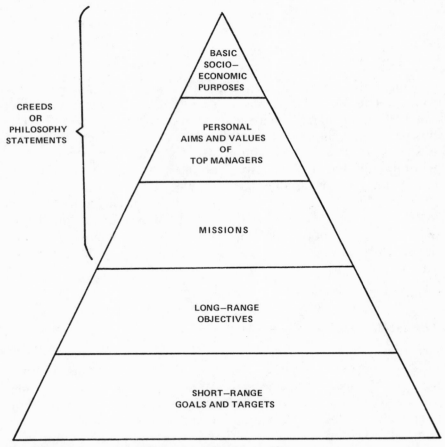

EXHIBIT 9–1:   The Network of Business Aims.

In the literature as well as in the practice of business aims there exists a paradox. On the one hand, there is recognition of the importance of aims. On the other, not many companies have well-structured networks of aims and those that do are generally not fully satisfied with them. The explanation of this paradox is simple: Developing a suitable network of aims is extremely complex; it is an area in which oversimplification has retarded better understanding; and it is unique for each business since it combines value judgments of managers with other elements of organizational operations.

Company Creed or Philosophy Statements

In recent years there has been a rapid increase in publicized statements of company purposes and missions. The documents are called creeds, policies, strategies, company purposes, philosophies, and, by their more critical observers, public relations beguilements. These statements generally express the basic purposes of a company and the beliefs of the chief executives. There is no uniformity in their content but the more complete ones generally include statements associated with the first three tiers in Exhibit 9–1,[3] as briefly explained in Exhibit 9–2.

Although it may be true that many written creeds or philosophies are designed to improve the public image of a company, they can be, and often are, the cornerstone of a company's direction and method of operation. Thomas Watson, Jr., chairman of IBM, emphasized the importance of company philosophy as follows:

> This then is my thesis: I firmly believe that any organization, in order to survive and achieve success, must have a sound set of beliefs on which it premises all its policies and actions.
>
> Next, I believe that the most important single factor in corporate success is faithful adherence to those beliefs. . . .
>
> In other words, the basic philosophy, spirit, and drive of an organization have far more to do with its relative achievements than do technological or economic resources, organizational structrue, innovation and timing. All these things weigh heavily on success. But they are, I think, transcended by how strongly the people in the organization believe in its basic precepts and how faithfully they carry them out.[4]

ITEM	PURPOSE OR VALUE STATED OR SOUGHT
Business mission	State thrust or grand design State market and product lines of business
Profitability	Dedication to profits
Interests to be satisfied and balanced	Devotion to public interest Devotion to interest of stockholders, employees, suppliers, and community
Quality	Seek high quality in products Stimulate high quality in management and employees
Efficiency	Seek low cost, high productivity
Atmosphere of enterprise	Good place for people to work Good company in which to invest Good company from which to buy
Observance of codes of conduct	Honesty Integrity Opportunity Leadership Fairness in all dealings Teamwork Development of employees Open opportunity for employees Preserve private enterprise system Be a good citizen Duty and loyalty Religious devotion

EXHIBIT 9–2. Brief Illustrative Resume of Table of Contents of a Company's Creed Statement. (Source: Adapted from George A. Steiner, *Top Management Planning* (New York: Macmillan, 1969), p. 145.)

What is included in the typical creed or philosophy statement rests significantly on the precepts, values, aspirations, and commitments of the chief executive of a business. The assumption of socioeconomic purposes and the determination of missions, for example, clearly may be based on or determined by the personal aims and values of top management. These groups of aims interrelate and overlap and, depending upon how they are stated, may be indistinguishable one from another.

Fundamental Socioeconomic Purposes

Enterprises are not isolated from the society of which they are a part. They are creatures of it and are nurtured and supported by it to accomplish specific purposes. They will survive only so long as they satisfy these purposes. One of the paramount purposes of organized business is to use economic resources efficiently in satisfying consumer wants. Implicit in fulfilling this purpose is the view that the more efficiently a business satisfies consumer wants at the right price, the higher will be the profit. Profit is a powerful motivation in the efficient use of resources. A fundamental purpose, therefore, for any business is to seek profit through effective and efficient use of resources.

A surprising number of company statements of basic purpose do not put profitability first. Some do not mention profit. But, whether mentioned or not it is implicit in company basic purposes. The profitability aim can take many forms:

> "Our purpose is to create profits sufficient to maintain the health and growth of the company."
>
> "The aim is to optimize profits."
>
> "A basic purpose of [our company] is to provide a high and growing record of earnings per share."
>
> "Our basic objective is to earn and pay dividends to our stockholders and to safeguard their investment."

Today society is demanding that larger corporations, particularly, continue to pursue this economic function but at the same time also undertake social programs to help society improve the quality of life. There is no consensus on what improving the quality of life means or whether it is something that corporations should address. Nevertheless, many large corporations do recognize this social demand in basic statements of purpose.

> "We believe in being a good corporate citizen."
>
> "We believe it is our responsibility to be a good neighbor by supporting community projects that will benefit the community."
>
> "We will constantly strive for good public relations by assuming our full share of responsibility in the communities in

which we operate. It is our duty to conduct our business so that society benefits by our activities."

"We recognize and will appropriately discharge our responsibilities for the welfare of our employees, the communities in which we do business, and society as a whole."

Basic purposes can be expressed in other ways, reflecting the personal interests of the top executives of a company:

"Our aim is to be the leading company in our industry satisfying in the highest technical sense the national security needs of the United States and its allies in space, air, land, and sea."

"We believe the first obligation of the company and the employees is to supply the public with the best modern utility service at reasonable rates."

Basic purposes can also include aims for management practices, such as the following:

"Our executives must be persons of talent, education, experience, and ability. They must be persons of common sense and understanding."

"We believe individuals should be rewarded according to performance and that to the fullest extent possible promotions should be made within the company."

Creeds and philosophies have always included observance of various ethical codes but this aspect of company purpose has been accentuated in recent years following the Watergate and foreign payoff scandals. Exhibit 9–2 identifies different groups of codes. The following are typical statements:

"We believe our individual and company relationships should be conducted on the basis of the highest standards of conduct and ethics."

"We believe in the application of the Golden Rule in all our dealings."

"We believe the success of our business depends upon the character and integrity of the people working in it."

Personal aims of top managers are, as said before, reflected in statements of basic purposes and missions. So important is a personal aim, however, that it deserves separate classification. Personal aims of top executives even though not always expressed orally or in written form may be and usually are powerful motivating forces to the top management and others in the organization who understand them. For example, a chief executive may have a personal aim of becoming financially independent at a particular time. The CEO's aim may be to build the largest company in the industry. It may be to have a better performance than the previous chairman with respect to sales, assets, profits, employees, or worldwide operations. It may be to build an organization in which the chief executive can satisfy his creative urge and talents.

Basic Missions

Mission statements identify the underlying design, aim, or thrust of a company. They may be expressed at different levels of abstraction. For example, they may be expressed as a grand design such as "Our business is service," which was for a long time the dominant expressed aim of American Telephone and Telegraph Company. Another is Du Pont's "Better things for better living through chemistry." When Vincent Learson was president of IBM his expressed grand mission was worded thus: "Our goal is simply stated. We want to be the best service organization in the world."[5] Voiced in this way such aims can be considered basic purposes or philosophies. They also may be considered public relations and/or advertising slogans. When taken seriously by management, however, they can be very significant. There are many people, for example, who believe that the grand design voiced by Learson was a primary reason for the great success of IBM.

Missions tend to be stated in product and market terms. For example, "Maintain a viable, growing business by developing, producing, and marketing engineered products and services to satisfy selected needs of utility, construction, and manufacturing industries."

Missions should be stated at least in both product and market terms. The reason is that specification of a product line of business without designation of market may result in too wide a mission scope. For example, to say that "we are manufacturers of airplanes" is virtually meaningless. A firm is in a very different business if it is a producer of commercial planes as compared with general aviation airplanes, or toy airplanes, or fighter aircraft. There is much more directive power to linking products and markets, such as "We are manufacturers of air conditioners for transportation vehicles."

Some companies ask their divisions to prepare mission statements with more content than this. Pillsbury, for instance, asks its divisions to prepare "charter" statements that include product and market, distribution systems, processing systems and technologies, relationships with other Pillsbury businesses, and anything unique about the division's business.

IMPORTANCE OF MISSION STATEMENTS

Mission statements, aside from providing general guides for strategic planning, have specific relevance to the formulation of program strategies and the nature of a business. Mission statements determine the competitive arena in which a business operates. They determine how resources will be allocated to different demands. They determine the size of the company. They make much easier the task of identifying the opportunities and threats that must be addressed in the planning process. They open up new opportunities, as well as new threats, when changed. They prevent people from "spinning their wheels" in working on strategies and plans that may be considered completely inappropriate by top management.

If devised appropriately, missions or revisions of missions can turn a company around. To illustrate from the past, I am convinced that the Baldwin Locomotive Works would still be alive and strong today had it said that its mission was to make tractive power for railroads, instead of steam locomotives. Buggy whip manufacturers might still be around if they had said their business was not making buggy whips but self-starters for carriages!

The D. H. Baldwin Company was a manufacturer of pianos from the 1890s to the 1960s. As a result of growing competition, especially from Japan, the company found itself in trouble. It discovered, however, that one lucrative part of its business was financing retail sales. This led the company to look at financial institutions as a new line of business. In 1968 it bought Empire Savings, Building & Loan Association, based in Denver. Today

D. H. Baldwin is "a multibank music company"—and very prosperous. More specifically, its mission reads:

> D. H. Baldwin Company is a diversified financial services holding company, with financial subsidiaries engaged in banking, savings and loan and insurance activities, and non-financial subsidiaries engaged in the manufacturing and merchandising of musical instruments.[6]

On the other hand, some companies have changed their missions with disastrous results. Two giant corporations that altered their basic missions to include computers were General Electric and RCA, both of which eventually retreated after substantial losses. Rohr Industries was a profitable company making ready-to-install aircraft engine pods. In the late 1960s the company decided to make rail cars for the San Francisco Bay Area Rapid Transit System and in 1972 it won a contract to build cars for the Washington Metropolitan Area Transit Authority. Both ventures were disasters and Rohr changed its mission again to eliminate these products and markets.

Two companies that faced the same environmental change but developed different missions to adjust to it are Gerber Products and Johnson & Johnson. For years Gerber Products said, "Babies are our only business." Then around 1972 it took a look at the projected baby population, which was destined to level off and decline, and said that "babies are our business." The company then proceeded to sell new products and services, such as baby clothing and insurance, to its old markets. Eventually the slogan was eliminated entirely. Johnson & Johnson, faced with the same environmental change, adopted a different strategy. It began to sell baby products to the adult population, who had used its products as babies.

WHAT IS THE RIGHT MISSION?

Whether a chosen mission is "right" or not can only be determined after the decision is made. The determination of a mission is based on judgment. As Vickers said: "The value judgments of men and societies cannot be *proved* correct or incorrect; they can only be *approved* as right or *condemned* as wrong by the exercise of another value judgment."[7] Sometimes it may appear that facts "dictate" the logic of a mission but there is no way to be certain the conclusion is "right" or "wrong" until after the fact. Rohr's mission change seemed logical at the time but events proved the change to be wrong.

Another case of misguided mission change was that of White Motor Corporation. In the mid-1950s White was a successful producer of heavy trucks. It was fearful of a takeover since its stock was selling at between $13 and $14 per share while the book value was $56. The company decided the best way to avoid being swallowed was to swallow. This led to an acquisition program that in the early 1970s led almost to bankruptcy. If the company had managed its acquisitions better, however, the change in mission might have been successful.

HOW ARE MISSIONS FORMULATED?

There is no standard approach to the formulation of missions. Mission statements are highly dependent on the values of the chief executive officer, however, and a mission statement is not likely to be changed without the direct intervention of the CEO.

Sometimes a mission change is the result of a great deal of conversation among top executives of a company. This was certainly the case with the decision to produce the L-1011. Following a disastrous experience with the Electra in the 1950s the Lockheed Aircraft Corporation completely eliminated a commercial airliner from its basic mission. The company had no written mission but the mission was generally understood by managers and did not include a commercial airliner. Then in the 1960s the company decided to produce a commercial, wide-bodied jet airliner, the L-1011. This change was made only after a great deal of discussion at the top and a final decision by the chief executive officer to go ahead.

When James McFarland became chief executive officer of General Mills he said:

> I asked myself what was expected of me as CEO. I decided that my role was really to build General Mills from a good into a great company. But I realized this was not just up to me. I wanted a collective viewpoint as to what makes a company great. Consequently, we took some thirty-five top people away for three days to decide what it took to move the company from "goodness" to

"greatness." Working in groups of six to eight, we defined the characteristics of a great company from various points of view, what our shortcomings were, and how we might overcome these.

Next, charters for specific divisions and groups were written in light of that meeting. They became the guidelines for a very successful company.[8]

In small organizations the CEO can and often does establish basic missions without much reference to others. Top managers of larger organizations, except in unusual instances, do not find this the best approach. Changing a mission or basic purposes in any significant way will likely necessitate major changes in the organization's operations, the interrelationships of people, the way in which people use their skills, and so on. Hence, precipitous changes, unless made in response to a crisis, are less likely to be successful than those that are gradually worked out by extended discussion.

After interviewing 100 top managers Brian Quinn suggested that managing significant changes is best done on an incremental basis. He found that in practice executives followed a sequence of steps. First, they recognized a need for change. Second, they sought to encourage the organization to acknowledge this need by commissioning study groups, staff members, or consultants to examine problems, options, contingencies, or opportunities posed by the sensed need. Third, they tried to broaden support through unstructured discussions, probing of positions, definition of differences of opinion, encouraging concepts favored by the chief executive, discouraging ideas not favored by top management, and so on. Fourth, they created pockets of commitment by building necessary skills or technologies within the organization, testing options, and taking opportunities to make decisions to build support. Fifth, they established a clear focus either by creating an ad hoc committee to formulate a position or by expressing specific ends that top management desired. Sixth, they obtained real commitment by assigning someone who would champion the goal and be accountable for its accomplishment. This last step can be expanded, for example, by including specific commitments in budgets and by making short-range operating plans.

Finally, the chief executive must insure that the organization is capable of responding to new opportunities and threats; in other words, that once a decision is made, the firm will not become locked in a fixed position. This process, says Quinn, "is a delicate art, requiring a subtle balance of vision, entrepreneurship, and politics."[9]

CONCRETENESS VERSUS GENERALITY IN MISSION AND PURPOSE STATEMENTS

Most business statements of purposes and missions are expressed at high levels of abstraction (this is especially so of purposes). Vagueness nevertheless has its virtues. These statements are not designed to express concrete ends but rather to provide motivation, general direction, an image, a tone, and/or a philosophy to guide the enterprise. An excess of detail could prove counterproductive: concrete specification could be the base for rallying opposition. Precision might stifle creativity in the formulation of an acceptable mission or purpose. Once an aim is cast in concrete it creates a rigidity in an organization and resists change. Vagueness leaves room for other managers to fill in the details, perhaps even to modify general patterns. Vagueness permits more flexibility in adapting to changing environment and internal operations. It facilitates flexibility in implementation.

How specifically a purpose of mission is stated is a matter of personal taste. If a company is engaged in "making chocolate-covered cherries" it would appear to be a valid expansion of mission to talk about "making chocolate candies." To extend the mission, however, to "being a processor of foods" would probably be going too far. Yet, a bronze plaque on the Lever House, London, proclaims: "The mission of our company, as William Hasketh Lever saw it, is to make cleanliness commonplace, to lessen work for women, to foster health, and to contribute to personal attractiveness that life may be more enjoyable for the people who use our products." This is a very broad mission statement but the company has been exceptionally successful. One reason for its success is that under this umbrella the company has developed a hierarchy of objectives formulated for each "stakeholder" group, functional area, and division. As one descends the hierarchy the more specific are the objectives.[10]

Generally speaking the further a company gets from its current products and markets the less likely it is to make a profit. The basic reason is that managers of the firm become less and less familiar with products and markets.

Disagreement at the top of an organization over basic purpose can cause trouble. This was one of the reasons for W. T. Grant's bankruptcy. As one executive reported: "There was a lot of dissension within the company whether we should go the K Mart route or go after the Ward's and Penney position. Ed Staley and Lou Lustenberger [two top executives] were at logger-heads over the issue, with the upshot being we took a position between the two and that consequently stood for nothing."[11]

SHOULD MISSIONS AND PURPOSES BE WRITTEN?

If there is general agreement among managers about mission and purpose statements, having them in written form may help to reinforce the commitment over time. On the other hand, when words are put on paper they can readily generate misunderstanding and contention.

For larger companies it would seem that the core purposes and missions will, when written, uniquely help crystallize their focus. It should be possible to develop a consensus around statements at reasonably high levels of abstraction. Nevertheless, too many statements written in too much detail might distort the focus. Written purposes and missions, when well prepared, not only have a benefit in directing the internal affairs of a company but also may improve the public's image of a company.

Very small companies do not have these needs for written purposes and missions. As they grow, however, consideration should be given to written purposes and missions.

Summary

In every organization there is a network of aims. The foundation for the building of this network is a formulation of the basic purposes and missions of the company. Specifying these basic purposes and missions is a very important function of top management.

Many companies prepare written statements of purposes and missions—called creeds or philosophies. There is no consensus about what such statements should include. Generally, they include a statement of the socioeconomic purposes of the company, missions (lines of business and markets), thrusts and characteristics of the company, managerial practices, relationships of the company to the community, and wishes of top management with respect to the adherence of business conduct to various codes of behavior. All of this is heavily dependent on the values, aspirations, and interests of the chief executive officer. Some companies prepare written statements for only part of this universe, such as codes of ethical behavior, or basic purposes of the company, or lines of business and markets served. Some companies have no written statements about these activities. In any event, if there is no written statement there usually will be an implicit understanding of purposes and missions.

Mission statements are often written as grand designs. These are at high levels of abstraction and may appear to be public relations or advertising slogans. Mission statements also frequently describe only the lines of business of the company and markets and customers to be served.

Carefully prepared missions have been the source of success of companies. Revised missions have turned companies around. On the other hand, poorly formulated missions have brought disaster to some companies.

Unfortunately, there is no way to determine what is the right mission except after the decision has been made.

Missions are formulated in different ways but always the chief executive officer is directly and deeply involved in the process. In larger organizations the process takes place gradually, with much participation from top managers. In some instances, however, the chief executive officer may decide upon a mission without consultation with others in the organization. This is most frequently the case in small companies.

Purposes and missions are most often expressed in broad, general terms. Vagueness in language at this level has many virtues. Specificity is more likely to cause difficulties than is vagueness.

The larger a company becomes the more advantageous are written statements of purposes and missions, which are available for general distribution within the company and often outside as well.

10 Developing Long-Range Planning Objectives

It is of the greatest importance for effective strategic planning that the broad, abstract, and often vague statements of purposes and missions, discussed in Chapter 9, be defined in more concrete terms. Statements such as "Our objective is to increase sales" or "Our purpose is to be a profitable company by making quality products" are not useful for planning purposes. Only when generalities are made concrete can people in organizations understand exactly what it is they are supposed to be trying to achieve. Only then will they be able to develop specific strategies and tactical plans to achieve the objectives set for them and the company.

In developing the network of aims the first step in clarifying broad purposes and missions is taken in the development of long-range planning objectives—the subject of this chapter. In later chapters the ways in which long-range objectives are further broken down into detailed goals and targets will be discussed.

The Meaning of Long-Range Planning Objectives

An objective in the lexicon of business aims used in this book refers to a desired or needed result to be achieved by a specific time. It is a value sought by an individual or a group in an organization. It is a specific category of a fundamental purpose and defines more concretely the purpose or a part of it. It is a desired future state of a business or one of its elements. Although the objective is to be achieved in the future, a specific period of time is assigned to its realization.

There is a continuum in the network of aims across which definitions shade into one another. At one end of the spectrum are basic purposes, at the other end are short-range goals, and in between are objectives. Some companies use the words purposes, objectives, and goals interchangeably, a practice likely to create semantic problems. Many companies and writers use the word goal in the same sense that the word objective is used here and they speak of objectives as being synonymous with purposes. Each company can legitimately define its own meaning in its own words but when definitions are settled they should be clearly understood throughout the organization.

Criteria for Objectives

Further clarification of the meaning of a long-range planning objective is found in guides for preparing objectives. Following are ten guides, presented in no particular order of importance. It should be noted, too, that they are not mutually exclusive.

SUITABLE

An obvious requisite for an objective is that its achievement must support the enterprise's basic purposes and missions. It must move the company in the direction identified by basic purposes and missions. An objective that makes no contribution to purpose is nonproductive. One that conflicts with purpose is dangerous. A positive contribution to purpose must be planned if the objective is to have more than a coincidental effect in that area.

MEASURABLE OVER TIME

To the extent practicable, objectives should state what is expected to happen in concrete terms and when. Planning is much easier when objectives are stated not in vague generalities but in such concrete terms as the following: "Our objective is to increase sales from $10 million this year to $50 million five years from now." Objectives can be quantified in terms other than dollars, such as quality, quantity, time, costs, ratio, percentage, rate, or specific steps to be followed. For example, a company may have as an objective the improvement of career opportunities during a three-year planning period. To quantify this objective the company can state:

> Procedures will be established to improve career opportunities in the company. Next year management training programs will be instituted for managers at all levels. During the second year a companywide program will be developed and installed to counsel employees on career paths. During the third year a program will be developed and installed to pay tuition of employees who wish to enter part-time educational programs.

Only when objectives are expressed in concrete terms for specified periods of time can their achievement be measured reasonably objectively.

FEASIBLE

Objectives should be possible to achieve. In setting objectives managers should not set unrealistic or impractical objectives.

Setting practicable objectives is not easy. There are many considerations involved in deciding upon a feasible objective. An objective must be set in light of what managers see happening in the industry—what competitors are likely to do and what is projected in economic, social, political, and technical aspects of the environment. Internal factors also must be considered such as managerial capabilities, forces that motivate or discourage employees, available capital, and technical innovative abilities. A feasible objective realistically reflects such forces and, with proper execution of plans, may be expected to occur in the time specified.

ACCEPTABLE

Objectives are most likely to be achieved if they are acceptable to people in the organization. An objective that does not fit the value system of an important manager is not likely to be pursued diligently. Try making a manager responsible, for instance, for developing a new product that the manager does not like. The objective certainly also ought to be acceptable in terms of the willingness of the company to incur the costs that its achievement might entail. Costs in this sense include not only financial resources but also managerial time, staff time, plant capacity, market share, and profits, at specific periods of time.

FLEXIBLE

It should be possible to modify the objective in the event of unforeseen contingencies. However, the objective ought not be wishy-washy; it should be firm enough to assure direction.

MOTIVATING

Generally, objectives that are out of reach of people are not motivating nor are objectives that are too easily achieved. For most companies, objectives that are a little aggressive, a little bit higher than likely to be reached, have motivating power. Research has confirmed that specific objectives increase performance and that difficult objectives, if accepted, result in better performance than do easy objectives.[1]

UNDERSTANDABLE

Objectives should be stated in as simple and as understandable words as possible. No matter how objectives are worded, however, managers who set them should take pains to make as sure as possible that they are understood by all who must try to achieve them. This may appear to be a gratuitous criteria but it is a very important one. One survey of pitfalls in planning concluded that misunderstanding of objectives was a major cause of complaint among managers.[2]

COMMITMENT

Once agreement is reached about objectives there should be a commitment to do what is necessary and reasonable to achieve them. In the case of a division manager, for example, there should be full commitment to achieving the objective. Also, if other managers have a responsibility for the achievement of the objective, they, too, should understand and accept their commitment to its achievement.

PEOPLE PARTICIPATION

Best results are achieved when those who are responsible for achieving objectives have some role in setting them. This is less true for very small organizations than, say, for large decentralized companies.

People who participate in setting objectives that they are to achieve are more likely to be motivated to reaching them than are people who have little input in this area. Involvement in objective setting also helps to meet the needs of people to use their skills in advancing the company interests as well as their own. Also, in large decentralized companies the detailed, intimate, substantive knowledge of managers and staff about their own operations is generally far greater than that of top managers. In such cases there are great advantages to both top management and the division managers in collaborating in the objective setting process.

LINKAGE

There are several aspects to linkage. First, objectives should be linked to basic purposes, as previously noted. Second, objectives in different parts of the company should be examined to see that they are consistent with and meet, in the aggregate, top management objectives. For instance, if individual divisions prepare objectives for their operations for sales and profits the aggregate of all divisions should fit top management's objectives for the entire firm. If this is not the case individual division objectives should be reexamined and/or efforts should be made to achieve top management objectives by other measures, such as acquisitions. Finally, within a centralized company or in a division there should be appropriate linkages among objectives. This point will be discussed later.

Conceptual and Operational Classes of Objectives

Theoretically, objectives should be set for every element of an enterprise that top management wishes to be the subject of plans. There is no standard classification of objectives or of the number of objectives that a company should have.

In practice, most companies have comparatively few long-range planning objectives. They generally set objectives for sales, profits, return on investment, margin, and share of market. Objectives for sales and profits are usually expressed in absolute numbers, percentages, or both. For example, the sales objectives may be expressed in absolute dollars for each of the next five years. Or, the objective may be expressed as follows: "Increase sales 15 percent each year over the next five years." Return on investment, margin, and market share are usually expressed in percentage terms.

Other areas in which objectives are often set include product development, productivity, diversification, minority hiring, facility replacement, labor content of product, industry ranking, management development, working conditions, employment levels, and social responsibilities. This does not exhaust the list and many subobjectives are possible in each category.

Peter Drucker has said that objectives are necessary for every area of a business whose performance and results directly affect the survival and prosperity of the enterprise. He identified the following areas as in need of objectives: market standing, innovation, productivity, physical and financial resources, profitability, manager performance and development, worker performance and attitude, and public responsibility.[3]

Larger enterprises have need for objectives in more areas than do smaller companies. The reason is that more people are involved who need guidance in decisionmaking, and many interests are concerned about objectives and the way they are to be achieved.

If an overall statement of purpose and philosophy does not

exist, or if it is very short, there is no reason wny the structure of objectives formulated in the planning process should not include aims that have no terminal point and that are classified as overall missions, creeds, or philosophies. Although one can draw conceptually clear distinctions within the network of aims, in practice it is not always necessary or desirable to do so.

Linking Objectives

Objectives and subobjectives should be closely related. This is so because in the actual operation of an enterprise there is a close relationship among the dominant economic objectives. For instance, an objective to maintain or increase return on investment equal to or above the industry average must be pursued in light of sales objectives, financial objectives, and objectives related to efficient use of resources. One cannot set one of these objectives without relation to the others. Depending upon where one starts, these objectives become subobjectives of each other. This is illustrated in Exhibit 10–1, which shows the dominant objectives of return on investment and the way other major objectives, as well as subobjectives, may be related to it. A more extensive tree of objectives could easily include other functions the objectives of which must mesh to get a desired return on investment.

LONG-RANGE OBJECTIVE	SUBOBJECTIVES	SUB-SUBOBJECTIVES SET IN THESE AREAS
MAKE A ROI OF 15% AFTER TAXES BY END OF 5 YEARS (SPECIFY FOR EACH YEAR)	INCREASE SALES TO $10,000,000 IN 5 YEARS	MARKET SHARE / ADVERTISING EXPENDITURES / NEW MARKET PENETRATION / REDESIGN OF PRODUCTS / DEVELOP NEW PRODUCTS FOR MARKET / BEGIN NEW R & D IN SELECTED AREA
	RAISE GROSS PROFITS TO $2,000,000 IN 5 YEARS	REDUCE OVERHEAD COSTS BY CONSOLIDATING FUNCTIONS / SELL OBSOLETE PLANT AND EQUIPMENT / REDUCE ADVERTISING OUTLAYS
	BUILD MODERN FACILITIES AND OPERATE THEM AT CAPACITY OVER NEXT 5 YEARS	BUILD NEW BUILDINGS / REPLACE TOOLS / IMPROVE PRODUCTION SCHEDULES / IMPROVE PLANT UTILIZATION RATES / INSTALL BETTER INVENTORY CONTROL / REDUCE DEFECTIVE PRODUCTS
	UPGRADE AND MAINTAIN A SKILLED WORK FORCE	MANAGEMENT TRAINING PROGRAMS / MANAGEMENT ADDITIONS / MANAGEMENT HIRING SCHEDULES / SKILL REPLACEMENTS

EXHIBIT 10–1: **Linking Business Objectives. (Source: George A. Steiner,** *Top Management Planning* **(New York: Macmillan, 1969), p. 162.**

Objective Setting Processes

In Chapter 4 four fundamentally different approaches to planning were presented—top-down, bottom-up, combination of these two, and the team approach. In very small companies the objective setting process is generally top-down but in most other enterprises it is either a combination of top-down and bottom-up or the team approach. In small companies and in strategic business units of large corporations the objective setting process is frequently a team effort.

In larger diversified companies a pure top-down model of objective setting would be unsuitable. First, top management does not have sufficient knowledge of all the businesses in the company to establish realistic goals. Second, the typical division manager would resent being handed an objective without an opportunity to discuss its feasibility. (One practical reason for this attitude is that objective setting is a very complex process involving all sorts of trade-offs, as will be noted later.) On the other hand, there are few if any top managements willing to accept divisional objective setting without top management review and approval. For these reasons the objective setting procedure in larger companies generally involves cooperation between top management and divisional managers.

In his study of fifty firms Dobbie found a wide variety of models that existed in practice between the pure top-down and the pure bottom-up approach to objective setting. He called them "dialogue models," a useful description of the process. Several objective-setting patterns appeared: First, as the companies became more experienced in planning, the relationship among managers and staffs in objective-setting became more complex; Second, the larger and more diversified the company, the more complex were the relationships; finally, companies that established corporate planning offices tended to emphasize a bit more top management direction over the setting of objectives.[4]

Methods Employed in Setting Objectives

A number of different methods are employed by businesses in establishing long-range planning objectives. The following are common practices, in no particular order of importance.

BASED ON PAST PERFORMANCE

A company may examine past performance and assume that past trends will continue into the future. To base objectives on such simple trend extrapolation is a naive approach.

TRENDS ADJUSTED FOR FUTURE FORCES

A more sophisticated approach is to extrapolate past performance into the future and then to adjust the trend line according to forces that can alter it. Such forces, to illustrate, are industry sales forecasts, market segment forecasts, new market opportunities, competitive threats, government regulations, product obsolescence, and company resources. Company resources include capital for expansion, new product development, worker productivity, and so on.

INDUSTRY TREND AND MARKET SHARE

A company can make a projection of industry trend and determine the share it wishes to capture.

RESOURCE UTILIZATION

Another approach is to calculate resources available to a company and determine possible and desirable utilization of them. For example, plant capacity will be calculated at a particular level. The greater the plant capacity used, of course, the lower the product cost per unit. Using all plant capacity will involve, of course, balance among other resources such as maintenance, employees, advertising and other promotion, and cash flow. If sales can be projected above plant capacity with any credibility then the company must determine whether it will expand. Some years ago Pendleton shirts were in great demand and the maker was faced with this question. The decision was made not to expand because the higher than normal demand was considered to be a fad, as turned out to be the case.

NEGOTIATION

In large decentralized companies division objectives are often set as a result of negotiaion between top management and division managers. When agreement on objectives is reached, plans to achieve them are then prepared.

TOP MANAGEMENT DICTATED

Top management can of course dictate objectives with or without documented analyses. There have been instances, for example, in which a chief executive said that the sales objective of his company was to grow at the rate of 15 percent a year, or some such number. There is nothing wrong with this approach if the chief executive has a feel for what is possible in his industry. Of course, the more such a dictated objective can be supported by rigorous analysis, the better. Also, it is not generally wise to announce that such a dictated objective will hold for a long period of time. Circumstances do change and the objectives may need revision.

ITERATION WITH STRATEGY

There is much iteration in the planning process, especially between objectives and strategy. This is as it should be because strategies may not be found to achieve stated objectives. On the other hand, in the search for strategies to reach an objective, a company may discover new sources of opportunity that will justify a higher objective.

RESULTS OF WOTS UP ANALYSIS

Through analysis of company opportunities, threats, strengths, and weaknesses managers and staff will identify alternative objectives and strategies from which firm objectives eventually will be established for the company.

FROM STRATEGIES

As noted previously the planning process may begin with strategies. Once creditable strategies are formulated it is easy to determine the objectives that will be achieved if the strategies are properly implemented.

ANALYTICAL TOOLS IN OBJECTIVE FORMULATION

Detailed studies of appropriate data and information may be used as a basis for formulating objectives. These can range for a sales objective, for example, from a simple analysis of salesmen's projections to computer based simulation and econometric models. What managers should know about such techniques is discussed in Chapter 15.

Trade-offs in Setting Objectives

Setting objectives is not a simple matter of determining one's wishes and announcing them. A manager can proceed this way but most managers go through an intricate process because numerous factors must be taken into consideration in setting objectives.

To illustrate, an increase in market share may require an expansion of plant and equipment. Every company, of course, has other uses for capital so this expansion would have to be made at the expense of something else. An increase in research and development to get a new product on the market may reduce current profits but enhance long-range profits. So, there may be a reduction of dividends today with the likelihood of higher dividends in the future. Is the trade-off worth it? A company may want to increase sales to maintain employment but to do so in a particular environment may mean price reduction and profit loss.

These illustrations make it clear that it is more than likely that most important objectives set by a company will necessitate trade-off analysis in which top management and lower level managers will be involved. Objectives are finally set after trying different combinations and permutations of objectives, strategies, and tactical plans. This is what is meant by iteration.

Summary

The planning process requires that general statements of missions and purposes be made more concrete by developing long-range objectives. When this task is done it becomes possible to plan specific strategies to achieve objectives and purposes.

Objectives should be suitable, measurable over time, feasible, acceptable, flexible, motivating, and understandable; they should also receive managerial commitment, be based on people participation in setting them, be limited in number, and be linked.

Theoretically, objectives should be set for every element in an enterprise of importance to management. Actually, this is too unwieldy a requirement and companies generally limit long-range objectives to sales, profits, return on investment, margin, and market share.

The larger an enterprise gets the more likely it is to have more long-range planning objectives.

In very small companies objectives are set by top management with little or no collaboration among managers. As companies grow in size and complexity the collaboration among managers in objective setting also grows. In large companies there usually is found an intricate set of relationships between managers and staff at headquarters and managers and staffs in divisions in setting objectives. The essence of this process is continuous dialogue until objectives are established by consensus.

One of the reasons for this continuous dialogue is that objective setting is done only after consideration of many combinations of elements in an organization. There are trade-offs among such factors as investment, market share, employment, and product price, which are settled when objectives are set.

11 Formulating Program Strategies

Once basic purposes, missions, and long-range planning objectives are established, the conceptual sequence in strategic planning is then to develop program strategies to achieve them. The subject of this chapter is the identification and evaluation of program strategies.

Overarching Considerations About Program Strategies

Before discussing how to identify and evaluate strategies, a few key dimensions of program strategies should be noted.

STRATEGY VERSUS TACTICS

In Chapter 2 it was pointed out that there is no consensus on words generally used in planning and that applies, of course, to the word strategy. As also noted in Chapter 2, in this book, program strategy refers to the acquisition, use, and disposition of resources for specific projects.

Program strategies shade into tactics. Along a spectrum with strategies to the left and tactics to the right there are clear distinctions between these two elements of planning. (For example, strategy is the framework within which tactical moves are made.

Strategy comes first. Tactics implement strategies.)[1] When the two come together on this spectrum, however, there is no sharp demarcation between them. One of the reasons for this blurring is an ends-means continuum. For example, a company may decide that it will establish a basic strategy of penetrating the European market by having a major division acquire a foreign firm that produces a product similar to its own. A tactic might be to acquire the foreign company by exchange of stock rather than by cash payment. To the division, however, this may be a strategy or, if one prefers, a substrategy.

NO CONSENSUS ON TYPES OF PROGRAM STRATEGIES

A comprehensive list of program strategies would be very long. Although there is no consensus on the classifications that might be used in such a listing, the following basic types of program strategies probably would receive general acceptance.

Product strategies would include such things as nature of the product line; new product development; product quality, performance, and obsolescence; dropping old products; and adding a product to the line.

Marketing strategies might include the following: distribution channels, marketing services, market research, pricing, selling and advertising, packaging, product brand, and selection of market areas.

Financial strategies would include such areas as divestment of unwanted assets, extent of customer credit, obtaining funds, financing basic research, and expenditures on facilities.

Strategies concerned with organization would embrace centralization versus decentralization, degrees of authority given to managers of decentralized profit centers, departmental staff organization, organization of the office of the chief executive, and matrix versus functional organizations.

Personnel strategies would concern union relations, compensation, management training, performance appraisal, rewards systems, and recruitment.

Strategies concerning public relations might include advertising policy, position of company on public policy issues, relationships with government regulatory agencies, and lobbying policy.

Social programs, a new area of strategy for many companies, particularly the larger ones, would include specific programs that the company wished to pursue, such as day-care centers, lending managers to local governmental units to help improve management practices, and contributions to charity.

COMPLEXITY OF STRATEGY FORMULATION

President Truman used to complain that even his most simple decisions created unbelievable complexities. This is the nature of a strategy. The apparently simplest strategies, such as doubling sales within five years, necessitate an extensive sorting out of alternatives. The alternatives need to be examined in terms of many variables—technical, financial, economic, production, marketing, human constraints, government policy (to mention but a few obvious ones)—and a variety of analytical tools. Then comes implementation, which of course must be considered before finally choosing the strategy. Throughout, the process mixes factual analysis with intuition and political considerations, using that phrase in its widest meaning.

UNIQUENESS OF THE PROCESS

The decisionmaking process for the most significant program strategies will vary from organization to organization and among programs in any one organization. Each process is unique because each involves a different mix of managerial value systems and judgments; personal, social, and political forces; interpersonal relationships; and individual managerial skills, attitudes, capabilities, motivations, and values.

NETWORK OF STRATEGIES

The identification of major strategies must entail the identification, and later evaluation, of substrategies. All strategies must be broken down into substrategies for successful implementation. A decision to expand plant capacity, for example, immediately raises a number of substrategy issues. Successful strategies turn out to be clusters of interrelated strategies.[2]

TRANSFERABILITY OF STRATEGIES

Successful strategies for one firm may not be successful for another. Consider, for example, what might happen to Revlon and Avon, or General Motors and Volkswagen, if they decided to exchange strategies. What is one manager's successful strategy may be another's poison.

STRATEGY FORMULATION IS AN ART

Although a good bit of progress has been made in developing analytical tools to identify and evaluate strategies, the process is still mostly an art. Some techniques used in strategy setting have great power in helping managers to make decisions but in all important strategic decisions the ability to ask the right question, the application of judgment, and the intuition of managers are the dominant determinants of the decision.

With these background considerations I turn now to some major approaches to identifying program strategies.

Approaches to Identifying Program Strategies

All of the following approaches to identifying program strategies can be pursued in a formal strategic planning process or they can be used individually outside a formal planning program. Some of them interrelate. A number of these approaches may be followed in the situation audit or flow directly from it. Some of them not only are useful in identifying strategies but also have power in evaluating strategies. They are not presented in any order of importance.

MAKING A STRATEGIC PROFILE

In this approach management will ask: "What are our strategies, implicit and explicit?" Once this question is answered, several more must be addressed: "Which strategies are still effective?" "Which ones must be changed?" "Where do we need new strategies?" Exhibit 11–1 shows the type of questions that might be raised in making a strategic profile. Such a profile might show, for instance, that one customer is purchasing a very large part of the company's output. Such a situation is potentially dangerous because the customer may suddenly decide to purchase elsewhere. Although this type of information should be general knowledge to top management, in the usual course of business it is not always

1. Identify and measure dominant product/market concentrations
   (a) Sales by customer classification
   (b) Sales by major product group
   (c) Sales by channel of distribution
   (d) Sales by price/quality category
   (e) Sales by geographic distribution
2. Identify and measure units and/or activities receiving the greatest deployment of company resources
   (a) Distribution of assets among units and activities
   (b) Cash flows produced by each unit and activity
   (c) Focus of company discretionary allocations
3. Identify and measure major competitive advantages by comparisons with major competitors
   (a) Market share
   (b) Product quality
   (c) Product price
   (d) Product customer acceptance
   (e) Profit margin
   (f) Plant capabilities
   (g) Managerial capabilities
4. Identify financial strategies
   (a) Debt/equity ratio
   (b) Current asset and liability ratios
   (c) Dividend distribution
   (d) Cash position
5. Determine personal strategies of key executives
   (a) Risk orientation
   (b) Time horizon
   (c) Entrepreneural
   (d) Functional orientation: production, sales marketing, finance, etc.
   (e) Consensus
6. Determine analytical profiles of strategies
   (a) Timing of evaluations of strategies
   (b) Methods of evaluating strategies

EXHIBIT 11–1: Identifying and Analyzing a Company's Strategic Profile. (Source: George A. Steiner and John B. Miner, *Management Policy and Strategy* (New York: Macmillan, 1977), p. 193.)

known by managers in a position to take action. Writing down
current strategies is useful in insuring that no important ones are
ignored.

EXAMINING THE PRODUCT-MARKET MATRIX

Exhibit 11-2 is a matrix that identifies major product and market strategies open to a company. A company, for instance, can
choose to stick with its current products in its present markets, or it
might decide to expand and diversify either by penetrating new
markets with present products or by developing new products for
current markets. In making a strategic decision to move in any one
or several of the directions in Exhibit 11-2 a broad range of substrategies will be open in each box. Managers should think carefully about the possibility that the further they move from current
products and markets the less likely they are to make a profit out of
the venture.

A somewhat different product and market matrix is shown in
Exhibit 11-3. A firm with a number of products can identify in

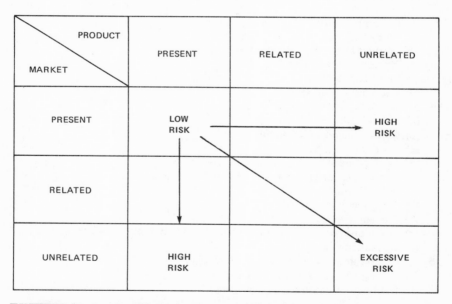

EXHIBIT 11-2:   Product and Market Matrix. (Source: George A. Steiner,
Strategic Managerial Planning **(Oxford, Oh.: Planning Executives Institute,**
1977), p. 18.)

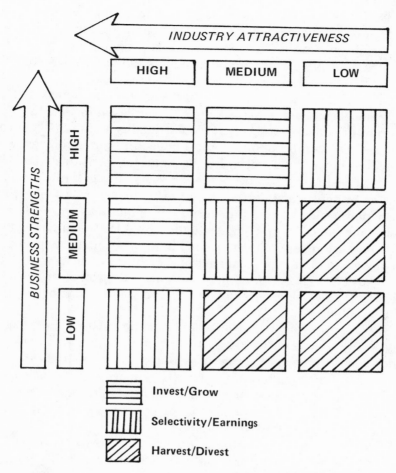

EXHIBIT 11–3: Business Strength/Industry Attractiveness Matrix. (Source: M. G. Allen, "Strategic Problems Facing Today's Corporate Planner"(speech before the Thirty-sixth Annual Meeting of the Academy of Management, Kansas City, Missouri, August 12, 1976), p. 9.)

which square the product falls. Different strategies will be suggested depending upon where the product is placed. For instance, if a product falls in the invest/grow area, a number of options are open to management. Thus, should the company increase investment in advertising and sales force to increase share on the assumption that the higher the share in an attractive market the greater will be the profit? or increase research and development? or yield on price to hold market share? If the product falls in the harvest/divest area these strategies make no sense. Possible strategies in this area might be to plan to exit from the business, or consolidate plants to cut costs, or prune product lines, or give up share to hold price and margin. Products falling in the selectivity/earnings area will raise different strategic issues.

Of course, strategic issues suggested in this matrix are not really so clear or so simply stated. One reason is that there are different dimensions to both market strengths and industry attractiveness. Depending upon which dimension is of significance the strategic choices will vary. For instance, dimensions of market attractiveness are size of potential sales, annual rate of sales growth, pricing, competitive structure, industry profitability, customer purchasing patterns, government regulations, ease of entry, environmental concerns, legal situation, and technical characteristics. Dimensions of company strength are market share, profitability, image, technology, managerial capabilities, distribution system, sales skills, service capability, patent protection, product efficiency, raw material availability, and ability to meet government regulations.

To illustrate the importance of such dimensions, a company may locate a product in the upper left-hand corner of the matrix, which measures market growth on one axis and market share on the other. The company may decide, however, to reduce its investment in the product and gradually phase out of that product for a variety of reasons: Government regulations are expected to increase with respect to the product; greater legal liabilities are expected to attach to the product; or the company may have other products with a higher potential rate of return where it wishes to place its capital.

A sharper focus on the identification of strategies will follow, of course, with a more precise meaning of market attractiveness and market strength. Companies should identify those characteristics of attractiveness and strength having the most importance to them and their products.

Exhibit 11–3 can be modified to clarify strategy identification in many ways. Exhibit 11–4 shows products in terms of next year's sales. Similar charts can be prepared for cash flow, market share, or assets employed.

The charts can be made more meaningful if market strength, for instance, is designated as being market share and shares are specified. Thus, low might be under 5 percent; medium, 5 to 15 percent;

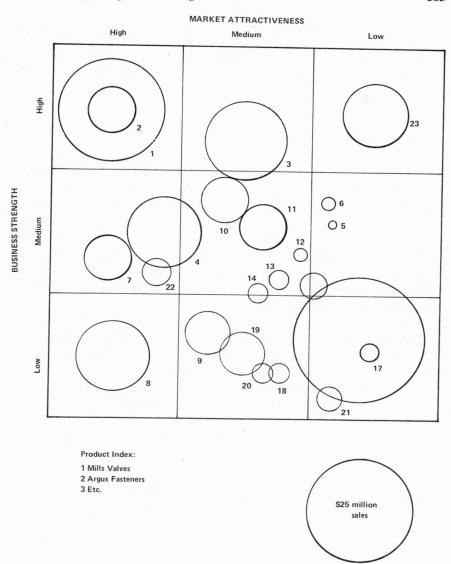

EXHIBIT 11–4: Stone Corporation Business Strength/Market Attractiveness Matrix.

and high, over 15 percent. Similarly, market attractiveness might be expressed in terms of sales growth and identified as follows: low could be under 3 percent a year; medium, from 3 to 7 percent; and high, over 7 percent. Of course, these numbers will differ by product and market.

EXAMINING PRODUCT LIFE CYCLES

Products pass through life cycles, pictured in Exhibit 11–5. Strategies identified as being worthy of further evaluation will vary depending upon the stage of the product life cycle. What makes sense in the market development stage, for instance, may be nonsensical in the maturity stage.[3]

Some companies, as shown in Exhibit 11–6, develop a scoring chart for evaluating strategies in terms of business attractiveness and company strengths. For example, each factor can be rated on a scale of one to ten (with one being low, poor, or worst). Upon the basis of such ratings alternative strategies may be evaluated. Of course, each company must decide what is being measured. For instance, what constitutes high and/or low sales potential? What constitutes a high or a low growth rate for the industry? Or, dropping down to company strengths in Exhibit 11–6, how does one measure a strong versus a weak technology base?

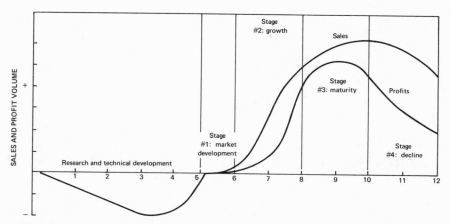

EXHIBIT 11–5: Product Life Cycle for an Industry. (Source: George A. Steiner and John B. Miner, *Management Policy and Strategy* (New York: Macmillan, 1977), p. 197.)

	PROJECT I Score	PROJECT II Score	PROJECT III Score
A. Business Attractiveness			
1. Sales/profit potential	_____	_____	_____
2. Growth rate (% year)	_____	_____	_____
3. Competitive situation			
Competitor reactivity	_____	_____	_____
Activity index of technology	_____	_____	_____
Patent position	_____	_____	_____
4. Risk distribution (segments)	_____	_____	_____
5. Opportunity to restructure an entire industry			
6. Special factors			
Ecology			
Energy	_____	_____	_____
Geography	_____	_____	_____
Other	_____	_____	_____
B. Company Strengths (Fit Factors)			
1. Capital requirements/availability	_____	_____	_____
2. Marketing capabilities	_____	_____	_____
3. Manufacturing capabilities	_____	_____	_____
4. Technology base	_____	_____	_____
5. Raw materials availability	_____	_____	_____
6. Skills availability			
Strong advocate	_____	_____	_____
Technical, legal, financial	_____	_____	_____
Other	_____	_____	_____

EXHIBIT 11–6: Strategic Business Planning Score Chart. (Source: D. Bruce Merrifield, *Strategic Analysis, Selection, and Management of R&D Projects* **(New York: AMACOM, 1977), p. 10.)** (Reprinted by permission of the publisher. Copyright © 1977 by AMACOM, a division of American Management Associations. All rights reserved.)

FINDING A NICHE IN THE MARKET

A superb strategy is to find a niche in the market that no one else is filling and that one's company can fill at a price customers cannot resist. This is a road to riches. To illustrate, shortly after World War II Marcel Bich decided to make disposable ball-point pens at a time when ball-points sold for about $12 and were supposed to last a lifetime. Societé Bic, the company built on this concept, today has about one-third of the world market for pens and has a market value in excess of $300 million.

Of course, success is not automatically guaranteed when a niche is discovered. The Franklin Mint, for example, found an unfulfilled demand for coins and metals produced specifically to be collected, but it took a substantial marketing effort to convince collectors that they had this need. Also, a niche once filled successfully naturally attracts competition, as Hugh Hefner of *Playboy* can attest.

Newman has described in detail a methodology to identify and exploit niches.[4] Basically it involves careful analysis of the market and the demand for a new product or service. Then actual and potential competition is studied. Finally, potential for success in terms of company strengths and weaknesses is assessed.

INVENTION

There are few if any better strategies than to invent something that becomes a generic name for similar products. Among long-time money-makers in this category are Coca-Cola, Dixie cups, Kleenex, Eveready batteries, Hershey's chocolate, Smith Brothers cough drops, and Kellogg's corn flakes. Not all inventions, however, have been instant successes. Indeed, most of them found it tough going at first.[5] For example, it took years for the Gillette razor to gain a strong following. Chester Carlson's invention of xerography, which eventually became the technical foundation for the spectacular success of Xerox Corporation, was rejected by a dozen or more large companies before finding support from the Battelle Memorial Institute.

COMPUTER MODELS

There are numerous computer models in use today that help managers identify strategies. For example, a financial simulation model will help managers answer "what if" questions. By using the model, they can determine what impact a dividend payment will have on cash flow, what impact a given expenditure will have on profits, or what the result on profits will be if a new inventory or customer service strategy is followed. Input-output models of the entire economy are used by companies to identify potentially growing or declining markets, which in turn help in identifying strategies. These models do not determine the strategy: they merely suggest possibilities.

IDENTIFYING STRATEGIC FACTORS FOR
BUSINESS SUCCESS

A valuable approach to identifying appropriate strategies is that
of asking and answering the question: "What are the strategic
factors responsible for the success of this company?" Research on
the subject has confirmed that certain strategic factors are correlated with the success of particular companies in particular industries and that managers in similar companies show a surprising
consensus on what they are.[6] For example, the production of
fail-safe equipment is a prime strategic factor for success in the
aerospace industry. A toy that delights children (and adults) is a
prime strategic factor in the success of a toy company. The ability
of automobile companies to meet federal emission and safety
standards is a new, dominant strategic factor for success in that
industry. Comprehensive lists of specific factors responsible for
success of larger firms have been prepared by Steiner and by
Guth.[7]

Cohn and Lindberg identified the following factors as bearing
critically on the survival and growth of small businesses:

> A cautious attitude toward growth. A concern for liquidity. A
> focus on providing wanted products or services and satisfying
> work while keeping costs lean. Establishment and maintenance of
> an open system of communication and decision making. Creation
> of a rational organization. Control over certain functions. Eco-
> nomical use of time. Control of owner-manager subjectivity.[8]

Much scholarly work has been done to pinpoint strategic factors
that will lead to success or possible failure in given circumstances.
To name but a few, the PIMS project (profit impact of market
strategies), now in the Strategic Planning Institute, has built a
massive statistical data base from over 1,000 business units. PIMS
has identified thirty-seven factors, arranged in seven categories,
that have a powerful and usually predictable influence on profitability. For instance, the data show clearly that the higher a market
share a company enjoys the greater will be its return on investment.[9] PIMS is used widely in industry today to identify and
evaluate strategies.

The Boston Consulting Group has studied intensively the well-
known learning curve effect—cost per unit drops with increased

production—and has come to a number of conclusions about preferred strategies. For example, early dominance of market is very important in building market leadership, which in turn results in a lower cost per unit as market share rises.[10]

Rumelt studied 273 companies with regard to the relationship between profitability and diversification strategy. He drew a number of important conclusions: Those companies were most profitable that diversified but related most of their activities to a core skill, competence, or resource. The least profitable were those companies that were vertically integrated raw material processors or were active in unrelated businesses.[11]

Space does not permit further elaboration of the detailed strategies that these studies suggest. Nor is it possible here to comment further on the growing literature concerned with strategic factors in business success.[12] Work in the field is voluminous and growing.

INTUITION

As discussed previously there is no superior approach to superb strategy identification than a brilliant intuitive mind.

LUCK

Many companies have found luck to be a source of successful strategies. Magic Chef is, for example, one company that lady luck smiled upon. For years this company made small, portable, heating units, a market that large producers like General Electric and Westinghouse found too small to be profitable. When the boom came after World War II in recreation vehicles and mobile homes Magic Chef found itself dominating that market for small heating units.

WOTS UP ANALYSIS

This approach was described at length in Chapter 8. It is mentioned here to complete the list of the foremost approaches to identifying strategies.

WHAT IS THE PROBLEM?

If a company is in difficulty, a direct approach that asks "What is the problem?" is one way to identify solutions. This is not as easy as it sounds because the problem usually turns out to be a cluster of problems and the key problem is not always obvious. The danger is to administer to symptoms rather than to the basic disease. For instance, a company showing increasing deficits has a problem. But what is the problem? The deficits are symptoms of something fundamentally wrong. Nevertheless, trying to identify the key problem or problems is an approach to formulating strategy.

GAP ANALYSIS

Gap analysis was discussed at length in Chapter 2.

FOLLOW THE LEADER

Some companies, particularly smaller ones in an industry dominated by one or several firms, may adopt a policy of following the leader. Large companies also often follow one another. Montgomery Ward followed Sears to the suburbs, a strategy successful for both. However, RCA followed IBM pricing policy for its computers with disastrous results.

ADAPTIVE SEARCH

Adaptive search is a phrase that I think Ansoff first used.[13] This approach formulates rules in gross terms and then successively refines alternatives through several stages as the generation of a solution proceeds. The method gives the appearance of solving the same problem several times over, but this is not the case. The solution is serial, each step builds upon but does not necessarily duplicate the preceding.

In adaptive search a major decision is made—for example, to diversify a product line. The next step would be to choose between diversification by investing in a research and development program and diversification by acquiring other companies. The third step would be to define the product areas for research, if that is the choice, or to select the industries in which the acquisitions search would proceed. Additional steps are obvious in this type of sequential decisionmaking.

SEARCH FOR SYNERGY

This approach attempts either to combine elements of an existing business or to add new elements that will in effect prove $2 + 2 = 5$. For example, a motel without dining facilities may decide that adding a restaurant will yield combined profits that those units operating independently could not realize.

OTHER APPROACHES

Some managers meet each day as it arrives and think about strategies solely in those terms. Brainstorming may be considered a variation of the situation audit. Trial and error has been used by some companies. The entrepreneurial and muddling through approaches were discussed in Chapter 7.

Evaluating Strategies

Once strategies are identified, they should be evaluated. Important program strategies are in a sense hypotheses to be tested. They are what the academic world calls unstructured problems. This means that there is no simple formula to produce a solution. As noted at the beginning of this chapter each program strategy problem and its solution is unique.

EVALUATION DOES NOT ALWAYS FOLLOW IDENTIFICATION

The conceptual steps in planning call for an evaluation of program strategies once they are identified but this does not always happen in the real world. There are many reasons why program strategies are not evaluated and implemented, a few of which are noted here simply to make the point.

Deciding upon program strategies is risky. If an executive takes a stand and the strategy turns out to be the wrong one a career may be jeopardized. In light of such risks executives sometimes prefer the safety of no decision.

Strategic decisionmaking is an art and as an art it is a creative process that requires knowledge and analysis different from that involved in short-term decisionmaking. As managers advance because of their skills in resolving short-range problems in narrow functional areas their capabilities in dealing with broad, unstructured problems may be neglected and they become hesitant to deal with them. Compensation systems of many corporations often inhibit strategic decisionmaking. As Gertsner noted: "Incentive compensation is often tied either to short-term earnings performance or to stock-price movements, neither of which has anything to do with strategic success."[14]

A NOTE ON STRATEGIC DECISIONMAKING
PROCESSES

Chapter 15 discusses in some detail the mental processes in and tools for decisionmaking in planning. Though the subject is covered earlier in this chapter, in previous chapters, and in Chapter 14, the following points deserve to be underscored: Strategic decisionmaking is very complex and is dominated by nonquantitative factors. Judgment is needed not only in making the final decision but also in determining the processes to be used in making the decision and the type of data necessary to guide decision. Robert McNamara, when secretary of defense and a strong supporter of quantitative methods in decisionmaking, addressed this point in testifying before Congress about his controversial TFX fighter plane decision:

> Fundamentally, we are dealing with a question of judgment. Granted there are specific technical facts and calculations involved; in the final analysis, judgment is what is at issue. . . . In this case we are faced with a situation in which judgments are pyramided upon judgments. . . . There is only one way I know to minimize the compounding error . . . and that way is to apply the judgment of the decision-maker not only to the final recommendation but also to the underlying recommendations and factors.[15]

A number of quantitative tools can help in decisionmaking but none can make the final decision. Again, Chapter 15 will discuss the applicability of different tools in the decisionmaking process. Here it is useful to note that data from the WOTS UP analysis provide important guides in decisionmaking. New statistical compilations such as those of PIMS, the Boston Consulting Group learning curve analysis, and Rumelt's relationships between profitability and organization are valuable guidelines. There are also rules of thumb that managers accumulate from their own and other's experience. As discussed in Chapter 15, managers can use many other analytical tools in decisionmaking, but their power generally diminishes the more important the strategic decision.

TESTS FOR EVALUATING STRATEGIES

In the final analysis the most effective universal approach to decisionmaking is to ask the right question at the right time. Exhibit 11-7 sets forth thirty-nine overarching questions that pose significant tests for both identifying and evaluating strategies. These are simple questions. Yet, if they are considered at the right time and given the proper weight they can prevent a disastrous decision or insure a decision with high prospects of being correct.

A few illustrations may serve to underscore the power of the list. The Ford Motor Company discovered too late that the answer to question 1, so far as the Edsel automobile was concerned, was negative, and the company lost several hundred million dollars. W. T. Grant did not ask question 2 and partly as a result went bankrupt. RCA did not ask questions 3 and 6 about IBM and as a result lost its computer business. The hockeystick approach noted in question 5 relates to a tendency to make optimistic projections, which curve upward rapidly like the end of a hockeystick, a few years into the future. Finally, Rolls-Royce failed to deal adequately with question 31 and went bankrupt. These are negative illustrations. Many companies that asked the right question from this list have done well.

Each company must identify the appropriate questions for the program under review. Once the questions are raised the implications become obvious. If the proper questions are not on the list then others pertinent to the issue at hand must be asked. Of course, more detailed questions fall under each of those in Exhibit 11-7.

On Combining Analytical Rigor, Intuition, and Judgment

To say that important program strategies are chosen for implementation on the basis of managerial intuition and judgment, rather than upon quantitative decision rules, does not mean that analytical techniques and rigorous quantitative evaluations are unimportant in the decision process. For instance, McNamara's comment reported earlier in this chapter is completely accurate in explaining the dominant position of intuition and judgment in a highly significant decision he made. Nevertheless, behind the decision were massive cost-benefit studies that relied upon vast quantitative analysis, including highly advanced computer calculations.

Question 24 in Exhibit 11–7 pertains to analytical tools that may be helpful in strategic decisionmaking. Wise managers will demand quantitative analysis that is pertinent to a decision but also will not make the decision solely upon the basis of the quantitative analysis when nonquantitative considerations are equally germane. The basic problem of managers in strategic decisionmaking is knowing how to combine quantitative analysis with their intuition and judgment. They must decide what analysis to make that is relevant and worth the price and what weight to give it in the final decision.

In considering the mix of analytical rigor, intuition, and judgment in decisionmaking it is important to observe that managers can have a variety of purposes in mind when asking for and using quantitative analysis in evaluating strategies. A generally understood purpose, of course, is to provide a solid basis for decisionmaking. Thus, for example, management may ask for a risk analysis of alternative strategies to help identify the most desirable one. A decision can be made on this basis when management has full confidence in the data and the analysis and when nonquantitative factors are relatively unimportant. If nonquantitative factors are persuasive, a rigorous risk analysis may narrow for managers the choices to which judgment must be applied in making a final decision. For example, as among four or five alternatives the risk in relation to profit may not be readily apparent without a computer based risk analysis. If staff analysis can show clearly that, say, two alternatives are far superior to all the others that conclusion should be of much help to management.

A. Is the Strategy Consistent with Environment?
1. Is your strategy consistent with the environment of your company?
2. Is your strategy acceptable to the major constituents of your company?
3. Do you really have an honest and accurate appraisal of your competition? Are you underestimating your competition?
4. Does your strategy leave you vulnerable to the power of one major customer?
5. Have you fallen prey to the hockeystick project syndrome?
6. Does your strategy follow that of a strong competitor?
7. Does your strategy pit you against a powerful competitor?
8. Is your market share (present and/or prospective) sufficient to be competitive and make an acceptable profit?
9. If your strategy seeks an enlarged market share is it likely to be stopped by the Antitrust Division of the Department of Justice?
10. Is it possible that other federal government agencies will prevent your achieving the objectives sought by your strategy?
11. Is your strategy legal and in conformance with moral and ethical codes of conduct applicable to your company?

B. Is the Strategy Consistent with Your Internal Policies, Styles of Management, Philosophy, and Operating Procedures?
12. Is your strategy identifiable and understood by all those in the company with a need to know?
14. Is your strategy consistent with the internal strengths, objectives, and policies of your organization?
15. Is the strategy under evaluation divided into substrategies that interrelate properly?
16. Does the strategy under review conflict with other strategies in your company?
17. Does the strategy exploit your strengths and avoid your major weaknesses?
18. Is your organizational structure consistent with your strategy?
19. Is the strategy consistent with the values of top management and other key people in the organization?

C. Is the Strategy Appropriate in Light of Your Resources?

Money
20. Do you have sufficient capital, or can you get it, to see the strategy through to successful implementation?
21. What will be the financial consequences associated with the allocation of capital to this strategy? What other projects may be denied funding? Are the financial substrategies associated with this funding acceptable?

EXHIBIT 11–7: Major Tests for Evaluating Strategies. (Source: George A. Steiner, *Strategic Managerial Planning* (Oxford, Oh., Planning Executives Institute, 1977), pp. 22–23.)

EXHIBIT 11-7 *(Cont.)*

Physical Plant
22. Is your strategy appropriate with respect to existing and prospective physical plants?

Mangerial Resources
23. Are there identifiable available and committed managers to implement the strategy?

D. Are the Risks in Pursuing the Strategy Acceptable?
   24. Has the strategy been tested with appropriate risk analysis, such as return on investment, sensitivity analysis, the firm's ability and willingness to bear specific risks, etc.?
   25. Does your strategy balance the acceptance of minimum risk with the maximum profit potential consistent with your company's resources and prospects?
   26. Do you have too much capital and management tied into this strategy?
   27. Is the payback period acceptable in light of potential environmental change?
   28. Does the strategy take you too far from your current products and markets?

E. Does the Strategy Fit Product Life Cycle and Market Strength/Market Attractiveness Situation?
   29. Is the strategy appropriate for the present and prospective position in the market strength/attractiveness matrix?
   30. Does the strategy fit the life cycle of the product(s) involved?
   31. Are you rushing a revolutionary product to market?
   32. Does your strategy involve the production of a new product for a new market? If so, have you really assessed the requirements to implement successfully?
   33. Does your strategy fit a niche in the market that is not now filled by others? Is this niche likely to remain open to you for a long enough time to return your capital investment plus a required profit?

F. Is the Timing of Proposed Implementation Correct?
   34. Is the timing of implementation appropriate in light of what is known about market conditions, competition, etc.?

G. Are There Other Important Considerations?
   35. Overall, can the strategy be implemented in an efficient and effective fashion?
   36. Have you tried to identify the major forces inside and outside the organization that will be most influential in insuring the success of the strategy and/or in raising problems of implementation? Have you given them the proper evaluation?
   37. Are the assumptions realistic upon which your strategy is based?
   38. Has the strategy been tested with appropriate criteria such as consistency with past, present, and prospective trends?
   39. Aside from the above questions, are there any others that are pertinent to an evaluation of this strategy?

Managers, however, may wish to have penetrating staff analysis for other reasons. A manager already may have made up his mind and merely want confirmation. Or, the manager has reached a final conclusion and wants staff analysis only to be sure that no major problem has been missed. Or, the manager may want staff analysis so that he can say, when presenting the decision to the board for approval, "All angles have been examined by staff experts."[16]

Summary

This chapter focused on methods to identify and evaluate program strategies. Before discussing these methods a few overarching considerations were examined to provide perspective.

1. There is no consensus on the meaning of program strategy, and program strategies shade into tactics.
2. There is no consensus on classifications and types of program strategies.
3. The strategy formulation process is very complex.
4. Each problem in identification and evaluation of important strategies is unique.
5. Successful strategies are clusters of interrelated strategies.
6. What is one person's strategy may be another's poison; strategies are not always transferable from one company to another.
7. Strategy formulation is more of an art than a science.

Major approaches to identifying strategies were noted as follows: making a strategic profile; examining the product and market matrix; examining product life cycles; finding a niche in the market; invention; computer models; identifying strategic factors for business success; intuition; luck; WOTS UP analysis; asking "What is the problem?"; gap analysis; follow the leader; adaptive search; and search for synergy. Playing it by ear, brainstorming, trial and error, muddling through, and entrepreneurship also were mentioned.

It was pointed out that evaluation of strategies does not always follow identification because there are factors that may inhibit managers in making strategy choice. But for those managers who are serious about evaluating program strategies there are many techniques available to help them. Nevertheless, the more important the decision the more dominant are nonquantifiable factors in it. Thirty-nine major tests for program strategies were presented to illustrate the significance of asking the right question as the universally dominant decision tool.

12 Medium-Range Functional Programming

The translation of strategic plans into current decisions takes place in two steps. The first is the preparation of medium-range functional plans and the second is the development from them of budgets and short-range tactical plans. This chapter concerns the first step; Chapter 13 will deal with the second.

The Role in Planning of Medium-Range Programming

The coordination of functional plans in the strategic planning process has a number of purposes. Medium-range programming will show how resources are to be deployed if strategies are to be implemented. When managers can show how effective use of resources will achieve strategies they then can certify that the strategies are creditable. If some resources are not available and cannot be acquired it becomes necessary to reexamine strategies and alter them to fit resource availability. If there happens to be an excess of some resources it is desirable also to revaluate strategies because changing them may permit better use of resources. When functional plans are interrelated with the satisfaction of managers they also provide a solid base for developing short-range tactical plans to ensure their implementation.

The usual time dimension for medium-range plans is five years. High technology companies and/or those with long research and production lead times tend to use longer time ranges. Smaller companies and those faced with rapidly changing and unpredictable environments tend to adopt a time frame for medium-range programming that is less than five years.

A company should adopt the time frame most likely to accommodate that integration of functional plans needed to secure the creditability of strategies they are designed to implement. This assurance, however, should be achieved without excessive costs incurred in the integration of too many functional areas over too long a period of time.

The Medium-Range Program Structure

There are many functional plans that theoretically should be integrated over the planning period. Complete planning would require that medium-range functional plans be prepared for every function, both line and staff, and for every product or service. Because of the enormous complexities of such integration no company tries to cover all functional areas. The sensible practice is to include only what is necessary and important to achieve the implementation of a limited number of strategies. To try to tie together all the activities of a company over a long period of time is to seek the impossible. Anyway, it is unnecessary and costly.

This does not mean that managers and staff who head functions not directly coordinated for the achievement of specific strategies need not make medium-range plans. All should do so. The degree to which they tie into the main body of plans, however, will vary. For example, a company with a large research and development staff that is responsible for introducing new products into the line and redesigning old products probably should have plans that relate directly to marketing and production. On the other hand, a small research staff that is maintained to do fundamental research that one day may result in new, important products for the company need not have plans that directly relate to the medium-range plans of the company.

Exhibit 12–1 is a simple illustration of how different functional plans may interrelate. It could be made more complicated by add-

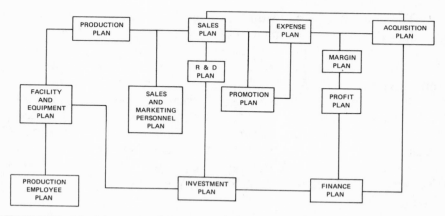

EXHIBIT 12–1: Medium-Range Programming of the Strategic Path. (Source: Suggested by Alfred Friedrich, "Planning in a German Steel Company," *Long Range Planning*, December 1972, p. 82.)

ing other functions such as raw material purchases and staff support programs—for instance, management information systems and public relations.

Variations in Practice

There are wide variations in the way in which companies ask managers and staff to prepare medium-range functional plans. (The words medium-range programs and/or plans are not universally used. Some companies refer to this part of planning as operational planning. Some use the words tactical planning. Some speak of program and project planning.) During the past decade the trend has been to move away from standard, rigid, and complete medium-range functional planning. Companies permit more flexibility in this area today than they did yesterday. Following are a few illustrations of current practices in divisionalized companies.

Some companies use prescribed forms for reporting medium-range functional plans. Exhibit 12–2 is a comparatively simple form that combines expected expenditures for various functional areas and the main parts of a profit and loss statement.

Most companies require divisions to translate functional plans into pro forma profit and loss statements. A simple form for preparing such reports is shown in Exhibit 12–3. Some companies also

ITEM	LAST YEAR	THIS YEAR FORECAST	NEXT FIVE YEARS				
			FIRST YEAR	SECOND YEAR	THIRD YEAR	FOURTH YEAR	FIFTH YEAR
SALES							
MARKETING EXPENDITURES							
ADVERTISING							
DISTRIBUTION							
UNIT PRODUCTION							
EMPLOYEES							
TOTAL							
DIRECT							
INDIRECT							
R & D OUTLAYS							
NEW PRODUCTS							
PRODUCT IMPROVEMENT							
COST REDUCTION							
NEW FACILITIES (TOTAL)							
EXPANSION PRESENT PROD.							
NEW PRODUCTS							
COST REDUCTION							
MAINTENANCE							
PROFIT AND LOSS SUMMARY							
TOTAL GROSS REVENUES							
COSTS OF OPERATIONS							
NET PROFIT BEFORE TAX							

EXHIBIT 12–2: Division Five-Year Functional Plans Form.

DIVISION: _____

	This Year	19__	19__	19__	19__	19__
SALES – UNITS						
GROSS SALES – DOLLARS						
ALLOWANCES						
NET SALES						
COST OF GOODS SOLD						
GROSS PROFIT ON SALES						
G & A EXPENSE						
SELLING EXPENSE						
ADVERTISING EXPENSE						
R & D EXPENSE						
TOTAL OPERATING EXPENSE						
OTHER CHARGES, NET						
INTEREST ON LONG-TERM OBLIGATIONS,						
OTHER						
INCOME BEFORE DEPRECIATION						
DEPRECIATION						
INCOME BEFORE OVERHEAD ALLOCATION						
ALLOCATION OF GENERAL OVERHEAD						
NET INCOME BEFORE TAXES						
RATE OF RETURN ON ASSETS						

EXHIBIT 12–3:   Financial Summary.

ask divisions to prepare pro forma balance sheets that would result from the implementation of the functional plans.

Some companies request their divisions to prepare detailed functional plans for all major functions for the first and second year of a five-year planning horizon. Less detail is requested for the third, fourth, and fifth years. Some companies ask for detailed plans for the first two years, nothing for the third and fourth years, and then only general trends for the fifth year. This approach inhibits extrapolation and helps focus the attention of managers and staff on short-range realities and longer range possibilities.

More companies are asking divisions to provide both quantitative and qualitative information about their medium-range functional plans. For instance, one company asks divisions to present their major strategies to headquarters. They are not asked to submit detailed functional plans but they are requested to sketch in qualitative terms the main paths by means of which strategies are to be implemented and objectives achieved. The divisions are asked, however, to present rather detailed financial plans in the form of pro forma income statements. In this firm the assumption is made that division managers have had considerable experience in planning and will coordinate functional plans not only to prepare more reliable income statements but also to test the validity of their strategies. Another advantage of this approach is that headquarters does not get bogged down in details and can concentrate on the most important issues—strategies, major functional plans, and financial results.

Some companies ask divisions to formulate their strategies and then develop tactical plans for each major strategy. The degree to which different functional plans are integrated varies among companies. In this approach, as in most others, divisions are asked to present income statements for the entire division.

Another company asks divisions to describe programs for implementing major changes in existing operations, the priorities that exist among alternative programs, and anticipated schedules for carrying out specific short-range plans. This company explains that typical programs to be covered are: products, pricing, sales programs, manufacturing methods, warehousing and distribution, physical facilities and equipment, location and space requirements, organization and personnel, finance and control procedures, data processing and record keeping, and purchasing.

Another company asks its divisions to submit strategic plans but not detailed medium-range functional plans. The divisions are supposed to interrelate new product development plans, marketing plans, facility and production plans, acquisition plans, and plans for organizational changes in order to insure that there is an integrated total division plan, that the needed resources are or will be available, and that they will be committed to the division plan. Only major items needed to implement strategies have to be reported to headquarters such as sales, market share, and new equipment. This company does ask the divisions to prepare a detailed financial statement and to indicate required capital expenditures.

Centralized companies, of course, have similar options in the development of their medium-range functional programming.

The structure of plans in either a decentralized or a centralized company will vary because of a number of considerations. For instance, the marketing plan will be central in a typical beer company. Production, raw material purchases, facilities, and so on, are geared to the marketing plan. Research and development may be central in a high technology company that depends upon its technology for competitive position. In an automobile company a number of functional plans must be carefully coordinated in an integrated plan—sales, production, facilities, research and development, material and component scheduling, employment, and finance. In labor-intensive companies facilities may be the central focal point from which other plans are developed.

Content of Major Functional Plans

There is no uniform structure of individual functional plans.[1] Therefore, the following descriptions are only illustrative of content. The plans are based on the assumption that for the company or division for which functional planning is to be done there will have been an established mission, long-range planning objectives, and strategies. In each functional area managers and staff must ask themselves what questions are of most importance in the implementation of strategies to achieve objectives and missions. As in the situation audit, the possible range of subject matter that could be addressed in each functional area is so broad that no company can examine it all. Hence, the subject matter of plans must be limited.

MARKETING PLANS

Although our interest in this section focuses on medium-range plans to implement strategies, it is useful to note that many companies define marketing plans as those that cover all aspects of planning as described in Exhibit 12–1. For that reason Exhibit 12–4 is presented to show the table of contents of a more or less typical marketing plan.[2] In the plan will be found the situation audit, master strategies (mission, long-range planning objectives), program strategies, medium-range functional plans, and short-range plans.

Marketing plans will vary with the nature of the product and services offered by a company, preferences of individuals in the company concerned with marketing, distribution systems employed, and so on. For instance, marketing plans for a consumer products company will focus heavily on advertising and sales promotion. Marketing plans for an aerospace company will focus on understanding the demands for its products and matching technology to meet them.

Medium-range plans identify specific functional actions required to implement strategies. Typically, this would include such activities as the field sales organization—size, structure, deployment; advertising; sales promotion; pricing, adding, dropping, modifying, branding, packaging, standardizing, and grading of products; market research; distributor or dealer activities; inventories; sales training; and technical services.

Although some companies insist on complete plans covering all products and markets there is a trend today for top managements to ask divisions only for data on dominant products and markets and to report with comparatively short statements. The assumption is made in many companies that those top managers who read marketing plans will have much background information about them that can be eliminated. Therefore, only the highlights of the plans are requested.[3]

Exhibit 12–4 lists contingency plans, a subject discussed in detail in Chapter 14. A survey of marketing plans reveals that very few companies have alternative plans to meet unexpected contingencies in the marketing area. The basic reason given for this lack is that it is difficult enough to get managers to prepare original plans let alone alternative plans. Rather than make contingency plans managers deal with uncertainty by altering original plans, when necessary, on a quarterly basis.[4]

NEW PRODUCT PLANS

Because of accelerating technology, rapidly changing consumer requirements and preferences, more intensive competition, reduced product life cycles, and high potentialities of product failure, new product planning is becoming ever more important. New product plans must be coordinated primarily with marketing, manufacturing, engineering, and finance plans. New product developments move through a series of steps each of which necessitates many detailed action plans. For example, the first step is the generation of new product ideas. This may involve brainstorming sessions, surveys of consumer requirements and preferences, or systematic new product research, to name a few approaches. Once

I. Information Base and Business Analysis
  A. General background economic indicators for past five years and future five years, such as GNP and its components, especially disposable consumer income; population growth; and commodity price trends.
  B. Data and analysis of past (three years), present, and projected (five years), as appropriate for:
    1. Total markets for each product.
    2. Characteristics of markets of interest to company.
    3. Sales potential and expected volume for each product and share of each market.
    4. Current posture for each product, including major strengths and weaknesses relating to product acceptance, distribution channels, promotion, and pricing.
  C. Data and analysis of competition, including for past and present such matters as:
    1. Share of market.
    2. Product acceptance.
    3. Future potential product, price, promotion, and channel distribution changes.
    4. Strengths and weaknesses of competitor marketing.
  D. Analysis of future changes in strategic factors for marketing success for each product and each market.
  E. Analysis of problems and opportunities in integration of the company's functions in supporting marketing.
  F. Conclusions pinpointing changes in the firm's environment, as well as those within the company, that constitute new and important opportunities or problems.
II. Marketing Charter and Objectives
  A. Define or restate the "charter" or "primary mission" of the company unit or product area covered by the plan.
  B. Objectives and goals concerned with volume, profit, and share of the market.
  C. Objectives and goals concerning main elements of marketing, such as product, promotion, channels, and pricing.
III. Marketing Strategies
  A. Product development
  B. Distribution techniques
  C. Pricing
  D. Promotion
  E. Profitability
  F. Share of the market
IV. Five-Year Plans
  (In this section are detailed functional plans for five years.)
  A. Product development
  B. Etc., as above

(Continued on facing page)

V. One-Year Detailed Plans
(Included here are the specific action steps necessary to accomplish marketing objectives, such as promotion, display, and support of other departments.)
VI. Financial Summary
A. Analysis of income, cost, and profit results (five years).
VII. Contingency Plans
A. Brief plans for alternative possible events.

EXHIBIT 12–4: Table of Contents of a Marketing Plan. (Source: Adapted from George A. Steiner, *Top Management Planning* (New York: Macmillan, 1969), pp. 532–533.)

a new product materializes there is a preliminary screening to test its likelihood of success. Following this step is a detailed analysis and evaluation of the product's potential. If the product passes this screening it then moves through development and further testing. Finally, it is launched on the market.

It should be noted that some new product plans may require detailed operating plans that extend well beyond the typical medium-range planning period. For instance, a producer of a commercial jet transport may have a medium-range planning period of five or seven years but the detailed plans for the airplane may extend ten to fifteen years in the future. The project plan for a new facility may also extend well beyond the medium-range planning period if it is to cover preliminary design, construction, and operation until revenues equal costs.

MANUFACTURING PLANS

Manufacturing plans may include all the activities required to produce products and/or services: facilities location, maintenance, and replacement; production; raw material and component purchases, scheduling, and storing; and manpower acquisition and employment. Some manufacturing plans also cover transportation and quality control, for example. In each of these areas, of course, there is a wide range of detailed action programs that could be included in a comprehensive listing of plan content.

FINANCIAL PLANS

There are different types of financial plans. One is the aggregation of all plans of a company to show the financial results of implementing them. Usually these are presented in typical income statement and balance sheet form. A second type of financial plan concerns the acquisition and control of needed financial resources to achieve the plans. This might take the form, for instance, of plans for common stock sale, long-term bond issues, better management of cash flow, and dividend payments. A third type of financial plan concerns capital allocations and may cover capital budgeting as well as general budgetary controls. Exhibit 12–5 is a form for showing facility requirements (plans). It includes important information submitted for facilities that represent proposed plans.

PERSONNEL PLANS

Among the functions that may be the subject of personnel plans are recruitment and placement; communications, including the company newspaper or newsletter; wage and salary administration; employee benefit programs, including insurance, pensions, and savings and credit plans; training and management development; labor relations and union negotiations; worker safety and fire protection; recreation for employees; and career planning for employees.

OTHER FUNCTIONAL PLANS

Other functional areas for which plans may be prepared would include diversification; organization; international operations; public relations; consumer affairs; governmental affairs; and information processing. Of course, this does not exhaust the list of possibilities.

Division _____   Date _____

Description of Item(s)

Reason for Expenditures

Cost		Classification of Expenses (Check One)	
Plant and Equipment			
Transportation and Installation		Expansion	
		Cost Reduction	
Total Expenditure		Necessity	
Less Salvage Value		Research and Development	
Total Cash Outlay			
Profit Improvement		URGENCY (Check One)	
Annual Added Profit			
Percent Return on Investment Annual Added Profit÷ by 1/2 Total Cash Outlay)		A	
		B	
Estimated Life of Depreciation		C	

Timing of Expenditure		Building and Equipment To Be Scrapped or Obsoleted	
19___ 1Q		Description	
2Q			
3Q			
4Q			
Total			
19___		Original Cost	
19___		Age	
19___		Book Value	
Total			

EXHIBIT 12–5:   Facilities Requirements.

Preparing Integrated Medium-Range Plans

A difficult problem in integrating medium-range plans, according to Hussey, is that it is easy to prepare a good argument to show that this task is impossible.[5] The sales forcast upon which marketing plans are based must rely upon cost of production estimates. Accountants will argue, however, that these costs cannot be estimated without knowledge of production output in terms of units, production capacity, production methods, and so on. Manufacturing managers may argue that these estimates are not possible without sales forecasts. Uncompromising positions in such matters will naturally lead to plans that do not mesh. There are many comparable instances in coordinated functional planning in which intransigent managers can create severe planning problems.

Integration of functional plans is further complicated by iteration among functional programs. For example, on the basis of past experience a given sales level may signify the need for so many employees. However, the costs of hiring additional employees may be considered too high by management. To reduce such costs managers may decide to purchase new machinery to increase productivity per man-hour and thus lessen the need for additional employees. Throughout the medium-range programming process hundreds of such trade-offs must be identified and choices made. Although past functional relationships are helpful in medium-range planning they are subject to change in light of future potentialities and are constantly altered in the planning process.

A number of organizational and procedural approaches exist to deal with these problems. The following are a few of the more commonly used ones.

One that is frequently used is the formation of a planning committee that prepares guidelines for the development of functional plans. The chief executive of a centralized company may be the chairman of this group, or the division general manager of a decentralized division may be the chairman. Members of the committee should be representatives from the functional areas whose plans are to be coordinated. The secretary of the group may be a staff planner. The work of such a committee will of course proceed through a number of steps because integration is not something that usually can be achieved in one sitting. Getting together those who are involved in planning has many obvious advantages.[6]

A variation of this approach asks each functional manager to prepare brief preliminary plans for his area and send them to other functional managers with whom coordination is essential. When each has had an opportunity to examine the plans a meeting is called to thrash out problems.

Another approach is to appoint one person, such as the director of marketing, to oversee the proper integration of plans.

Another possibility is for the chief executive of a centralized company, or the division manager of a decentralized company, to assume the coordination responsibility. One variation of this approach is for the chief executive to appoint a staff director to work with him and the functional managers in such a way that the chief executive will have the participation of functional managers but make the basic decisions concerning plans.

Some Guides in Developing Integrated Functional Plans

Experience with integrated functional planning has yielded a number of lessons that can help in the development of more effective plans. A few of the key ones are reviewed here.

First, top management must determine the degree of interrelationship that will exist between strategic plans and medium-range plans, among medium-range plans, and between medium-range and short-range plans. The relationship can be loose or tight. For example, an advertising program for a nondurable consumer product planned for five years from today need be specified only in broad terms and related only loosely with sales, engineering, production, and so on. On the other hand, a plan to construct a nuclear power plant must be laid out in the greatest detail for perhaps ten to fifteen years ahead. There is no formula to give the proper balance over the planning time horizon between precise detail and close interrelationships and broad estimates and loose interrelationships.

If planning relationships are too tight and too detailed, there may be a lack of interest in planning and a stifling of creativity among lower level managers. On the other hand, if the relationships are too loose the result may be much the same because lower level managers will not be sure they are performing in conformance with the wishes of top management and as required to implement effectively other functional plans. Striking the right balance is a matter of managerial style, the nature of the subject of planning, and the structure of the business.

Second, attempts to coordinate completely all functions into an integrated plan are ill-advised. The lesson of experience, as noted previously, is to integrate only those functions that must be coordinated. Also, the further out in time the less is the need for close coordination.

Third, plans should be kept as simple and short as possible. In the past, the tendency was to prepare elaborate and detailed functional plans. Marketing plans, for instance, sometimes were 100 or more pages long. Companies today prepare much less elaborate plans and request that they be presented in simple terms.

Fourth, line managers in each functional area should be responsible for their plans and should get deeply involved in their development. Furthermore, their functional plans should be prepared with an eye toward other functional plans and not independently of them. Functional managers have dual roles. They must prepare plans for their areas that are in conformance with their views and yet they must prepare these plans in harmony with plans of other functional areas. This balancing act is not always easy. It cannot be done unless managers are closely involved in planning.

Fifth, functional managers should prepare their plans for an area over which they have authority. Their plans should not cover activities in other organizations and other managers should not prepare plans for them. An exception of course is plans made by top management that affect the entire organization.

Sixth, attention must be given to avoiding extrapolation. When planning is done on an annual cycle there is a tendency for managers and staff to extrapolate from last year's plans to get the plan for the year ahead. Thus, if a company makes five-year medium-range plans, there is a tendency for managers and staff to calculate the fifth year's plan by extrapolation from the previous year's plan rather than to rethink the entire five-year plan. This tendency reflects the fact that planning is difficult and time-consuming; managers, impatient to get back to today's business, will take shortcuts in planning if they can. (Another type of extrapolation is to extend the annual budget into the future. This approach, too, must be avoided.)

Seventh, managers should be given as much flexibility as practicable in the development of their plans and in reporting them to higher levels of management. Managers in functional areas should be expected to include in their plans the most important actions required to implement strategies and to relate properly their activities to other functional plans. Flexibility should be minimized, however, in reporting the financial results of plans. Some uniformity is necessary so that the financial implications of plans can be aggregated and evaluated easily.

Eighth, only high priority actions should be covered in functional plans. Clearly, including too many actions leads to too much detail, which in turn leads to excessive planning burdens and greater possibilities for conflicts among plans. There unfortunately is no formula for deciding the priority actions to be included in each functional plan.

Summary

This chapter described the role of medium-range functional programming in the strategic planning process. This part of planning is significant because it establishes the creditability of strategic plans and provides the base for effective implementation of strategic plans.

It was pointed out that there is no one way to do medium-range functional programming. Variations in the medium-range programming structure and in approaches to developing such plans were reviewed. Also, there is little uniformity in the content of medium-range functional plans although, as noted in this chapter, there are fundamental questions concerning each one that should be asked and answered.

Finally, a number of guidelines based on experience were presented. Keep the interrelationships among functional plans as simple as practicable and neither too tight nor too loose; stick to as few functional interrelationships as practicable; keep the plans as simple and short as possible; involve line managers in planning in their areas of responsibility; make sure plans follow organizational lines;

avoid extrapolation; give managers as much flexibility as possible in developing and describing their plans; and make sure that only top priority questions are raised and answered in each functional plan so as to avoid excessive detail.

13 Translating Strategic Plans into Current Decisions

No company ever made a nickel of profit by making plans; profit flows from the implementation of plans. The aim of strategic planning, as discussed earlier, is to formulate superior strategies and to implement them effectively. The first step in translating plans into decisions to implement them was discussed in Chapter 12. This chapter will narrow the focus and discuss the second step, the preparation of tactical plans to guide current decisions and actions to implement strategic plans. Budgets are the primary technique used in this process and therefore the chapter will devote most attention to them. Other tactical programs to guide current actions will be briefly discussed. The third and final step in implementation concerns controlling and motivating people to take actions in conformance with plans. This subject will be treated in Chapters 16 and 17.

Budgets

Budgets are integrating methods to translate strategic plans into current actions. They are guides to action. They set standards for coordinated action and they provide a basis for controlling performance to see that it is in conformance with plans. Implicit in these descriptions are three overlapping functions: planning, coordinating, and controlling. Before describing these functions in more detail I shall review the structure of budget systems.

Budget Systems

Like strategic planning systems budget systems must be fitted to the unique characteristics of an organization. Since each organization differs from all others so will budget systems. Most companies have sales and expense budgets but there universal practice ends.

A simple budget system is shown in Exhibit 13–1. In this system an annual budget for income and expense is prepared first. The detailed budgets for both income and expense are prepared next, as shown in the exhibit. The results of operations are then reflected in financial statements.

Details within each of the master budgets shown in Exhibit 13–1 will vary from company to company in classification and detail. For instance, in a large manufacturing company there may be dozens of classifications of budgets in the manufacturing area, each of which may be extensively subdivided. In small companies the whole system may be very simple, with few budgets and few classifications in them.

In Exhibit 13–1, the budgets noted under marketing are identified to illustrate that in each of the areas shown in the chart there are many subbudgets. To illustrate further, in a large company, the manufacturing master budget may be broken down into production units for every product, raw material requirements for every product, inventory for every product, direct labor schedules and expenses for every classified task (assembly, fabrication, modeling, etc.), managerial salaries, maintenance, new facilities and tools, and miscellaneous supplies. Each of these classifications may be further broken down into sub-subgroups. For instance, new facilities and tools may be divided into brick and mortar of various types and different types of tools.

Some of the budgets may cover an entire year, whereas others may be made for three-month periods, one-month periods, or weeks.

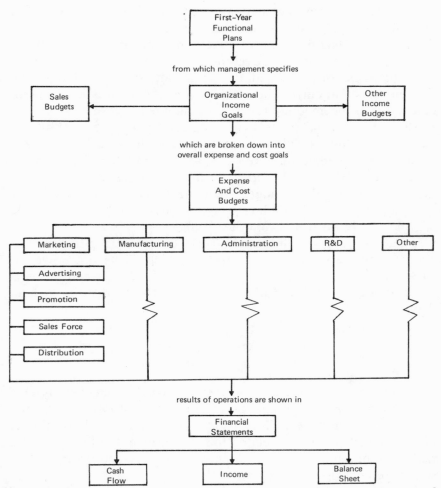

EXHIBITS 13–1: A Simplified Development and Structure of Operating Budgets.

BASIC MANAGERIAL PURPOSES OF BUDGETS

More should be said now about the three managerial functions of budgets, namely, planning, coordinating, and controlling.

Budgets are designed to improve planning. They force managers to direct attention to the formulation of goals and the way in which they are to be implemented. Pressure is put on managers to express the ends they seek in quantitative terms. Once the ends are quantified budgets necessitate the specification of the means to achieve them. The first year of a medium-range plan should establish a solid base for the development of current budgets but it generally does not provide all that is needed for annual budgeting. The reason is that current budgets involve much more detail than is developed in the medium-range programming process.

Budgets are a means to help managers coordinate operations. Exhibit 13–2 illustrates how budgets are coordinated. In this chart, production, raw material purchases, and direct labor requirements are coordinated with anticipated sales. In more comprehensive budget systems other budgets may be included: manufacturing expense, inventories, building services, advertising, maintenance, cash flow, administrative overhead, and so on.

Finally, budgets facilitate managerial control over performance. Budgets themselves do not control anything. They do, however, set standards of performance against which actions can be measured. More will be said about this aspect of budgeting in later chapters.

LINKAGE

Reference was made to the fact that current budgets are related to medium-range programs, especially the functional plans prepared for the first year. Managers must determine how closely annual budgets are to be related to the figures in the first year of a medium-range program plan. Managers are divided on the issue. Some prefer a tight linkage and others a loose linkage.

In a system with a very tight linkage, the numbers in the annual budget will be the same as those in the first year of the medium-range plan. Where linkage is loose the annual budget will be made within a framework established by the medium-range plan.

Those who favor tight linkage argue that it gives realism to plans. It shows, they say, a commitment to implementing plans that are realistic. Tight linkage shows the importance of planning to managers and assures credible plans.

Those who argue against tight linkage say that it creates budget myopia. They say that if managers know their budgets are to be identical with the first year plans of the medium-range programs their eyes will be focused exclusively on the first year of the

SALES BUDGET FOR YEAR

Product	Units	Price	Total Sales
1	20,000	$20.00	$ 400,000
2	30,000	30.00	900,000
3	50,000	15.00	750,000
4	5,000	50.00	250,000
	105,000		$2,300,000

PRODUCTION BUDGET

	Products			
Description	1	2	3	4
Quantity	20,000	30,000	50,000	5,000
Ending Inventory	5,000			
Total Required	25,000	etc.		
Less				
Beginning Inventory	3,000			
Required Production	22,000			

RAW MATERIALS UNIT

	Products				
Material	1	2	3	4	Total
St. (lbs.)	10,000	5,000	2,000	1,000	18,000
Cu. (lbs.)					
Al. (lbs.)		etc.			

RAW MATERIALS PURCHASES BUDGET

Material	Prod.	Inv. End.	Total	Less Beg. Inv.	To be Purchased	Price	Cost
St. (lbs.)	18,000	8,000	26,000	6,000	20,000	$150	$3,000,000
Cu. (lbs.)		etc.					
Al. (lbs.)							

DIRECT LABOR BUDGET

Product	Quantity to be Produced	Standard Labor Hours Per Unit	Total Standard Labor	Budget at $5 Per Standard Labor Hour
1	22,000	2	Hours	$220,000
2				
3		etc.		
4				

EXHIBIT 13–2: Illustration of Budget Coordination. (Source: George A Steiner, *Top Management Planning* (New York: Macmillan, 1969), p. 300.

medium-range planning horizon. Tight linkage, as a result, will produce planning fixation in the short range. Little if any longer range thinking will take place.

These arguments will have different applications in different companies. It is possible to use a tight linkage and have managers think creatively about the longer range future. To achieve this result, however, will require managers who are capable of and completely sympathetic to strategic planning as discussed in this book, together with a top management committed to seeing that the company has an effective strategic planning system.

One observer put the problem of linkage this way:

> A budget is a document of restraint and control, whereas a plan is an assertive, strategic, forward-looking document. These are very different approaches. However, the approaches must be reconciled to give operating creditability to planning, and to work a meaningful degree of action into the planning process. Obtaining the benefits of linkage without succumbing to its pitfalls is a difficult problem which cannot be resolved on a purely intellectual level.[1]

Degree of linkage will depend upon such factors as managerial capabilities, as noted previously; the size of the firm; the way in which plans are prepared; perceived purposes of planning; capital intensity; and environmental turbulence. For example, in a small company in which plans are made by the team approach and in which coordination of functions is critical there is likely to be tight linkage. In large companies, on the other hand, with rapidly changing technology and economic-environmental forces, the linkage is likely to be looser. In capital-intensive companies that are growing slowly and in which management is greatly concerned about current operational efficiency the linkage is likely to be tight.

FLEXIBILITY

The essence of budgeting is to put a dollar sign on an activity and freeze it. As environmental conditions change, however, it may not be wise to keep the frozen budget. On the other hand, it may be administratively impossible constantly to revise budgets as circumstances change. How can flexibility be injected into budgeting?

First, a company can use supplemental budgets. This method is employed mostly with budgets that establish limits on expenditures. If a capital expenditure budget of a division turns out to be too low, for example, a supplement can be requested and added to the original budget.

Second, alternative budgets can be devised. A company may establish a budget for what it considers to be the most probable conditions. If there is a possibility, however, that sales may be lower, then alternative budgets may be developed for, say, 5 percent, 10 percent, and 15 percent under estimate.

Third, management can accept flexibility. Some large companies prepare highly detailed budgets for each of the divisions for each month of the calendar year and the budgets are not altered except under the most unusual circumstances. The reason is that varying the budgets with changes in environment may be administratively too costly. Under such circumstances, top management's review of operations and appraisal of divisional management performance are based less upon the original budget than upon the original budget as it should be modified by actual events.

Fourth, the company can use variable expense budgets. Variable budgets are made to insure proper coordination of activities as changes take place in sales. They are schedules of cost of production that tell managers what levels of critical activities actually should be as changes occur in sales and output volume. They permit managers to realize a dynamic integration as events require deviations from planned output. Exhibit 13–3 shows a variable budget and what should have happened, as compared with what did happen, when volume changed. Shown in the table is the output and cost budget for the first quarter of the year. Notice how the fixed, semivariable, and variable costs relate to the forecasted output. Effective variable budgeting depends upon identification of these costs and a reasonable understanding of how each changes with different output volumes. In the bottom part of Exhibit 13–3 is shown what actually should have happened when volume dropped 10 percent to 720 units. Variable costs should have dropped 10 percent; semivariable costs, 7 percent; and fixed costs, not at all. Actually, neither the variable nor the semivariable costs dropped enough, as is shown in the last two columns.

When variable budget schedules are accurate and reports are prompt it is possible for managers to insure a continuous, planned

FIRST QUARTER
OUTPUT AND COST BUDGET

Month	Units	Direct Labor & Materials	Property Taxes	Supervision	Production Total Costs
J	800	$ 640	$100	$280	$1,020
F	1,000	800	100	300	1,200
M	1,200	960	100	320	1,380
Total	3,000	2,400	300	900	3,600

RESUME OF PLANNED AND ACTUAL OPERATIONS FOR JANUARY

Item	Budgeted for Original Program	Budgeted for Actual Volume	Actual Costs at Actual Volume	Variance
Production (Units)	800	720		-80
Costs:				
Variable	$ 640	$576	$ 630	$ +54
Taxes	100	100	100	0
Semi-variable	280	260	270	+10
Total	1,020	936	1,000	+64

EXHIBIT 13–3: **Illustration of Variable Budgeting in Operation. (Source: George A. Steiner, *Top Management Planning* (New York: Macmillan, 1969), p. 302.)**

integration of operations as changes take place in sales and production volume.

Project Plans

Project plans are made for the pursuit and completion of a concrete activity such as plant construction, an acquisition program, penetration of a new market, or the development of a new product. Strategies and tactical plans related to such projects are incorporated in the strategic planning process, from strategy formulation through medium-range programming and budgeting. Two important characteristics of project plans are of relevance here. First, as noted previously, they have a time span that is determined by the implementation time of the project itself. This may be much longer than the medium-range time horizon. Second, they generally contain far more detail than is found in the typical medium-range functional plan as well as in the typical operational budget. As a result, short-range project plans complement the budget process as a mechanism to implement strategic plans.

Management by Objective

Peter Drucker is credited with creating the idea of management by objective (MBO).

> Each manager, from the "big boss" down to the production foreman or the chief clerk, needs clearly spelled-out objectives. These objectives should lay out what performance the man's own managerial unit is supposed to produce. They should lay out what contribution he and his unit are expected to make to help other units obtain their objectives. Finally, they should spell out what contribution the manager can expect from other units toward the attainment of his own objectives. Right from the start, in other words, emphasis should be on teamwork and team results.[2]

He pointed out that these objectives should be set in light of both short-range and long-range considerations. From the time these words were written in 1954 until today MBO has been introduced into more and more organizations, both private and public.

Like strategic planning MBO systems vary from company to company.[3] In some companies, with very elementary budget systems, MBO may carry an important responsibility for implementing strategies to achieve the overall objectives of a company. In companies with well-established and sophisticated budget systems MBO may be a vital complement to budgets in implementing strategies.

Budgets are concerned with actions needed to implement plans. They are used primarily by managers who are clearly identified as links in the implementation process. However, MBO has a wider concern. It is concerned with achievement of corporate objectives but it is more comprehensive in scope than are budgets. For example, objectives in an MBO system for a chief executive may be to develop a better climate in the organization to make possible more effective strategic plans, to become more involved in community affairs in order to improve the image of the company, or to speak out more aggressively in a fashion to help reduce general public antipathy toward business. A division manager may have budgets to guide his or her actions but they may be complemented by other objectives in an MBO system such as improving methods to identify and train the manager's replacement, developing a better system to survey technological threats, or encouraging employees to develop more interest in community affairs. Objectives such as these cover the entire range of managerial activities. An MBO system should help to highlight the more important managerial activities and to integrate management functions in a consistent and logical fashion.

Since a great deal has been written about MBO only a few additional comments about it will be made here.[4] Although the basic concept of MBO is simple, MBO is difficult to introduce and perfect in an organization. This system is designed to facilitate planning and the implementation of plans. It also has wider purposes, such as to motivate people to help achieve organizational aims, to improve problemsolving and decisionmaking in a company, to facilitate performance appraisal, and, in general, to improve management so as to achieve more efficiently and effectively the aims sought by an organization.

Because of the many problems associated with MBO it is not as likely to facilitate efficient and effective implementation of strategies as will a well-conceived system of budgets and tactical plans. Nevertheless, an appropriate MBO system should complement a well-conceived short-range planning system in insuring superior implementation of strategies and more effective achievement of overall aims.

Zero-Base Budgeting

Zero-base budgeting (ZBB) was first used in industry by Texas Instruments in the early 1970s but it was not until later in the decade that the method received widespread attention in business and government.[5]

To oversimplify, ZBB is a method to insure that all expenditures are reviewed in a budget process, that all expenditures are tested in a cost-benefit analysis, and that only higher priority expenditures are approved. This idea is not new with ZBB, but most budget processes do not make such a review.

In budget systems there is a historical base of expenditures (administrative expenses, for example) necessary to conduct ongoing activities that are essential to the operation of a company and its subunits. In too many instances the assumption is made that activities in this historical base are being performed efficiently, are necessary to the achievement of overall company aims, and are projected in the budget year to be cost effective (that is, benefits are greater than costs). These expenditures therefore are included in budgets each year with little or no review and with small incremental increases to take account of inflation, expanded activity, and so on.

Some items in the historical base should be eliminated, some reduced, and some retained. But which ones? The ZBB process seeks to help managers make this determination on a logical basis. Therefore, ZBB is not so much a technique to further the implementation of strategies as it is a method to control costs better.

The definition of ZBB by one of its architects is as follows:

> A planning and budgeting process which requires each manager to justify his entire budget request in detail from scratch (hence zero-base) and shifts the burden of proof to each manager to justify why he should spend any money at all. The approach requires that all activities be analyzed in "decision packages" which are evaluated by systematic analysis and ranked in order of importance.[6]

As does traditional budgeting, ZBB begins with the development of overall corporate aims, strategies, and medium-range functional plans. The second step is to identify so-called decision packages. Decision packages identify a discrete activity. For example, a cost center; a group of people; a particular product, project, or service; a program to reduce costs; and a capital expenditure.

Third, alternative ways of operating to achieve given ends are identified for each package. For example, a decision package may be identified as market research. Alternatives would be to continue the operation as is, eliminate it, or change it. For instance, research could be done by an outside consultant, the staff could be reduced, or research could be done by subdivisions.

Fourth, a decision is made about the level of effort below which the end desired cannot be achieved. For example, if the decision is made to keep the research unit in its present position in the organization the minimum may be to reduce it to one professional person. Then, additional increments of service and cost are developed. For instance, if one more person is added, the cost and benefit will be evaluated. If two more persons are added, again, the cost and benefit will be calculated. The result will be for each increment a decision package.

Decision packages can then be ranked, in a fifth step, in priority order on the basis either of a cost-benefit analysis or of a subjective evaluation.

In a sixth step the manager at the next level gets the packages. This manager can compare the rankings with package rankings from other units under his jurisdiction. When they are aggregated by priority this manager may determine which packages will be authorized and which eliminated. This manager, in turn, will prepare decision packages for his operations and pass them along to the next higher level of management until the process reaches either the chief executive or a budget committee or both.

This method of budgeting is not applicable throughout the budgeting system. In manufacturing, for example, the sales forecast and technology will determine the mix of different levels of output. Standard cost accounting will provide the expense numbers for budgeting so there will be no need for ZBB. However, ZBB is applicable to areas in which standard cost accounting is weak, such as services, staff functions, and research and development.

There are some obvious advantages in using ZBB. To name a few, it forces careful evaluation of ongoing costs and relates them to benefit. It links resource allocations with results. It facilitates decisions in resource allocations. It should result in cost savings.

On the other hand, ZBB has some limitations. It is not applicable to the same range of operations as a traditional budgeting system. And it may complicate the budgeting process. For example, making cost-benefit analyses may be difficult and controversial. The problem in making cost-benefit analyses is aggravated when goals are not concrete and understood. As in strategic planning and budgeting it is not easy to determine precisely what the appropriate ZBB system is for a company, yet, if the system is not appropriate it will not operate effectively.

Other Tactical Plans

A number of tactical plans aside from those already discussed should be noted. For example, GANTT milestone charts schedule tasks, such as the development of a product. More complex interrelationships of tasks can be scheduled in network charts. It bears repetition that budgets do not set standards only in financial terms. Many different physical budgets or standards can be set up, such as output per man-hour, tons of coal purchased, or component purchases. Of course, sequences of steps can be prepared to guide all sorts of activities.

Summary

Short-term budgets, the main subject of this chapter, are devices to express planned intentions in quantitative terms, to coordinate different functional operations of the firm, and to provide a means for measuring performance and permitting proper control of operations. They are therefore a significant means to translate strategic decisions into action.

There is no one way to design a budget system for a company since each system must be designed to suit the characteristics of each company. One simple systems design was presented in the chapter.

Budgets may be tightly or loosely linked to the first year of medium-range functional programs. The merits and disadvantages of these two approaches were presented.

Budgets made for an extended period of time, say, one year, should not remain unchanged when environment alters. A number of ways to make budgets flexible were presented in the chapter.

Other complementary methods to translate strategic plans into current actions are project plans and management by objective, both of which were discussed briefly in the chapter. Finally, zero-base budgeting was discussed. Zero-base budgeting is a new set of buzz words for an old idea, namely, reevaluate completely all budgets and do not blindly accept without analysis a historical base of ongoing activities. Also, ZBB provides a cost-benefit analysis that permits managers to allocate funds against the highest priorities. Zero-base budgeting is more suitable for administrative type programs, such as services, than for manufacturing programs. Finally, it was noted that a variety of tactical plans complement budgets in well-conceived short-range planning systems to implement strategies.

14 Contingency Planning and Alternative Futures Explorations

In recent years, as pointed out previously, the business environment has been turbulent. Unexpected events have occurred, economic forecasts have proven inaccurate, and new forces have appeared that, at the very least, have raised puzzling questions about their impact on business and what management ought to do about them. Succinctly, uncertainty about the evolving environment of business has increased rather than diminished. All this, of course, makes managers uneasy about their formal strategic plans and their implementation. To help cope with environmental uncertainties managers today are making contingency plans and are having staffs prepare studies of alternative futures. These two types of planning are the subject of this chapter.

Contingency Planning

NATURE AND PURPOSE OF CONTINGENCY PLANNING

Formal strategic planning is based on events that have a high probability of occurring—the most likely happenings. However,

229

there are less likely conditions that could create serious difficulties for a company if they actually occurred. These are the subject matter of contingency plans. Very simply, contingency plans are preparations to take specific actions when an event or condition not planned for in the formal planning process actually does take place.

The fundamental purpose of contingency planning is to place managers in a better position to deal with unexpected developments than if they had not made such preparations. By failing to anticipate certain events managers may not act as quickly as they should in a critical situation and the event may create more damage that it otherwise would have. Contingency planning should eliminate fumbling, uncertainty, and time delays in making the needed response to an emergency. Contingency planning also should make such responses more rational.

An additional advantage of contingency planning is that it forces managers to look at dimensions in the environment other than probable events. This endeavor, together with their experience in strategic planning, should make them more adept at dealing with unexpected turns of events. Events dealt with in a contingency plan are not likely to take place precisely as set forth in the plan. Hence, even with contingency plans a manager may be forced to improvise.[1]

DISADVANTAGES OF CONTINGENCY PLANNING

A possible problem with contingency planning is that it may stimulate negative attitudes in the minds of managers. Many contingency plans deal with pessimistic possibilities, such as lower sales, profits, or share of market than expected. Dwelling on such potentialities can generate negative thinking, pessimism, and fear, attitudes not consonant with the enthusiasm and optimism effective management should have.

Just the reverse, however, may take place. If managers have contingency plans they may be overly optimistic in their strategic plans because they know what to do if the planned objectives and goals are not met.

Contingency plans also may generate fear and uncertainty in an organization if they are revealed. For instance, a contingency plan to reduce employment in the event of a sales decline may cause morale problems among employees.

IDENTIFYING THE SUBJECT OF CONTINGENCY PLANS

The subject of a contingency plan should be one for which the probability of occurrence is considered lower than for events included in the planning process; one the actual occurrence of which will cause serious damage, especially if not dealt with quickly; and one the company can plan ahead to deal with swiftly if the event occurs.

The range of events and conditions fitting these characteristics is very wide for most companies. Thus, companies must identify those few contingencies for which plans will be made. Generally, the subject of contingency plans is deviation from expected sales growth or profit levels. But there are many other possibilities: the introduction of a product by a competitor that will take away a firm's market; a fire in a critical facility; the loss of a key manager; union activity; "takeover" threats; government regulations; prices of purchased materials; interest rates; new technology; capital availability; and availability of specific raw materials.

In this first step of contingency planning the subject must be identified and an estimated probability placed on its occurrence. A pragmatic approach to identification is simply to ask this question: "What if . . . ?" "What if we suddenly lose the customer who today is purchasing 30 percent of our total output?" "What if a fire shuts down our only ball bearing plant, whose output is indispensable in the production of our electric motors?" The most serious eventualities can be identified in this way, and probabilities must be attached to them. Then those events are identified for which detailed plans should be prepared.

Both the degree of criticality and the degree of probability must be considered and which one is overriding is a matter of choice. Some events with low probability must be addressed because of their criticality. For instance, assume that a product has a competitive advantage because it uses a patented bearing produced in only one of the company's plants. The sudden loss of that plant could be disastrous if no plans existed to meet that contingency. Though a plant is fireproofed and well protected it could still burn down. Here is a case of low probability but high criticality.

Contingency plan subjects should be selected with reference to the impact on the firm of an occurrence. The estimate of potential impact can be made in financial terms, competitive position, employee availability, or a combination of such considerations.

DEALING WITH "WHAT IF" QUESTIONS

The next step in contingency planning is to develop strategies and tactical plans to deal with the possible occurrence of each event selected for planning. The objective here is to neutralize or offset as much as possible the effects of the event when and if it occurs.

Alternative strategies should be identified and evaluated in light of the anticipated nature of the event and the company's capabilities and constraints in dealing with it. The result may be a decision to take advance action as well as to set forth strategies to be followed at the time of the event. For instance, in the case of the ball bearing plant, the company may decide to stockpile some bearings immediately to ease the impact of the loss of the plant. It may decide to set up a second source, or it may make arrangements with another company to acquire the needed bearings. Such strategies may not completely offset the damages of the loss of the plant, and additional strategies may be formulated to be implemented at the time of the plant loss.

Strategies should be as specific as possible. For instance, a company may develop a contingency plan to be implemented in the event of a drop in sales below a certain point. Strategies such as "reduce employment," "reduce advertising expenses," or "delay construction" are too broad. They should specify: "If sales drop 10 percent below expectations our net income will decline by $10 million. In order to reduce this loss by 50 percent it will be necessary to defer the programmed expansion of plant Y, to reduce the number of employees to 1,000, and to cut variable production costs in proportion to the sales decline." Comparable strategies can be prepared to offset income loss by 75 or 100 percent.

If a company is to be prepared to implement such strategies it must have tactical plans at hand. In the foregoing case of the 10 percent drop in sales, tactical plans must be made to reduce employment, to defer construction, and to cut variable costs.

In sum, answering the "what if" question entails formulation of strategies for advance actions and actions in response to the unexpected, and of tactical plans to implement the strategies. When appropriate, and to the extent practicable, the expected results of such actions should be calculated—in financial terms, as noted with respect to the ball bearings, or in other meaningful measures such as market share, capacity, and available manpower.

TRIGGER POINTS

Contingency plans may specify trigger points or warning signals of the imminence of the event for which the plan was developed. For example, if a plan is prepared to deal with a 10 percent decline in sales below estimate there will be warning signals. Sales may fluctuate daily, weekly, or monthly. What will trigger the implementation of the plan? To illustrate, one company with a contingency plan of this type specifies that the plan is to be implemented when sales are 10 percent below estimate for two consecutive months.

In some cases, a fire, for instance, the trigger point is the event itself. But in others the point at which the plan should be implemented is not so clear. In those cases trigger points should be specified in the contingency plan.

The contingency plan should thus indicate the type of information to be collected and the action to be taken at the trigger point. Also, it is a good idea to assign specific responsibility to someone to collect the relevant information and to keep informed whoever makes the decision to implement the contingency plan.

CONTINGENCY PLAN DETAILS

There is no standard concerning the detail in which contingency plans are developed. Some plans may be no more than a few ideas in the mind of a chief executive about what action should be taken in response to a specific occurrence. Other contingency plans may be more elaborate, specifying what will be done if sales fall below a certain level.

There are no standard formats for contingency plans. It would seem appropriate to hold the level of detail to a minimum but also to include enough detail to provide suitable guidance to action when required. Conceptually, the more critical the plan the more detail. And, the shorter the available reaction time the more detail.

VOLUME OF CONTINGENCY PLANS

O'Connor interviewed fifty-eight executives whose companies did contingency planning and concluded: "Most companies emphasize that no more than a half dozen critical events—those that would have a significant impact on the financial and strategic goals of the company—should be selected for contingency planning."[2] This is probably a wise guide. Too many contingency plans can take too much staff and executive time to prepare. Contingency plans, according to O'Connor, should be made for really critical events, not merely troublesome ones.

EXPERIENCE WITH CONTINGENCY PLANS

O'Connor reported that among the companies she surveyed that did contingency planning none reported having to put any of their plans into effect in 1976 although several did so in 1975. It is not known whether this finding reflected a changing business climate or better planning. Very few of these companies had contingency plans prior to 1974.

Generally, when contingency plans are written they relate directly to short-range operating plans and not to long-range strategies. This is logical since the immediate response to a crisis must be made in short-range specific actions. Such contingency planning shades into variable budgeting, which of course has been standard accounting practice in many companies for years.

If, however, the short-range actions contemplated in the contingency plan have longer range strategic implications of importance, reformulation of long-range strategies should be made at the time the contingency plans are formulated and become part of them. When the contingency becomes reality top management may decide to redo its entire strategic plan. If, however, strategic changes are not too drastic the reformulation can be made in the next planning cycle. It probably is a good idea to consider the long-range strategic implications of immediate actions spelled out in the contingency plans. Otherwise, managers, in their desire to deal aggressively with an emergency, may lay the base for a future crisis.

In most companies contingency plans are prepared after the strategic planning cycle is completed. Undoubtedly, however, in many companies the data examined in the normal planning process yield information valuable in contingency planning.

O'Connor reported that managers in those companies doing contingency planning frequently complained that contingency planning is worthless without a good base plan. They believed that if a choice had to be made between contingency plans and first-rate strategic and action plans there is no contest—forget contingency plans. But, managers should not make that choice. With all the problems associated with contingency planning, and there are many, contingency plans should be made to deal with potentially highly critical events whose timing is uncertain and whose occurrence could seriously hurt the company if swift action were not taken.

Finally, as with strategic planning, contingency planning will assist managers in dealing with crises for which no contingency plans have been prepared.

Futures Explorations

Managers today are asking for a variety of environmental searches for use in the regular strategic planning process and for speculation about events beyond that time period. These searches, analyses, research studies, or projections, I lump together and call futures explorations.

The nomenclature in this area of planning is very loose and definitions vary greatly among different writers. I present Exhibit 14–1 to clarify the words used in this discussion.

We have already discussed at length the types of forecasts used in the regular strategic planning process. As pointed out in Chapter 8 they cover economic, technological, social, and political areas of concern to a company in completing its strategic plans. These are indicated in area B of Exhibit 14–1.

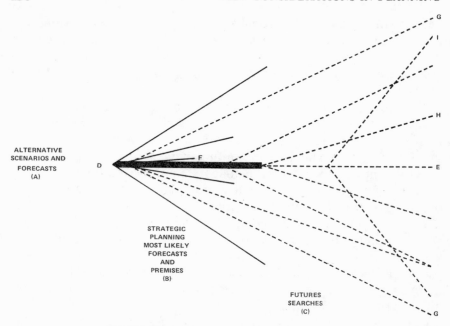

EXHIBIT 14–1:   Futures Explorations.

In recent years managers in many companies have felt the need to have projections other than the single case forecasts typically used in the formal planning process.[3] These (area A) are divided into two categories as shown in Exhibit 14–1, namely, those done for periods of time within the regular planning time horizon (area D bar line) and those done for periods extending beyond the regular planning horizon (area C in Exhibit 14–1).

The distance of lines on the chart from line DE is meant to indicate scope of the projection. A short distance (F) illustrates narrow scope, such as a forecast of interest rates. A great distance (G) illustrates a broad survey, such as scenarios of the future characteristics of the U.S. economy. Exhibit 14–1 says, therefore, that broader futures explorations are generally found in studies of the distant future. Sometimes the time period covered by long-range studies of the future overlap with the standard planning horizon, as indicated by line G. Sometimes they extend beyond the planning horizon in a continuous line (H) and sometimes there is a discontinuity (I). Lines above DE are meant to indicate optimistic projections, or projections better than the most likely ones used in the regular planning process. Lines below are meant to indicate more pessimistic projections than used in the regular planning process.

NATURE AND PURPOSE OF ALTERNATIVE SCENARIOS AND FORECASTS FOR THE PLANNING PERIOD

The word scenario first became popular as an approach to making projections with the publication of Kahn and Wiener's book *The Year 2000*.[4] This book defined scenarios as "hypothetical sequences of events constructed for the purpose of focusing attention on causal processes and decision-points. They answer two kinds of questions: (1) Precisely how might some hypothetical situation come about, step by step? and (2) What alternatives exist, for each actor, at each step, for preventing, diverting, or facilitating the process?"[5] As amply demonstrated in the book the scenarios are narratives, descriptions, or word pictures of future potential societies.

The word scenario continues to mean what Kahn and Wiener said it did but it has been stretched to include much narrower alternatives such as circumstances that might produce sales above or below a probable forecast. Thus, at one end of the definition are broad, societal hypothetical conditions at some future time; at the other end are comparatively short-range hypothetical projections of narrow phenomena.

Although the development of alternative scenarios and forecasts is not new in corporate planning (some companies used this methodology in the 1950s) there has been renewed interest in making these projections. One reason is that in the turbulent environments of recent years managers have been increasingly confronted with unforeseen events. In addition, they have found that forecasting is not an exact art; many forecasts have turned out to be wrong. Contingency plans have been prepared to deal with such uncertainties. Managers also have asked for alternative projections to help them understand and deal with uncertainties in the environment.

Alternative scenarios and forecasts will give managers a wider range of possibilities against which they can test policies and strategies. Managers are given a broader vision of alternative events, which may in turn help them to see better the things to be avoided or facilitated, as the case may be. The awareness of managers is raised; their outlook is broadened.

Alternative scenarios and forecasts also provide fertile ground for identifying events that might become the subject of a contingency plan.

Alternative scenarios and forecasts also serve to stretch the imagination of managers and staff. They force staff and managers to deal with details and interactions of forces that might be missed in single case projections. Their preparation and contemplation stimulate thinking about future environments and the possibilities in them for finding new opportunities and identifying hitherto unforeseen threats.

Studying scenarios should improve the ability of managers to conceptualize, to see broad patterns, generalizations, and interrelationships of systems. This is in contrast to concentrating on day-to-day details of a narrow scope. The higher in an organization a manager rises the greater a conceptualizer, generally, he must be. Thus, managerial participation in scenario building and/or study of the results of futures explorations can be considered a managerial training program.

BUSINESS EXPERIENCE WITH ALTERNATIVE SCENARIOS AND FORECASTS

Unfortunately there is no comprehensive survey of what industry is doing in this area. The available data seem to show increasing reliance on alternative scenarios and forecasts as an aid to business planning.[6]

RANGE OF ALTERNATIVE SCENARIOS AND FORECASTS IN THE PLANNING PERIOD

Probably the most common type of projection is the high-low scenario or forecast, alternative projections of the most likely cases used in the formal planning process; they concern such trends as sales, profits, market share, and inventories. For instance, a company may ask: "What circumstances might cause a sales level 15 to 20 percent below the most likely forecast?" "What forces may bring about a level 15 to 20 percent above the most likely case?"

Or, "Develop a scenario of the best possible environmental future and the worst possible situation for our company five years from now." This request may be narrowed to focus on the best and the worst with respect to sales, profits, or market share.

Other economic alternative scenario and forecast subjects are the gross national product, inflation, interest rates, energy, raw material supplies, competition, housing starts, and foreign imports of steel. Each of these factors could be the subject of an alternative survey, or a research study might include different combinations of them.

There are other subjects, of course, covering technology, changing social values, government regulation, potential legislation, labor union activities, the outcome of presidential elections, weather, foreign political and social changes in specific nations, and demographic changes, to name but a few.

Ideally, it would seem desirable for a manager to design strategies that fitted all three types of scenarios and forecasts— high, low, and probable.[7] In practice, however, this is possible in only a few instances.

TRENDS TOWARD VERY LONG-RANGE FUTURES PROJECTIONS

In the 1970s there has been an enormous increase in futures explorations extending out ten, twenty, thirty, or more years.[8] Interest in the distant future has been centered more in universities and service organizations than in business; however, interest is developing rapidly in the business world.[9]

TYPES OF ALTERNATIVE FUTURES SEARCHES USED IN BUSINESS

Futures analyses beyond the planning period can cover topics similar to those noted earlier for the planning period. Generally, however, they are considerably broader. General Electric, for example, has an ongoing project for evaluating changing social values that might affect the company in the 1980s and beyond. Mobil Oil Corporation has a long-term project concerned with the supply and demand of energy in general and hydrocarbons in particular in the year 2000 and beyond. Another company has one staff person assigned to the task of identifying pitfalls and possibilities for the company in the year 2000.

Though some studies cover only specific topics most of them are very broad. They ask open-ended questions such as: "What's out there (in a ten-, twenty-, or thirty-year period) that may affect our company that we should know about?"

TYPES OF ALTERNATIVE FUTURES SEARCHES USED IN GOVERNMENT

Government agencies have made much wider use of futures research than has business. Many of these studies have been very broad, extending to the year 2000 and beyond. The state of Hawaii, for instance, established a Commission on the Year 2000 to study choices open in the distant future, to make people aware of them, and to make legislative recommendations.

The Environmental Protection Agency commissioned the Stanford Research Institute to prepare alternative futures for the period 1975–2000 that would be useful in developing environmental policy planning. The result was a comprehensive report setting forth a number of alternative futures for our society.[10]

PURPOSES OF ALTERNATIVE FUTURES SEARCHES

The purposes of alternative futures searches in both industry and government are comparable. They are mind-stretching exercises for executives and their staffs. They make people more aware of possible events in the future that may influence management decisions. They should serve, I believe, to ease the anxieties of executives about the future. The known is less frightening than the unknown. By taking a longer view managers in business may be able to make better decisions in a shorter planning time horizon, such as three or five years. Both legislators and administrators in government should be able to make better current decisions the more they know about future possibilities. This may be more of a hope than a reality but it is a possibility that ought not be ignored. Other purposes and benefits to managers and staff in developing alternative scenarios and forecasts covering the regular planning period also are applicable here.

DEVELOPING ALTERNATIVE FUTURES EXPLORATIONS

To begin with it must be noted that alternative futures explorations can be too expensive for a small company to develop itself. However, for a small company there is a vast literature that may serve to stimulate futures thinking in executives.[11]

Many of the futures exploratory studies used in business are made in corporate planning departments. But a number of companies have appointed staff specialists to do this. Some have created separate departments to make these studies.[12] Many companies, at both headquarters and in the divisions, set up ad hoc committees, teams, or task forces to make futures studies. These groups are often organized with interdisciplinary and interdepartmental representation. Many companies like to have their managers involved in these groups. Some companies appoint "environmental watchers" to keep track of the changing environment.[13] Many consulting firms specialize in futures studies.[14]

The forecasting tools mentioned in Chapter 8 are complemented by a vast range of new methodologies used in futures research. Space does not permit discussion of these methods but a large literature exists on the subject.[15]

I would guess that for sweeping alternative scenarios the most frequently used method is interdisciplinary analysis of forces and the development of estimates of how they may intertwine at some future point of time. This is library research that is done on the basis of interdisciplinary knowledge, guided by judgment and intuition. The Delphi technique, also widely used, is a method to probe expert minds in a series of interviews from which some consensus is sought. Those participating in the experiment usually do not know who else is involved.[16] Exhibit 14–2 is a model showing how the General Electric Company prepares some of its scenarios.

Summary

As a result of the turbulent environment of the past few years managers have been faced with unforeseen events and have found that some forecasts upon which plans were based proved to be inaccurate. To help in dealing with such uncertainties they have

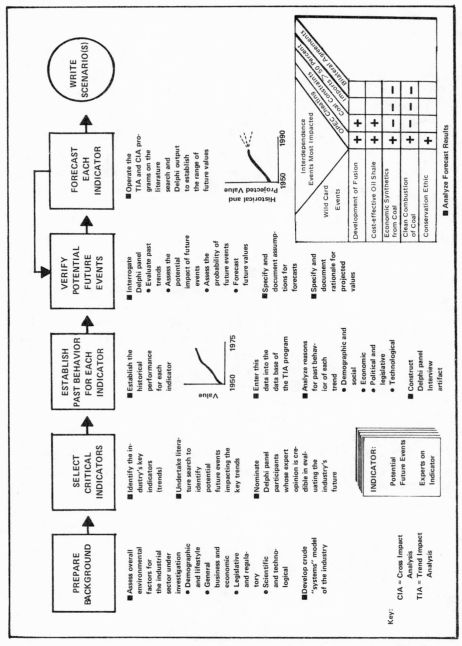

EXHIBIT 14-2: How Scenarios Are Constructed at General Electric Company. (From Rochelle O'Connor, *Planning Under Uncertainty: Multiple Scenarios and Contingency Planning* [New York: National Industrial Conference Board, 1978], p. 8. Used by permission.)

added contingency plans to their planning process. They also have increased their use of alternative scenarios and forecasts. Such futures explorations have been prepared for use in the regular planning process but some cover periods of time well beyond the typical planning horizon, often to the year 2000.

The possible range of subjects for both contingency plans and futures explorations is very wide. Most of the subjects used in business, however, are economic. Nevertheless, more companies are developing such studies for technological, social, and political conditions of concern to the company.

Contingency plans specify actions that management can pursue if an event not considered in the regular planning process actually occurs. Such planning also helps train managers to deal more promptly, and with more certainty, with unforeseen contingencies for which no advance plans have been prepared.

Futures explorations for time periods well beyond the planning period are important in helping managers become better conceptualizers and to be more aware of possibilities in the environment that may help or injure the company.

Futures research has escalated much more rapidly in universities, service organizations, and government than in business, but it is being adopted increasingly by business. The movement is widespread, has considerable thrust, and has produced a vast literature on methodology and hypothetical scenarios.

15 The Executive View of Analytical Techniques for Planning

Managers have available a large number of techniques that may be used in making decisions in the planning process. What should a manager know about these techniques? On the one hand, it certainly is not necessary for an executive to be skilled in the technology of all analytical tools that could conceivably be used in the planning process. On the other, it would be disastrous for a manager to depend completely upon staff specialists for decisions about the use of analytical techniques. Between these two poles is a middle ground of knowledge that managers should have. This chapter describes that area.

The Palette of Planning Analytical Techniques

The palette of planning analytical techniques is a rich assortment of methods to help managers make decisions. The range is from intuitive techniques to automatic quantitative decision tools such as inventory replenishment formulas. It is not feasible here to describe and explain the use of each of the most important techniques, let alone all of those that are usable in planning. So, the discussion is only illustrative.

OLDER NONQUANTITATIVE TECHNIQUES

This category includes creativity, judgment, hunches, intuition, and reliance on experience. These approaches can be used by people individually or collectively. Group analysis can be developed through such techniques as brainstorming, project teams, and Delphi.

Other older nonquantitative techniques include simple decision chains and tables, asking the right question, listings, rules of thumb, problem design, simple problemsolving steps, organization per se, policies and procedures, and general knowledge of the field in which a decision is to be made (e.g., law, economics, physics, sociology, and production).

OLDER QUANTITATIVE METHODS

Outstanding in this class are accounting systems and models such as the overall accounting system, balance sheets, profit and loss statements, cash flow analysis, accounting ratio analysis, break-even analysis, budgets of all types, cost controls, and special systems. Also included are return on investment formulations—ratios such as profit return on assets or profit return on stockholder equity—and present value rates of return such as discounted cash flow analyses or simple present value calculations for capital investments.

Quantitative forecasting methods include trend extrapolation, exponential smoothing, correlation analysis, econometric models, input-output analysis, and multiple regression analysis.

Another class of quantitative methods consists of critical paths such as PERT/Time and PERT/Cost models, milestone charts, and decision trees.

NEWER COMPUTER BASED MODELS

Included here are newer mathematical techniques and the adaptation of older techniques to computers. The idea of a model has long been used by engineers and scientists. Aerospace engineers, for instance, develop mock-up models of an airplane to study its characteristics in various physical environments. A model is a simplification of reality by means of which reality can be studied comparatively easily. A computer based model, like the airplane mock-up model, is a simplification of reality by means of which various complex relationships can be studied. For instance, a financial simulation model will interrelate the most significant financial functions of an enterprise; managers can then manipulate the model to determine what would happen in real life if they made a particular financial decision. Many different types of computer based models can be used in the planning process.

Computer based simulation models are the most extensively used models in planning today. The most popular ones are financial models. Yet the computer can simulate anything from the entire production process of a company to subelements of that process, such as inventory replenishment.

Older techniques of forecasting such as correlation analysis are frequently used in computer based models to project future trends. As noted previously, PIMS is a new computer based model used extensively in decisionmaking in planning and is fundamentally a correlation analysis. Cost experience curves perfected by the Boston Consulting Group can also be classified similarly since they rest on calculations of declining cost per unit based on past experience.

Some computer based models permit managers to make assumptions about conditions under their control, or changes assumed in environment, to see what the impact will be. This is the case, of course, with econometric models. Financial simulation models permit managers to ask "what if" questions—" What if we cut dividends in half?" The model will explain the impact on cash flow, stock price, etc.

Most of these models are called deterministic as distinct from probabilistic. The latter type models permit managers to express probabilities and derive probable results from the model. In risk analysis, for example, managers may introduce into the computer their probabilities concerning such matters as market size, market share, market growth rate, operating costs, and so on. From this will be calculated probable rates of return on investment.

OTHER TECHNIQUES

In this group are lumped complex methods combining many different techniques. In mind, for example, are cost-benefit analyses, social science research, corporate planning systems, and program budgeting.

This brief classification by no means exhausts the list of methods available to decisionmaking in the planning process. As brief as it is, however, it makes clear that the range of techniques is wide; that classifications overlap; and that these techniques, especially the advanced mathematical ones, raise perplexing problems about their use for managers who lack expert knowledge in this area. Before addressing the last point I shall comment on the uses of these different techniques in theory and in practice.

Uses of Advanced Quantitative Methods in Decisionmaking

The literature on decisionmaking, which is written mostly by academicians, strongly supports an expanding and valuable role for advanced quantitative techniques in decisionmaking. Indeed, some believe that top level decisions will be made in the near future almost wholly by quantitative methods. There are others, however, who believe that top level decisions will continue to be made essentially on the basis of qualitative techniques. The latter group accepts the idea that parts of the decisionmaking process may involve quantitative models. To what extent are advanced quantitative methods being used at the top decisionmaking levels of corporations?

SURVEYS OF COMPUTER BASED MODELS

Only spotty surveys of the use of quantitative models have been made but they make clear that although usage has expanded considerably it is far below the level advocates of quantitative methods believe to be desirable. Let us look at the results of surveys and then examine some of the reasons for the comparatively low usage.

A few years ago Naylor and Mansfield sent 1,881 questionnaires to companies that they had identified as using, developing, or planning to develop some form of corporate planning model.[1] They received 346 replies, from which they derived the following conclusions:

Seventy-three percent said they were using or developing corporate planning models. This contrasted with 20 percent (of 323 respondents) who said they were using or developing corporate planning models in 1969.

The most popular model being used was the simulation model. Sixty-two percent said they used such a model. The most popular uses of the simulation model were, in declining order of importance, cash flow analysis, financial forecasting, balance sheet projections, financial analysis, pro forma financial reports, budgeting, and sales forecasts.

Most models (94 percent) were in firms with sales over $500 million. Only 10 percent were in firms with sales under $100 million.

Models were mostly used to evaluate policy alternatives (79 percent). Other reported uses were financial projections (75 percent), long-term planning (73 percent), decisionmaking (58 percent), short-term planning (56 percent), preparation of reports (47 percent), goal setting (46 percent), analysis (39 percent), and confirmation of other analyses (35 percent).

The corporate planning department was named as being responsible for corporate model development more often than any other department (27 percent), compared with finance (16 percent) the next highest, and operations research (15 percent) the next highest.

Not surprisingly, the vice-president of finance was the person most often named as receiving and using output from the models. The president, however, was a close second (55 percent to 46 percent).

Other surveys confirm the fact that although corporate computer based models are growing in usage it is the simulation model that is most popular.[2] Other models are a distant second in popularity, and sophisticated probabilistic models like risk models are very infrequently used.[3]

WHY ARE NOT COMPUTER BASED MODELS USED MORE?

In dealing with this question there are several perspectives that should be clarified. First, simulation models are being used more frequently but reliance on other models is disappointing to model advocates. Second, the incidence of model usage is greatest for lower level decisions. Models are infrequently used in decision-making at the top levels of organizations. When used they are generally devoted to exploring financial alternatives. Finally, most concern about model use is directed toward the top of the organization; accordingly, the reasons for comparatively low use of models will be focused there.

A number of writers have devoted attention to this question and most of them would, I believe, agree with the following major considerations.[4]

First, many strategic decisions are not readily amenable to quantification. As noted previously, the more important the decision and the higher up in an organization at which it is made the less quantitative data influence the outcome. For example, it is difficult to conceive of any computer model being particularly useful to a chief executive officer who is trying to formulate the basic mission, thrust, and philosophy of an enterprise. Even decisions about more specific strategies, such as the location of a plant, are generally based ultimately upon forces not readily quantified. Political as well as social factors are involved. Personal commitments may be important. Executive judgment about the changing environment may be weighted more heavily on the decision scales than staff computer based estimates. The point is that models are usually one-dimensional in the sense that they focus solely on economic numbers whereas higher level decisions must take into consideration noneconomic factors, and generally the noneconomic factors are more important in the decision than are the economic factors.

Furthermore, zealots who insist that decisions be made on the basis of quantitative logic assume that decisionmaking in an organization is rational in their terms. What is rational to one person may be irrational to another. A company may decide not to pay dividends for what management considers to be rational financial reasons. A stockholder, however, may not think the action is rational. This suggests that what is rational may be determined by the best selection of means to achieve an objective that is acceptable to the value system of the evaluator or the test the evaluator chooses to apply. The test of rationality of means also is determined by the same value system.

Different disciplines look at rationality in diverse terms. Rational action to a classical economist is that which maximizes profits. Quantitative scientists tend to view rationality in terms of optimizing output per unit of input. Behavioral scientists view rationality in terms of human psychological needs. Lawyers see rationality in terms of legal precedent. A chief executive of a company may test rationality in many terms other than economic ones although economic considerations are dominant in most decisions.

Even when a decisionmaker sets out to make rational decisions on the basis of whatever scale of values he chooses to use there are problems in being rational. Janis and Mann in a brilliant book discussed a number of psychological forces that may lead to miscalculation, such as "cognitive defenses, situational anxiety, acceptance of fear-arousing warnings, obedience to authority, selective exposure to persuasion, determinants of self-control, bystander intervention, reliance on reference groups, delay of gratification, risk-taking behavior, and psychological preparation for future stress."[5]

For these and other reasons there frequently are conflicts between the disciplinary logic of analytical techniques, including the strategic planning system, and the realities of managerial decision-making. Odiorne has captured this conflict in what he calls the "logic of theory" and the "logic of practice" as follows:

> The logic of theory arranges the stages of decision as an orderly, rational process, moving from the setting of objectives to the determination of the final course of action to be taken. It has symmetry, logic and a beginning and an end. The logic of practice is made up by the time and interest of the executive, his pressures, and the day-to-day judgments on numerous decisions which he goes through in a single day. He makes a fragmentary judgment on a single part of a larger problem, then awaits further developments. He seldom has time to stick with one major problem to carry it through two or more stages of action. If the problem has "high priority," he may spend more time on that matter. Usually he must await other's actions, and accordingly, turns his attention to the currently required stage of another of the numerous problems with which he is dealing. The admixture of actions he takes comprises the logic of practice. He is more like a juggler than a weight lifter.[6]

Second, managers are not usually faced with simple choices that can be resolved with concrete numbers. This point is implicit in the observations made earlier but may be amplified in another direction. Choices often involve trade-offs, the resolution of which frequently demands a blend of quantitative and qualitative considerations. In mind are trade-offs such as full product line versus concentration on one or a few products; current profits versus future profits; preserving present market share versus costs to increase share; growth versus stability; in-house versus acquisition methods to expand; maintenance of price versus losing market share; and reducing price versus holding market share. In reality, the trade-offs involve multiple factors.

Third, managers are faced with high uncertainty. No one can foresee the future with certainty. Generally speaking, the more important the decision the less certain will be the outcome. In light of uncertainties about future events managers are not likely to make major decisions solely on the basis of a set of data.

Fourth, managers do not take time to participate in model building and as a result tend to distrust the output of the model. Most managers are extremely busy dealing with problems that must be resolved immediately. They respond to many concurrent problems that are resolved under continuous pressures. In such circumstances there is little incentive to become engaged in the development of a computer based model. If they do not understand how the model is developed and how it works they will be skeptical of its results.

Fifth, top managers tend to trust their intuition over mathematical models. This is especially so, of course, when they do not completely understand how a model is constructed and works and what assumptions are made in it. Managers who have prospered by trusting intuition are not about to rely on a black box whose operation is mysterious to them. Furthermore, there are inherent limitations to models that raise doubts about reliability in the minds of managers. In the Naylor and Mansfield study respondents listed shortcomings of computer models (in descending order of mention): not flexible enough, poorly documented, too much input data required, inflexible output format, took too long to develop, running cost too high, development cost too high, model users cannot understand model development, analytic process not understandable, output not detailed enough, not user oriented, results obviously inaccurate, and output too detailed.[7]

In light of such considerations it is not surprising that top managers favor simulation modeling to explore alternatives. The more complex and sophisticated computer based models are used as only one factor in decisionmaking at top levels and not ususally a significant one at that.

Should and Will Computer Based Models Be Used More?

The answer to this question is certainly in the affirmative. The reason why they should be used more is that they can be important ingredients in decisions for which they are designed to be helpful. It is also likely that they will be used more because more managers have studied computer based models in universities. The extent to which they will be used more, however, will depend upon the ways in which managers direct their use. There are lessons from experience to help managers better to use the various analytical techniques applicable to planning. The most important ones are discussed in the remainder of this chapter.

Guides for Managers Using Analytical Techniques in Planning

The following guides, as the heading says, are for managers, in contrast to specialists in the use of quantitative analytical tools. A good bit has been written in recent years by these specialists about how they can and should function to improve the value of their techniques to managers.[8] This literature will prove valuable to those managers who are interested in developing a more penetrating understanding of how quantitative techniques may be made more useful to them.

DO NOT UNDERESTIMATE THE IMPORTANCE OF OLDER NONQUANTITATIVE TECHNIQUES OF DECISIONMAKING

In recent years there has been a tendency in academic circles as well as in business to glorify newer quantitative decision methods and to underplay intuition, judgment, and creativity.[9] There certainly is nothing wrong with using quantitative methods whenever they are appropriate. This should not, however, lead to an underestimation of the creative processes in decisionmaking in planning. As noted earlier there is no other way to make decisions in some critical parts of the planning process, such as the formulation of basic organizational missions, thrusts, and purposes. Throughout the entire planning process, including implementation, the contributions of intuition, judgment, and creativity should not be underestimated.

Many other nonquantitative techniques are valuable in the decisionmaking process in planning, a range of which have been discussed previously. The point made here is applicable to them— do not underestimate their significance.

DO NOT UNDERESTIMATE THE POWER OF OLDER QUANTITATIVE TECHNIQUES IN DECISIONMAKING

Older quantitative techniques also are valuable in decisionmaking. There is great power, for example, in using the company accounting system to aid decisionmaking. To illustrate, past and current ratios of cash to current liabilities or of profits to assets employed, debt-equity ratios, and so on, are powerful decisionmaking tools. The accounting system can also be used as a base for making projections of importance, such as cash flows.

DO NOT UNDERESTIMATE THE POWER OF NEWER QUANTITATIVE TECHNIQUES

The human mind has severe limitations in dealing with quantitative consequences of change in one or more variables on other variables in complex systems. Quantitative tools are powerful aids to managers in such situations. For instance, suppose a railroad wishes to move ten freight cars among five different locations at the least total possible cost. This is a problem with which the human mind cannot easily deal without technical help. A computerized linear programming model will yield the answer rapidly. A primary reason for the popularity of financial simulation models lies in the fact that they can provide instantaneous answers to questions that the human mind cannot answer very quickly. Real-time computer based models of production processes can give quick answers to the impact of changes of raw material inputs, component shortages, new orders, and so on.[10]

Models such as these save time in analysis. Moreover, they are often more reliable than intuitive judgments.

DO NOT OVERESTIMATE THE POWER OF
NEWER QUANTITATIVE ANALYTICAL TOOLS

On the other hand, there are limitations to all quantitative methods. Many decisions made in the planning process simply are not amenable to mathematical techniques. Also, of course, the quality of the output of quantitative models will depend heavily upon the quality of the assumptions on which they are based. Managers must always question the methodology of the techniques, the assumptions on which they are based, and the credibility of the results.

It goes without saying that no matter how accurate a set of data may be there are many other considerations that usually must be held in mind in any particular case before a decision is made. For example, a return on investment calculation may show a much higher figure for project A than for project B. Project B is chosen, however, because it fits the product line, which is not the case with project A. It is easy for managers to come to rely too heavily on quantitative data as a substitute for careful thought.

DO UNDERSTAND THE STRENGTHS,
WEAKNESSES, AND APPROPRIATE
APPLICATIONS OF TECHNIQUES TO BE USED
IN PLANNING

Managers do not necessarily need to be experts in the mechanics of quantitative techniques to use them properly any more than they need to understand the technology of the combustion engine to operate an automobile. But managers do need a working knowledge of each major technique—its nature, how and where it can and should be used, and its strengths and weaknesses at the point of use. They should know how the technique is operated, the types of data employed, the forces to which data output is most sensitive, and the significance of the output to the decision being made.

Executives, for instance, must have a variety of forecasts at hand in developing plans. It is important that they have an understanding of the different types of forecasting methods that may be applied in particular situations, as well as of the strengths and weaknesses of alternative methods in contributing to the decisions to be made. Costs of getting the forecasts with different methods should, of course, be related to the value of the data developed.[11] Some forecasting methods are very costly so managers should give constant attention to the cost-benefit equation.

Furthermore, managers should have an understanding of the assumptions underlying a forecast. With such knowledge the manager will know which forces are most likely to alter significantly the forecast. The executive will therefore be in a position to monitor events of most concern to the validation of the forecast. The executive should also contemplate what actions to take in the event that the forces under review do not develop as projected.

Altogether, therefore, an executive need not be a specialist in making forecasts. But he should know which forecasting methods are most appropriate to the problems at hand, how they are prepared, and which forces to watch to avoid unacceptable surprises.[12]

Managers must also know the uses of various techniques. For instance, a short-term forecast of sales may be used to schedule production and should therefore be as accurate as possible. A long-range forecast, however, is not intended to predict the future. It is, rather, a base for developing strategies and tactical plans. It is a force for making managers and staff think about the future and prepare proper responses to it. In each planning cycle the forecast will change as environmental conditions change. In this light, long-range forecasts should seek to capture major trends rather than attempt to be precise. The point should be underscored that managers need to know a good bit about the analytical tools they use and not depend upon specialists in this area.

DO MAKE SURE TO CHOOSE THE RIGHT
PROBLEM TO SOLVE

The most pertinent question to a manager is not so much how to do things right but how to find the right things to do. A manager

runs a far greater risk of missing the problem than of missing a
reasonable solution. It seems so elementary to emphasize that
solutions to problems, no matter how elegant, are useless if they
solve the wrong problem. But, as Drucker pointed out, "the most
common source of mistakes in management decisions is the emphasis on finding the right answer rather than the right question."[13]
A primary job of management is thus to find the right problem and
to define it. Then and only then is it appropriate to search for the
proper techniques to analyze the problem.

DO DETERMINE WHAT INFORMATION IS
NEEDED AND HOW MUCH

Information gathering is expensive and time-consuming. Cost
savings in analysis can be made if managers determine what types
of information are needed and how much. This, of course, is not
always easy because informational needs may evolve with the
development of the decision process. It is not always clear in the
mind of a manager what information to ask staff to get. Also, as
Exhibit 15–1 shows, a manager is not always sure he will get what
is requested. Despite these difficulties—perhaps because of them
—-managers ought to try to define what and how much information is needed.

Winston Churchill is reported to have highlighted one aspect of
this managerial problem in an incident when he was opposition
leader in the late 1940s. He asked a young aide for data on infant
mortality that he might use in debates in Parliament. The aide
gathered voluminous statistics on the subject for Sir Winston.
Churchill did not use the data in the debates and later, when asked
by the aide why he did not use them, he said: "Young man, if you
wish to become a member of Parliament there is something you
need to know about statistics. When I ask for statistics about the
rate of infant mortality I want proof that fewer babies died when I
was Prime Minister than when anyone else was Prime Minister.
These are political statistics."

The point is that managers and not staff use statistics in decisionmaking. But both managers and staff must have a good idea
of what is wanted from the information gathering and analytical
task if it is to be of use to managers.

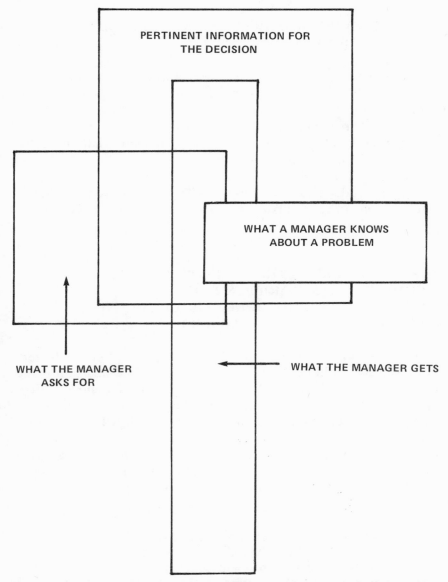

EXHIBIT 15–1: Conflicting Perceptions of Relevant Decision Data. (Source: Suggested by Joseph Francis Aguilar, *Scanning the Business Environment* (New York: Macmillan, 1967), p. 7.)

DO DETERMINE WHEN PRECISION IS NEEDED
IN MEASUREMENT

Staff experts tend to seek precision in data gathering and to spend as much time as they can in getting it. This can be expensive. Fortunately, however, managers very frequently do not need great precision in statistical inputs to their decisionmaking. Once a problem has been identified rough estimates of relevant data often are enough to advance the decisionmaking process.

Managers should therefore determine when precision in statistical data is needed and when it is not. Clearly, precision should not be sought when the results do not alter managerial choices significantly.

DO MAKE SURE IN THE DEVELOPMENT OF
COMPUTER BASED MODELS THAT THE
OBJECTIVES FOR THE MODEL ARE CLEAR AND
RELEVANT DATA ARE AVAILABLE

Before a computer based model is developed certain fundamental questions should be asked and answered: What decision is the model designed to influence? Who is going to use the model? How important is the model likely to be in influencing the decision? Are relevant data available for the model? How much will the exercise cost?

These guides seem elementary but many computer based models in industry have failed to address such questions with the result that hundreds of thousands of dollars were wasted.

DO MAKE SURE IN BUILDING COMPUTER
BASED MODELS THAT MANAGERS WHO ARE
TO USE THE MODELS PARTICIPATE IN THEIR
CONSTRUCTION AND HAVE A THOROUGH
UNDERSTANDING OF THEIR USES

Experience amply demonstrates the importance in having managers rather than expert model builders supervise the construction of models. In this way the purposes of the model will be clearly in line with managerial requirements rather than technical objectives. These two ends are not the same. By participating in model building managers will understand how the results of the model are achieved. They will understand the assumptions made and the procedures that are performed. This is important because, as noted earlier, managers will mistrust what they do not understand and they will know less about models that they have not been involved in developing.

To neglect this lesson can be costly: The model may have to be abandoned before it contributes to managerial decisionmaking.

DO START COMPUTER BASED MODEL BUILDING SIMPLY

When computer based models are first developed in a company they should be as simple as possible but still able to influence decisionmaking. Sophisticated, complex models are not likely to be used by managers unfamiliar with this technique.

As one observer put it: We should not be surprised if a manager "prefers simple analysis that he can grasp, even though it may have a qualitative structure, broad assumptions, and only a little relevant data, to a complex model whose assumptions may be partially hidden or couched in jargon and whose parameters may be the result of obscure statistical manipulation."[14]

Once managers have used and understand simple models the models then may be made more sophisticated. Generally speaking, it is better that managers seek more sophistication than that staffs lead them into greater complexity.

THE MANAGER IS HIS OWN BEST ANALYTICAL TECHNIQUE

Managers have numerous staff experts to help them in their decisionmaking—economists, management scientists, accountants, lawyers, and engineers, to mention but a few. In the final analysis these specialists do not make the decisions, managers do. Experts are recognized for their competence in one narrow area of knowledge, and often expert opinion differs significantly. Managers must learn how to understand, appraise, and use the contributions of experts.

A biographer of Winston Churchill said:

> He was always deeply interested in techniques of all kinds and listened avidly to experts and professionals, imbibing all they told him with a rare accuracy and grasp. But he never fell a victim to the black magic of specialist infallibility. It was the task of specialists and experts to supply the weights and measures; it was for him to assess them and to reach conclusions.[15]

This managerial assessment process does not depend solely on intuition. Important, too, is some knowledge about the personality and competence of the practitioner of the discipline. The manager, in developing superior assessment powers of diverse disciplines focused on the managerial decisionmaking process, is his own best analytical technique.

Summary

This chapter described the palette of analytical tools that may be employed in the strategic planning process and focused on what managers should know about them.

It was pointed out that the more advanced mathematical techniques are being used more at top management levels but far less than advocates of these techniques believe is desirable. The main reasons for this situation were presented: Many strategic decisions are not amenable to quantification; managers are not usually faced with simple choices that can be resolved with concrete numbers; managers are faced with great uncertainties that defy reliable forecasts; managers do not take the time to participate in building quantitative decision models; and managers trust their intuition over mathematical models.

Experience provides a number of guides for managers using analytical tools in planning. The most important ones were reviewed:

Do not underestimate the importance of older nonquantitative techniques.
Do not underestimate the power of older quantitative techniques.

Do not underestimate the power of newer quantitative techniques.

Do not overestimate the power of newer quantitative analytical tools.

Do understand the strengths, weaknesses, and appropriate applications of techniques to be used in planning.

Do make sure to choose the right problem to solve.

Do determine what information is needed and how much.

Do determine when precision is needed in measurement.

Do make sure in the development of computer based models that the objectives for the model are clear and that relevant data are available.

Do make sure in building computer based models that managers who are to use the models participate in their construction and have a thorough understanding of their uses.

Do start computer based model building simply.

The manager is his own best analytical technique.

IV Implementing Plans

16 The Nature and Design of Control Systems

In Chapter 13 I discussed the translation of strategies into current decisions through the development of budgets and other tactical plans. A final step in implementation concerns the control of individual behavior to insure the achievement of the tactical plans and the aims upon which they are based. Budgets, tactical plans, rules, regulations, and so on, do not in themselves implement plans. It is only when activities of individuals are directed toward the achievement of enterprise aims, guided partly through these techniques, that strategies are really implemented. This involves the entire process of management. Of course, so large a subject cannot be treated adequately in this short book. A useful purpose will be served, however, in underscoring the nature and design of control systems and the human aspect managers need to consider in dealing with individuals in the control process. These two features of implementation are the subject of this chapter and the next.

The Scope of Management Tasks in Implementation

Before plans can be implemented, there must of course be plans. Paralleling the development of plans and/or following the preparation of plans, it is necessary for managers to take many actions before they can be implemented. For instance, the entire organization of the enterprise must be appropriate to the tasks, size, and thrust of the company. Key tasks and sequences of steps to be performed to implement plans must be determined and communicated. Those responsible for specific tasks must be identified and they must have a thorough understanding of what they are supposed to do. There must be assurance that resources, both physical and human, are available or will be at hand, when needed, to facilitate implementation of plans. Motivation and incentive systems must be set up. Appropriate systems to coordinate effort and guide individual activity must be devised and installed. This refers, of course, to budgets, tactical plans, and other guides to action. The entire management information system must be designed to make sure that managers have the knowledge needed to assess whether individual performance is in line with plans and, if not, what should be done about the matter. Training programs to improve managerial and worker capability in making and implementing plans should be designed. Overall, a managerial leadership that will guide effectively the effort of all individuals in achieving the aims of the enterprise must be assured.

All of these managerial responsibilities are intertwined. They are not serial. The point to be underscored is that control techniques (except automatic ones) do not control anything. It is the entire process of management that guides, coordinates, motivates, and controls human endeavor and determines the effectiveness and efficiency with which plans are implemented. These managerial activities must reflect attitudes, motivations, responses, and so on, of individuals in organizations. Put in these terms, developing control techniques and using them to implement plans involves a wide range of considerations relating to the management of people in organizations.

The Meaning of Control

The word control is used here in the sense of managerial control that seeks to insure that performance conforms to plans. Such control involves a process of evaluating performance and taking corrective action when performance differs from plans. This process involves three basic steps—establishing standards, measuring performance against standards, and correcting deviations from standards.

Types of Controls

Classified by use there are controls to standardize performance, conserve assets, standardize quality, limit authority without top management's approval, measure performance, and so on.[1] Newman classified controls into three basic types. First are steering controls, which are designed to detect deviations from a standard and to permit corrective action before an operation is completed. For example, trajectory measurements were made immediately after the moon spacecraft takeoff and corrections were made long before the vehicle reached the moon. Second are yes-no controls, which specify that approval is required before a next step can be taken. Finally, there are postaction controls, which measure results after an action is completed.[2] Control system design of course reflects the basic type of control management has in mind. Most of what is said in this chapter refers to the first type.

The Basic Control Process

ESTABLISHING STANDARDS

The control process begins with plans. In the planning process, as noted previously, there is a continuous narrowing of detail from broad strategies to specific tactical plans. These tactical plans establish goals, targets, and standards (which words will be used synonymously here) to guide the fulfillment of strategic plans.

Managerial decision is important at this point in choosing and defining specific standards to guide action. The key to determining what standards will be set is the answer to the question: What is it that management wishes to measure? Standards cannot be set for everything so choices must be made about those key activities that managers wish to monitor continuously.

Managers should keep in mind Pareto's law in choosing standards.[3] This law says that in a group of elements the most important ones are a small proportion of the total. Thus, a firm may find that 5 percent of its employees account for 90 percent of total absences, or 80 percent of its income is derived from 5 percent of its customers. The more concrete and specific the standard is, the easier it will be to measure performance against it. This is not to say that all standards must be specific. Actually, not all activities that management wishes to monitor can be expressed in concrete terms. For example, a plan to improve managerial training is not readily expressed in numbers.

MEASURING PERFORMANCE AGAINST STANDARDS

There are many important facets to the measurement of performance. First, how much variation will constitute a reason for taking corrective action?

Second, managers must be on the alert to determine whether standards should be altered. As changes in environment take place it may be necessary to correct standards before looking at performance. Variable budgets, discussed in Chapter 13, are designed to do precisely this.

Third, management must develop the proper type of reporting and information system to appraise, compare, and correct performance. This aspect of control opens up a vast subject because it concerns not only control but all other aspects of management as well. So far as control is concerned the management information system must identify those points in a manager's area of responsibility the surveillance of which will permit the manager to exercise the appropriate control over employee performance in achieving the targets for which the manager is responsible. This is a complex design problem because it must be responsive to a manager's needs, knowledge, preferred methods to get and use information, the standard under review, and so on. The less concrete the standard against which performance is measured the more difficult is the information system design problem.

Control reports will vary much at different levels in the organization. The chief executive officer, for instance, will want reports concerned with whether the missions and objectives of the company are still adequate, whether critical parts of the strategic plan are being implemented (e.g., acquisitions, divestment, new product development, and progress of new facility construction), and whether current operations are satisfactory.

The executive vice-president will want much more penetrating details about the operations of the enterprise. The focus of lower level managers will be narrower.[4]

Fourth, the power of computers in facilitating control must be mentioned.[5] The computer, when properly designed, installed, and operated is an extremely efficient method by which to acquire information promptly and accurately. Today, for example, computer based real-time information systems are widely used in getting reports about actions when they take place.

Fifth, getting reports that compare actual results with desired results may be useful for certain types of information but quite inadequate for others. When managers are appraising the overall performance of other managers, a comparison of financial results of their area of operation with predetermined objectives is a needed base for evaluation. For many other types of activities, however, what is required is advance warning, or predictors of results. This is future oriented, feedforward, control.[6] Managers do not want to find out that sales last month were 10 percent under what was desired. They want to know today that sales next month may be 10 percent under standard unless some action is taken to counter the trend. Really effective control requires accurate prediction.

Much ingenuity is needed to find useful predictors. Forecasts provide one type of forewarning. Networks, such as scheduling flows of activities, may serve to flag future difficulties when a particular milestone is not reached. A sales manager may use a composite of field visits, customer inquiries, complaints, returned merchandise, and so on, to foresee future deviations from plans.[7]

EVALUATING PERFORMANCE AND TAKING CORRECTIVE ACTION

Measurements of past performances and predictions of things to come alert management to what is going on or likely to happen but do not determine what should be done. There are two phases to this activity. The first concerns the evaluation of the warning signals and the second relates to managerial decision about any remedies for correcting deviations from standards.

Proper evaluation of signals is important. Some methods to

predict future events may not be entirely reliable and considerable judgment may be required to prevent precipitous action. For example, a sudden increase in the sale of a product may indicate a fad and not a long-lived increase in consumer demand. To take action on the current jump in sales could lead to excessive over-capacity, rising costs per unit, and declining profits.

Once a manager decides that corrective action is required, the issue then joins the entire process of management. Revision of plans may be required. New standards may be needed. New leadership may be in order. Better motivation of employees may be desired. And so on. Although control may be identified as a key function of managers it cannot be performed without simultaneous actions among other functions.[8]

SOME LESSONS OF EXPERIENCE IN
DEVELOPING CONTROL SYSTEMS

From what has just been said it is clear that designing an effective system of controls is not a simple matter, especially in a larger corporation. Long experience with control systems has produced a number of lessons that should help managers develop more effective systems. Since budgeting is central to most control mechanisms some of the more outstanding lessons of experience with respect to budgets will be presented. These lessons, without exception, are also applicable to all control systems that seek to implement plans.

Developing and properly using a system of budgeting is not an easy task and yet it is crucial for effective strategic planning. Among the lessons of experience in developing effective budgeting systems the following stand out, not in any particular order of importance.

First, there must be top management support. No budgeting system can realize its potential value without the unqualified support of top management.

Second, there must be a clear-cut organizational structure in the firm. For a budgeting program to be most useful all managers must understand their authority and responsibility, their relationships with superiors and subordinates, and their relationships with other organizational units. This is necessary to make sure a budget does not cover more, or less, than the legitimate activities of each manager. To do so lessens its value as both a planning and a control tool.

Third, the budget system should form part of an effective, companywide planning program. The budget system is the cutting edge of planning. It is part of the planning process, but not all of it. To take long-range plans and translate them into quantitative budgets that insure current coordination among functions, and integration with longer range programs, is the essence of good business planning.

Fourth, responsibility for the budgeting system must be fixed and understood. Although the ultimate responsibility is top management's, in all but the smallest companies this task is given to someone else, usually a controller or a budget director. Again, everyone concerned should know what is going on and who is supposed to do what. An important problem in achieving effective budget preparation and control is collecting, organizing, disseminating, and evaluating information. In larger companies the procedures for operating the system are usually detailed in a manual of instructions.

Fifth, budgets should not dominate decisions. This means, for example, that the system must foster mutual understanding, trust, and common sense in using budgets. Managers should feel that requests for deviations from budgets to give deserved merit increases, for instance, or to take advantage of a new opportunity for improving profits, will be sympathetically received by top managers. It means that no department will fail to cooperate with another for solely budgetary reasons. It means that there is general understanding that, as events change, more dominant company goals may be thwarted by a rigorous adherence to budgets. I am not suggesting that budgets not be administered with firmness. Rather, they should be administered in such a way that the larger purposes of a company are served as changes take place or new considerations arise that cannot be accommodated within current budgetary limits.

Sixth, accounting jargon should be held to a minimum. Although budgets are not entirely accounting instruments there is much accounting in the structure. Better budgeting nevertheless does not flow from more esoteric language.

Seventh, care should be taken to insure that the budgeting system does not become too complex, too cumbersome, and too restrictive. Budgeting is a mechanism for delegating authority, and if budgetary restrictions are too detailed and too confining for the exercise of discretion, managers will experience frustration, then resentment, and finally inertia. Budgets are tools for management, not management itself.

Eighth, better results are achieved if budgets have clearly stated standards upon which basis performance is to be measured.

Ninth, proper understanding of the purposes and limitations of budgets must be created throughout the firm. Budgets are tools to facilitate the achievement of the highest aims of a company. They are not, as some lower level managers sometimes are made to feel, clubs to frustrate people. They are not pressure devices designed to goad people to higher performance. If, for instance, a person is capable of selling fifteen units but the supervisor thinks he will sell only ten, the lower figure should be put in the budget if for no other reason than it is a better basis for linking production, raw material purchases, and so on. If a manager thinks a salesman can sell five more units, motivation should come through means other than lifting the salesman's budget.

Tenth, some understanding of and attention to budget games-manship should ferret out practices that should be much reduced or eliminated.

Eleventh, there must be participation in the development and use of budgets. People generally do not like budgets, probably because most people do not like to be controlled. One powerful technique to make the restraints of budgets acceptable is to provide for proper participation of people in making budgets that provide standards for their performance. This point will be examined in more detail in Chapter 17.

Twelfth, the budgetary system should be economical. There are several senses in which the word economical is important. To begin with, the fewer the controls to achieve an effective result the better. The budget system should be kept as simple as practicable. An excess of controls is more likely to create confusion and frustration than to improve control. Drucker has wisely noted that managers should ask themselves this question: "What is the smallest number of reports and statistics needed to understand a phenomenon and to be able to anticipate it?" Once that is settled they should ask: "And what is the minimum of data regarding this phenomenon that gives a reasonably reliable picture?"[9]

A second important aspect of economical controls is cost. It is very easy to build expensive reporting requirements (especially with computers) whose costs are far beyond their value to managers. The cost-benefit equation should be constantly kept in mind in designing and using control systems.

Thirteenth, budgets must be meaningful. Budgets should be established only for the important things management wishes to monitor, measure, and understand.

Finally, there is no one ideal budgeting system suitable for all organizations. The unique characteristics of a company, including management style, size, purpose, and problems, must enter into this system design.

Control Systems in Large and Small Companies

It is worthwhile to note differences in control systems between large and small companies. In very small companies comparatively few budgets and other tactical plans are required because managers are in daily communication with one another and their employees. Production processes, marketing forces, cash flow analysis, and so on, tend to be much simpler than in a larger organization and therefore easier for managers to monitor without elaborate reporting systems.

In large organizations, however, communications problems among managers at all levels become more and more intractable as the organization grows. Increased difficulties arise in coordinating efforts. The organization is subject to more threats and requires a wider network of scanning techniques to foresee the threats. The result is, of course, that control systems in larger organizations are much more complex than in smaller companies.

Summary

This chapter began with the observation that controlling human activities to achieve plans involves the entire process of management and an understanding of the nature of human beings.

It was noted that there are many different types of control systems to implement plans. The one discussed in the chapter concerned the establishment of standards for performance, the evaluation of performance in light of standards, and the taking of action to correct deviations from standards.

Lessons of experience in the formulation of budget systems were examined with the assertion that they are applicable to other systems designed to control performance to implement plans. The lessons were as follows:

There must be top management support.

There must be a clear-cut organizational structure in the firm.

The budget system should be planned and integrated into the strategic plan.

Responsibility for the budgeting system must be fixed and understood.

Budgets should not dominate decisions, that is, they should not replace managerial judgment.

Accounting jargon should be held to a minimum in budgets and budget reports.

Care should be taken to insure that the budgeting system does not become overly complex, cumbersome, and restrictive.

Better results will be achieved if budgets have clearly defined standards against which performance is to be measured.

Proper understanding of the purposes and limitations of budgets must be created throughout the firm.

The more sporty aspects of budget gamesmanship must be avoided, such as spending a cash surplus the last few days of the budget year to secure a higher base for next year's bargaining.

There must be widespread participation in the development of budgets.

The budgetary system should be economical.

Budgets must be meaningful.

The budget system must fit the unique characteristics of the company.

Finally, it was noted that control systems in small companies are simple compared with those in large companies.

17 The Human Dimension in Implementation

Managers who wish to achieve effective control of operations to implement plans must grasp the design characteristics of control systems as well as the human dimension involved therein. Managerial control systems in themselves control nothing.[1] People must take action.

The behavioral aspect of the control process has not received the attention it deserves. Research in recent years has added much to our knowledge in this area but there are still gaping holes in our understanding of the many ways in which individuals react to control systems.[2] The purpose of this chapter is not to summarize what is or is not known about this subject. It is rather to make a few comments solely for the purpose of underscoring the place and significance of the human element in plan implementation.

The chapter begins with a few observations about human behavior that affects the entire control process. Different human responses in the main elements of the control process will then be noted.

Resistance to Control versus the Search for Order

Much of the literature dealing with human reactions to control dwells on the resistance of individuals to control. However, say some scholars in the field, people are more interested in seeking to establish order upon which basis they can build satisfying systems of behavior in their interpersonal relationships.[3] If this is so, why do so many writers on the subject speak of resistance to control? The answer is that changing from one set of interpersonal relationships to another creates behavioral problems. As one of the early writers on human behavior in organizations put it: "Any move on the part of the company may alter the existing social equilibrium to which the employee has grown accustomed and by means of which his status is defined. Immediately this disruption will be expressed in sentiments of resistance to the real or imagined alterations in the social equilibrium."[4] This will be recognized as the same underlying force giving rise to antiplanning biases. In addition, however, are many other factors that influence human reactions to controls.

People respond to controls in different ways; some welcome them and others do not. The degree of resistance or acceptance will vary with many factors such as the level of control in the organizational hierarchy, the degree of participation in setting standards and evaluating them, the nature of communications systems, the comprehensiveness of the control system, how performance is evaluated, how people perceive the control system, the reward and punishment system, the subject of control, and the quality and style of management.

Controls can generate more resistance than acceptance, but that is not necessarily to be expected. People can be motivated not only to accept controls but also to achieve above-average goals with enthusiasm.

Managerial Control Strategies

Managers must devise control strategies to suit their particular circumstances. And the strategies they choose can have a powerful impact on individual motivation. To illustrate, the Likerts classified management systems as follows. At one extreme is "system 1," in which the motivational forces are essentially punitive, that is, fear, threat, and occasional reward. There is slight reliance on instilling a desire to achieve or on developing a sense of personal worth and importance. In such systems the controls are centralized at the top of the organizational hierarchy. Individuals working in such a system will have predictable behavior toward the controls. They will not be motivated to achieve aggressive goals and they will distort reports of performance to score as high as possible under the circumstances.

At the other extreme is "system 4," which encourages and supports individual involvement in decisionmaking implementation. Rewards for performance are based on a compensation system developed through the participation among those involved. There is full recognition of individual achievement. In such systems concern for control functions is felt throughout the organization, there is strong pressure on individuals to report accurate information about performance, and all motivational forces tend to support strong efforts to achieve high organizational goals.[5]

At one end of this spectrum of strategies is reliance on so-called extrinsic rewards (or penalties) such as pay, promotion, job security, recognition from the supervisor, and more interesting work. At the other end more reliance is placed on intrinsic rewards, which come from within the individual. The organization cannot give them, unlike extrinsic rewards, but it can stimulate them. Motivation springs from self-satisfaction in good performance.

The proper mix of these strategies for a particular situation will produce the best results. For instance, for several years I nailed hardwood floors under an incentive system that paid so much per square foot of flooring. The system seemed equitable and it never occurred to me that it was anything but just. On the other hand, such a control system applied to a group of engineers who are given responsibility for designing a new satellite would be completely inappropriate.

Both extrinsic and intrinsic incentive systems have their place. Where tight control is needed on routine tasks the extrinsic strategy may be preferred by both management and workers. Where managers rely on intrinsic rewards to motivate people they may lose control over their behavior. Furthermore, if managers do not formulate specific goals, their subordinates may relax and set lower performance levels.

Unfortunately, there is no simple formula to determine the proper mix of strategies for achieving the optimal implementation of plans. Many alternatives exist, and what will work best in one setting at one time may not be effective in the same setting at another time and place. The best that can be done is to be as aware as possible of the human element and the way it interacts with control designs. In the remainder of this chapter some lessons of experience that address the question of effectiveness will be presented.

An Overview of Participation in the Design and Implementation of Control Systems

The amount of participation that is possible and desirable differs among management levels and the individuals involved. At the top management level one finds in more and more companies today a continuous participation of executives in the decisionmaking process. At the supervisory level, where operations take place within narrow decision constraints, the opportunities for, and value of participation, are much more limited.

The actual degree of participation depends much upon the superior and the subordinate. Superiors not only must be trained and willing to deal with subordinates but also must provide the opportunity for doing so. The subordinate also must be interested in participation and must understand that participation does not mean the transfer of the superior's authority. In the end the superior may be forced to modify or reject a suggestion of the subordinate. Overall, there must be mutual understanding and trust or participation will not be effective.

If participation between the subordinate and the superior in developing budgets is perfunctory, if subordinate suggestions are not taken seriously, and if the arrangement is a sham, the results will be negative. There is substantial evidence that good results will be achieved only if the character of participation is related to the values, skills, and expectations of the people involved.

Levinson added a dimension to this point when, in speaking about management by objective, he observed:

> The reason is that although people are told that they have opportunities to set their own objectives, in fact they merely are given a limited range of choices within those established by their superiors and often must modify their own objectives to meet the expectations of management. The objectives they have defined may not be truly theirs, but they are nevertheless compelled to put their own cheese (goals) at the end of the maze. If they do not run the maze well enough to get the cheese, they are then criticized for not

meeting their own objectives. I would have no objection to people being told what they are being paid for and the conditions of promotion. I object to their being manipulated into pretending those objectives are necessarily theirs or that they have set them.[6]

An effective budgeting system requires that plans and budgets be made and reviewed at all levels of management through a superior-subordinate face-to-face relationship. In an effecting system there is guidance from the top and actual development of plans and budgets from the bottom—a balance between the top-down and the bottom-up approach to planning and budgeting.

Strategies and Behavioral Response in Goal Setting

Many studies confirm the view that there is a positive relationship between participation in the budget process and motivation to achieve the goals that are set.[7]

Lawler and Rhode suggested that participation in standard setting is likely to reduce resistance for several important reasons. First, people have a chance to shape the control system to fit their interests better. Without participation they have no opportunity to inject their views and needs into the systems design and this can be threatening to individuals. Second, resistance to control systems may be based on false information about how the systems are designed, the appropriateness of measures of performance, and performance evaluation methods. Participation and effective communications in the organization can eliminate or significantly reduce such causes of dissatisfaction and resistance.[8]

Participation will not always reduce resistance. As noted earlier, participation has to be perceived by the individuals as being appropriate, honest, and meaningful. Participation in setting standards for performance is likely to be more effective when the organization has a strategy of widespread participation of people throughout the decisionmaking process.

If participation in setting standards is so important, why is it not universally applied? One reason is that superiors do not always trust subordinate employees to establish suitably difficult standards. Employees often provide invalid data about what they can accomplish in order to make sure their performance will look good. In some instances superiors have such pressure on them for higher performance that they cannot afford to negotiate lower standards with employees. In these situations the quality of participation tends to be rather low. The result is resistance by employees toward what they may perceive to be unrealistic standards.

Not everyone wants to participate in the goal setting process nor is it always appropriate that they should do so. If resistance to goal setting is to be reduced, in the absence of participation, it is necessary that goals be clear, reasonable, and meaningful and that rewards be directly and openly tied to performance so that there is incentive to achieve them.

Participation in goal setting has some drawbacks. People will tend to seek acceptance of goals that are lower than they can achieve, especially if compensation is tied tightly to goal achievement. This obviously is in their self-interest. Or, they may seek more funds than are needed to achieve a given end simply to provide a cushion in the event of unforeseen difficulties.

Individuals will tend to try to meet standards on which their rewards are based because it is in their interest to do so. As a consequence, it is crucial for managers to establish the "right" standards. If a salesperson's performance is evaluated by number of calls made, there will be many calls and few sales. If it is measured only on the basis of sales there may be larger sales but disgruntled customers and lower profits. Customers may be pressured into buying products they do not really want or be promised services and benefits that cannot be delivered. The net result will be cancellation of orders, perhaps a permanent loss of customers, and reduced profits.

If goals are to be considered meaningful by people, they must have certain characteristics. For example, the goals should focus on significant areas of organizational needs. They must be expressed in terms that are clear and operational. The individual must believe the goals are reasonable. Finally, compensation should be tied to performance in an understandable fashion.

Hard to achieve goals will motivate individuals if they participate in setting them. Their acceptance and motivation to achieve will be greater if they have a strong inner commitment to the goals. This is more likely the greater the congruence between personal and organizational goals. Even so, such goals must not violate perceived norms of behavior of the group in which they are effective. If there is conflict the individuals in the group are more likely to conform to peer pressure to achieve group goals than to strive to meet organizational standards.

Carroll and Tosi found that difficult goals were related to strong achievement efforts only among those managers who were self-assured, who were mature, and who associated closely their performance with the reward system. Managers who were less mature and experienced and who had low self-assurance displayed less effort in goal achievement.[9]

What is a meaningful standard for one manager may be irrelevant for another. A vice-president in charge of several divisions may believe that holding maintenance costs within budgetary limits is meaningful. To a supervisor, however, who sees the need for additional maintenance to improve the productivity of a machine under his jurisdiction, such a standard may be considered irritating at best and irrelevant at worst. Perceptions, of course, could be just the other way around.

Goals that are not clear tend to be resisted and/or ignored because individuals do not know what is expected of them. On the other hand, goals that are too precise and give individuals little or no leeway in meeting them also may be resisted.

If people have performance goals set for them and lack confidence in the qualifications of those setting the standards, hostility toward both the goals and the goal setters may arise.

People who have studied control systems agree that goals that are too high or too low are not motivating. If they are too low people will lean on their oars in meeting them. If they are too high they will see them as unrealistic and feel little obligation to try to achieve them. Furthermore, excessively high goals will tend to generate hostility. Goals that are tough, a little aggressive, but achievable, seem to be best.

Measuring Performance against Standard

A good bit that has already been said relates to measuring performance against standard. A few other observations, however, deserve inclusion here.

When extrinsic rewards are tightly tied to performance people will often present invalid data if they can get away with it, the reason being that they gain by doing so. The literature is filled with stories of one department sending shoddy products to another department to get higher ratings of product shipped, of services to customers unfulfilled in order to save expenses, and so on.[10]

If people feel manipulated by a carrot-and-stick approach to motivation they will fight to preserve their self-esteem. They will unionize, featherbed, manipulate performance data, and in other ways try to control their work environment. In order to get high performance ratings, workers will tend to stick to the strict rules of the control system. They become reluctant to make exceptions. Such action constitutes a form of bureaucratic behavior that injects rigidity and inefficiency into operations. For instance, in order to make a monthly quota of output both supervisors and employees in a job shop may ignore requests of a salesman to fill the urgent demands of an old customer because it is more efficient for them to stick to job lots that yield high per unit output. This is one way to lose valuable customers.

In measuring performance, individuals want the relevant aspects of their behavior evaluated. If they are evaluated on the basis of measures that they feel are not particularly appropriate or that do not include all the criteria they deem relevant, they will have little confidence in the evaluation process. Their dissatisfaction is increased if they believe that the person evaluating them is not competent to do so or is hostile to them.

Control systems are more respected by individuals when they are allowed to make corrections in their performance before someone else steps in to do so. This is the great virtue of steering control systems described in the preceding chapter. If the goal is accepted by individuals in such a system, then feedback on performance is seen to be an aid in achieving suitable performance. Critical path and milestone charts, for example, permit such experience.

Who steers is crucial. If the steering is done by someone outside the unit in which work is performed the measurement and demand for corrective action may be irritating and therefore resisted. Self-regulation is much better received. Thus, steering controls should be implemented as close to actual operations as possible.[11]

The reporting system for deviations from a standard should obviously be appropriate and timely. Premature and unreliable measurements can cause all sorts of troubles. For example, if quality of product output is a standard for measuring performance, the measurement and timing of action is important. If the product is mass-produced, random sampling of quality is in order. Premature action taken when the first product is detected that reveals poor quality not only may create inefficient operations but also may generate cynicism and hostility in the machine operator.

Correcting Deviations from Plan

Again, much that has been said earlier in this chapter relates to the correction of behavior to conform to plans. A few additional points may be made, however. The extent to which individuals resist or welcome directions to change performance varies a great deal with respect to the individual and what is being controlled. Some employees are comfortable with a superior who tells them exactly what they should do; others resent such supervision. Some will accept strict supervision for tasks that warrant close monitoring but will reject close managerial surveillance where it does not seem to be necessary.

Correcting deviations in performance brings into focus the entire task of management. Managers can correct performance by changing measures. Perhaps deviations can be resolved by a change of plans. A manager may eliminate poor performance by reorganizing the company, by hiring new people, by retraining present workers, by changing job assignments, and so on. To correct deviations from plans, therefore, involves all of the functions, tasks, and responsibilities of managers. To go back to the first chapter, planning is inextricably interwoven into the entire process of management. This means not only the making of plans but also their implementation throughout the organization.

Summary

Control systems must be designed and operated with full knowledge of the human considerations that are involved. Managers have available a number of strategies that can be employed to achieve optimal effectiveness of control systems. This chapter illustrated some of them.

Unfortunately for the manager, there is no simple and easy way to determine precisely which control strategy will be most effective in a given situation. This chapter presented a number of lessons of experience that may be applicable in particular situations.

V Evaluating and Reenergizing the System

18 Dangers to Avoid in Strategic Planning

Not all organizations that have developed formal planning systems are completely satisfied with their systems or results. One reason for this dissatisfaction is that they have made mistakes in setting up, doing, and using their systems.

Almost three decades of experience with formal planning systems have taught many lessons about what ought to be done and what should be avoided for effective planning. A number of these lessons already have been discussed. This chapter brings together the most significant dangers that experience tells us should be avoided if planning systems are to be effective.

A Survey of Planning Pitfalls

Several years ago I sent a questionnaire concerning planning pitfalls to 600 companies and received 215 usable replies.[1] Over 33 percent of the replies were from companies with sales over $1 billion but 7.4 percent had sales under $50 million; exactly 5 percent had sales between $50 and $99 million. Thus, the distribution was skewed toward larger companies although smaller companies were represented.

It was my intent to get responses from a representative group of chief executives, division managers, and managers of headquarters staffs. Unexpectedly, however, most companies decided to have only the corporate planner complete the form. Thus, 75 percent of the replies were from corporate planners, which created another bias in the results. Despite these biases I believe the results of the survey still have value.

A principal purpose of the survey was to determine whether or not a list of fifty pitfalls, which I had identified and which are shown in Exhibit 18–1, really covered most or all of the major traps that experience indicated should be avoided for successful planning. Respondents were asked to add to this list, and a number of additions were suggested.[2] They were either modifications of pitfalls identified in Exhibit 18–1 or subsets of them. The respondents confirmed my conviction that Exhibit 18–1 includes the most important traps, both conceptually and operationally, that must be avoided if a formal planning system is to be effective. There are, however, some reservations to this observation that should be explained.

First, the list of pitfalls is incomplete because it does not include the entire management process associated with planning. As pointed out in Chapter 1, strategic planning is inextricably interwoven into the entire process of management. The list isolates only the more significant pitfalls to be avoided in getting the system of planning started, in understanding the nature of strategic planning, in doing planning, and in using the plans once they are prepared.[3]

Second, there are other pitfalls in planning such as selecting the wrong subject to examine, or making the wrong type of analysis of the information at hand, or drawing the wrong conclusions from reliable data. Planning can easily fail if such mistakes are made. For instance, it is a serious error to assume that a simple linear extrapolation of past sales data will provide acceptable forecasts for planning. A formal planning system will be accused of failing if a company goes through the process and formulates the wrong strategy for implementation, to illustrate another dimension. This result may or may not be the fault of the planning system. The point here, however, is that many mistakes can be made in planning that relate to methodology, decisionmaking processes, and individuals' thinking that are not explicitly shown in the list of fifty pitfalls.

Third, any company at a particular point in time has many choices about how to avoid the errors shown in Exhibit 18–1. This is another way of saying that each of the pitfalls encompasses a wide range of possible actions any one of which may have a high or low applicability to a given situation. For example, the first pitfall—"Top management's assumption that it can delegate the planning function to a planner"—has many subleties associated with it. It is a fundamental mistake to delegate the entire planning function to a planner. On the other hand, a chief executive must get some help from staff. How much planning responsibility a chief executive can or should delegate to staff depends upon many circumstances, as discussed in Chapters 4 and 5.

Executives and staff must search for and understand the pitfalls discussed here and then determine whether or not, and how much, they are applicable to their particular situation.

Parenthetically, it is worth noting that many of the pitfalls are obvious. Many are not. Some may be considered counterintuitive. They will be ignored by management at great risk to the effectiveness of their planning systems.

Ten Major Mistakes to Avoid

Respondents to the survey mentioned above were asked to rank what they considered to be the five most important pitfalls. From this ranking I developed a list of the most critical pitfalls that respondents thought should be avoided, presented in Exhibit 18–2 in descending order of importance.

Respondents to the survey were also asked whether or not they were satisfied with their planning systems. They reported much more satisfaction than dissatisfaction, as shown in Exhibit 18–3.

Those who completed the questionnaire were also asked whether they had become significantly ensnared in any of the traps. Without exception those companies that answered affirmatively for any of the snares identified in Exhibit 18–2 were more dissatisfied than satisfied with their planning systems.

Comments on the Ten Major Mistakes to Avoid

In previous chapters a good bit was said about some of the top ten mistakes. Consequently, only brief comments will be made here.

"Top management's assumption that it can delegate the planning function to a planner." The chief executive of a company must

A. PITTFALLS IN GETTING STARTED:

1. Top management's assumption that it can delegate the planning function to a planner.

2. Rejecting planning because there has been success without it.

3. Rejecting formal planning because the system failed in the past to foresee a critical problem and/or did not result in substantive decisions that satisfied top management.

4. Assuming that the present body of knowledge about planning is insufficient to guide fruitful comprehensive planning.

5. Assuming that a company cannot develop effective long-range planning in a way appropriate to its resources and needs.

6. Assuming that comprehensive corporate planning can be introduced into a company and overnight miraculous results will appear.

7. Thinking that a successful corporate plan can be moved from one company to another without change and with equal success.

8. Assuming that a formal system can be introduced into a company without a careful and perhaps "agonizing reappraisal" of current managerial practices and decision-making processes.

9. Ignoring the power structure of a company in organizing the planning process.

10. Failure to develop a clear understanding of the long-range planning procedure before the process is actually undertaken.

11. Failure to create a climate in the company which is congenial and not resistant to planning.

12. Failing to locate the corporate planner at a high enough level in the managerial hierarchy.

13. Failure to make sure that the planning staff has the necessary qualities of leadership, technical expertise, and personality to discharge properly its responsibilities in making the planning system effective.

B. PITFALLS RELATED TO A MISUNDERSTANDING OF THE NATURE OF STRATEGIC PLANNING:

14. Forgetting that planning is a political, a social, and an organizational, as well as a rational process.

15. Assuming that corporate comprehensive planning is something separate from the entire management process.

EXHIBIT 18–1:   Fifty Common Pitfalls in Formal Strategic Planning.

EXHIBIT 18–1 *(Cont.)*

16. Failure to make sure that top management and major line officers really understand the nature of long-range planning and what it will accomplish for them and the company.

17. Failing to understand that systematic formal planning and intuitive (opportunistic, or entrepreneurial) planning are complementary.

18. Assuming that plans can be made by staff planners for line managers to implement.

19. Ignoring the fact that planning is and should be a learning process.

20. Assuming that planning is easy.

21. Assuming that planning is hard.

22. Assuming that long-range planning can get a company out of a current crisis.

23. Assuming that long-range planning is only strategic planning, or just planning for a major product, or simply looking ahead at likely development of present product. (In other words, failing to see that comprehensive planning is an integrated managerial system.)

C. PITFALLS IN DOING STRATEGIC PLANNING:
I. Managerial Involvement

24. Top management becomes so engrossed in current problems that it spends insufficient time on long-range planning, and the process becomes discredited among other managers and staff.

25. Long-range planning becomes unpopular because top management spends so much time on long-range problems that it ignores short-range problems.

26. Failure to assume the necessary involvement in the planning process of major line personnel.

27. Too much centralization of long-range planning in the central headquarters so that divisions feel little responsibility for developing effective plans.

II. The Process of Planning

28. Failure to develop company goals suitable as a basis for formulating long-range plans.

29. Assuming that equal weight should be given to all elements of planning (i.e., that the same emphasis should be placed on strategic as on tactical planning, or that the same emphasis should be accorded to major functional plans).

30. Injecting so much formality into the system that it lacks flexibility, looseness, and simplicity, and restrains creativity.

EXHIBIT 18–1 (*Cont.*)

31. Failure to make realistic plans (e.g., due to overoptimism and/or over-cautiousness).

32. Extrapolating rather than rethinking the entire process in each cycle (i.e., if plans are made for 1971 through 1975, adding 1976 in the 1972 cycle rather than redoing all plans from 1972 to 1975).

33. Developing such a reverence for numbers that irreverence for intuition and value judgments predominates the thinking going into planning.

34. Seeking precision of numbers throughout the planning horizon.

35. Assuming that older methods to choose from among alternatives should be discarded in favor of newer techniques.

36. Assuming that new quantitative techniques are not as useful as advertised.

37. Doing long-range planning periodically and forgetting it in between cycles.

III. Creditability of Results

38. Failure to develop planning capabilities in major operating units.

39. Failure of top management and/or the planning staff, to give departments and divisions sufficient information and guidance (e.g., top management interests, environmental projections, etc.).

40. Attempting to do too much in too short a time.

41. Failure to secure that minimum of system and information to make the process and its results creditable and useful.

D. PITFALLS IN USING STRATEGIC PLANS:

42. Failure of top management to review with departmental and divisional heads the long-range plans which they have developed.

43. Forgetting that the fundamental purpose of the exercise is to make better current decisions.

44. Assuming that plans once made are in the nature of blueprints and should be followed rigorously until changed in the next planning cycle.

45. Top management's consistently rejecting the formal planning mechanism by making intuitive decisions which conflict with the formal plans.

46. Assuming that because plans must result in current decisions it is the short run that counts and planning efforts as well as evaluations of results should concentrate on the short run.

47. Failing to use plans as standards for measuring managerial performance.

EXHIBIT 18-1 *(Cont.)*

---

48. Forgetting to apply a cost-benefit analysis to the system to make sure advantages are greater than costs.

---

49. Failing to encourage managers to do good long-range planning by basing reward solely on short-range performance measures.

---

50. Failing to exploit the fact that formal planning is a managerial process which can be used to improve managerial capabilities throughout a company.

---

assume responsibility for planning and must get involved in it. How much of this task the chief executive delegates and how much responsibility he assumes will depend upon the executive, the experience the company has had with planning, staff capabilities, and many other factors. The lesson is clear, however: Complete delegation of planning to staff is the road to planning failure.

"Top management becomes so engrossed in current problems that it spends insufficient time on long-range planning, and the process becomes discredited among other managers and staff." There must, of course, be a proper blend of short- and long-range planning. Everyone recognizes that most managers are faced with excessive demands on their time, not the least of which are urgent, short-range problems. This fact of life, however, must not lead to the neglect of long-range strategic planning. To do so is likely to lead to poor short-range decisions.

"Failure to develop company goals suitable as a basis for formulating long-range plans." I was surprised to see this mistake listed so high so I queried a number of respondents about it. It turned out that in many companies objectives were set only in broad terms, such as "make the best acquisition possible" or "optimize profits." Other companies set unrealistic objectives for growth, profits, share of market, and so on. In other companies there appeared to be problems of clarification and/or agreement between central headquarters and divisions. In some cases divisions wanted headquarters to specify objectives for the divisions but headquarters would not do so. The results were frustration in trying to plan. Long-range objectives, as pointed out in Chapter 10, should be concrete and well understood. Failure to meet these requirements inevitably creates problems in strategic planning.

"Failure to assume the necessary involvement in the planning process of major line personnel." Line managers at lower levels in an organization will not spend time on projects that they do not believe top management is thoroughly committed to doing. Exhor-

Rank	Pitfall Number	Description	Times Ranked					Number of Times Ranked 1 to 5
			1	2	3	4	5	
1	1	Top management's assumption that it can delegate the planning function to a planner.	31	9	2	4	2	48
2	24	Top management becomes so engrossed in current problems that it spends insufficient time on long-range planning, and the process becomes discredited among other managers and staff.	13	7	10	8	9	47
3	28	Failure to develop company goals suitable as a basis for formulating long-range plans.	8	16	6	6	10	46
4	26	Failure to assume the necessary involvement in the planning process of major line personnel.	4	5	7	10	4	30
5	47	Failing to use plans as standards for measuring managerial performance.	3	7	8	7	4	29
6	11	Failure to create a climate in the company which is congenial and not resistant to planning.	8	7	4	5	3	27
7	15	Assuming that corporate comprehensive planning is something separate from the entire management process.	3	7	8	6	3	27
8	30	Injecting so much formality into the system that it lacks flexibility, looseness, and simplicity, and restrains creativity.	2	6	5	4	7	24
9	42	Failure of top management to review with departmental and divisional heads the long-range plans which they have developed.	3	3	4	10	4	24
10	45	Top management's consistently rejecting the formal planning mechanism by making intuitive decisions which conflict with the formal plans.	5	5	3	3	7	23

EXHIBIT 18-2: The Ten Most Important Pitfalls to Be Avoided as Ranked by Respondents (N = 150)

Degree of Satisfaction	Number of Responses	Percentage of Responses
1. Highly satisfied	21	10.0
2. Above-average satisfaction	72	34.1
3. Average satisfaction	68	32.2
4. Some dissatisfaction	21	15.2
5. Highly dissatisfied	18	8.5
Total sample	211	100.0
N.A.	4	—

EXHIBIT 18–3: **Degree of Satisfaction with Reported Planning Systems.**

tation by top management to others in the organization to get on with strategic planning is not enough. Some years ago Kirby Warren identified tests that managers applied when planning was first introduced in organizations to determine what their response would be.[4] These tests are still valid. Warren said that before managers did much of anything they took a wait and see attitude. In this period they applied four tests to chief executive commitment.

First, "Who is chosen to be the director of planning and how is he or she treated?" If a strong, capable director is chosen and is treated with respect and is welcomed by top management the first test is passed.

Second, "How much direct backing does the president give longer-range proposals?" If top executives focus on the short range other managers will conclude that long-range thinking is a waste of time. This signal makes clear what the chief executive's commitment to strategic planning is—no matter what is said.

Third, "What is management's response to strong and weak planning efforts?" What happens when a manager presents a poorly conceived strategic plan but an excellent operating performance? On the other hand, how does management react when a manager presents a first-rate strategic plan, well thought out and creditable, along with a poor short-term performance? If the first manager is praised and the second is criticized there will be little managerial effort given to long-range strategic planning in this company.

Finally, "How much emphasis is given to long-range planning in determining bonuses and promotions?" In a previous chapter it was pointed out that if a manager is evaluated solely on the basis of the short-term bottom line there will be little or no long-range strategic thinking. In Chapter 11 it was noted that General Electric

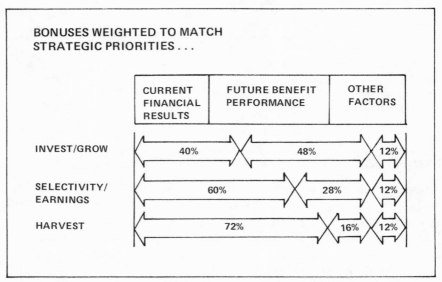

BONUSES WEIGHTED TO MATCH
STRATEGIC PRIORITIES . . .

	CURRENT FINANCIAL RESULTS	FUTURE BENEFIT PERFORMANCE	OTHER FACTORS
INVEST/GROW	40%	48%	12%
SELECTIVITY/ EARNINGS	60%	28%	12%
HARVEST	72%	16%	12%

EXHIBIT 18–4: General Electric Company Bonus Calculation. (Source: Michael G. Allen, "Diagramming GE's Planning for What's Watt," *Planning Review*, September 1977, p. 8.)

evaluates managers partly on the basis of what they do with products under their jurisdiction located in different parts of the market strength/market attractiveness matrix. The GE bonus weighting system is illustrated in Exhibit 18–4.

"Failure to create a climate in the company which is congenial and not resistant to planning." This is an important issue that was explored at length in previous chapters. No further discussion will appear here.

"Assuming that corporate comprehensive planning is something separate from the entire management process." This point, too, was covered previously, especially in Chapter 1.

"Injecting so much formality into the system that it lacks flexibility, looseness, and simplicity, and restrains creativity." One common mistake some large centralized companies make is to prepare a planning manual and make it applicable to all divisions, irrespective of size, planning capabilities, culture of the organization, and so on. Divisions, like companies, need a planning system to fit their unique characteristics. My observation is that fewer companies fall into this trap today than previously.

"Failure of top management to review with departmental and divisional heads the long-range plans which they have developed."

If top management does not review plans or does not tell managers who prepared plans that they have been reviewed, managers will believe top management does not care about their planning efforts. Review and feedback by top management to managers making plans are essential.

"Top management's consistently rejecting the formal planning mechanism by making intuitive decisions which conflict with the formal plans." Whenever a company falls into this error it means that the top manager is in effect delegating the planning function to someone else and if plans do not sit well with the top executive they are rejected. It means insufficient involvement of the top executive in the planning process. If plans are rejected very often in such a situation they are not likely to be prepared with care. On the other hand, a planning system must incorporate the intuitive judgments of managers—including top executives—throughout its development. Formality and intuition, however, should be balanced. The pattern should not be one of rigid, sequential steps whereby lower level managers complete their planning and top executives then accept or reject. This pattern is not likely to produce the best results from lower level managers especially if the typical experience is top level rejection.

Other Major Mistakes to Avoid

Many writers in recent years have addressed themselves to reasons for the failure of planning.[5] For the most part the reasons given duplicate or are subsets of one or more of the fifty pitfalls shown in Exhibit 18–1. It is worthwhile, however, to comment on some of them because they do highlight specific mistakes that can result in poor planning.

In a study of 350 companies in Europe and the United States Ringbakk found ten major reasons for the failure of planning:

1. "Corporate planning has not been integrated into the firm's total management system."
2. ". . . lack of understanding of the different dimensions of planning."
3. "Management at different levels in the organization has not properly engaged in or contributed to the planning activities."

4. "The responsibility for planning is often wrongly vested solely in a planning department."
5. "In many companies, management expects that the plans as developed will be realized."
6. ". . . in starting formal planning too much is attempted at once."
7. "Management fails to operate by the plan."
8. ". . . extrapolation and financial projections are confused with planning."
9. "Inadequate inputs used in the planning."
10. "Many companies fail to see the overall picture of planning. They get hung up on little details."[6]

Most of Ringbakk's causes of planning failure directly relate to one or more of the pitfalls shown in Exhibit 18–1. Some are not readily identified with my pitfalls because they are subsets. Some have been mentioned in previous chapters. They all are important and should be kept in mind by managers.

Hans Schollhammer and I used the same questionnaire that included the fifty pitfalls noted in Exhibit 18–1 and surveyed Japan, Canada, England, Italy, and Australia.[7] The top ten important mistakes to avoid generally were identified by respondents in these countries as the same ones U.S. respondents listed. In some countries other of the fifty pitfalls were high on the list. For instance, in Japan pitfall 43 was in fifth place—"Forgetting that the fundamental purpose of [planning] is to make better current decisions." In England pitfall 27 was ranked fourth—"Too much centralization of long-range planning in the central headquarters so that divisions feel little responsibility for developing effective plans." In Canada pitfall 27 was ranked sixth; number 43 was ranked seventh.

Summary

In this chapter a comprehensive list of mistakes that must be avoided in formal strategic planning was presented and the more important of these errors were identified. The reader should not assume, however, that those warnings discussed in this chapter as being the most critical to heed are the only significant ones. Any of the fifty pitfalls, and other subsumed in the list of fifty, may be dominant in a particular situation.

19 Evaluating the Planning System and Maintaining a High Payoff

Managers should try to develop as effective a planning system as possible. Good strategic planning and good management go together, a combination that leads to successful business operations. Poor planning not only leads to poor decisions but wastes time and effort on the part of managers and staff.

This chapter explores the question of how managers can measure the effectiveness of strategic planning systems? The discussion focuses on the organization that has developed a comprehensive, formal planning system over a period of time. Nevertheless, the measures of planning effectiveness examined herein can be applied to any planning system after appropriate modifications.

On Measuring Planning System Performance

Two points should be made at the outset. First, comparatively little has been done to develop tested measures of planning system performance. Second, and partly a cause of the first point, effective planning systems result from the proper synthesis of management style; managerial intuition; logic and analysis; organization culture;

and planning processes, tools, and techniques. In a sense, therefore, appraisal of planning effectiveness shades into overall management appraisal. Formal, structured management performance appraisal systems for many years have been a conventional part of the management of business organizations.[1] Comparatively little has been included in these appraisal systems, however, to evaluate the effectiveness of the corporate strategic planning system.

Actually, the state of the art of measuring the effectiveness of strategic planning systems is elementary. This chapter will suggest a few approaches to measurement.

A Questionnaire

Exhibit 19-1 is a questionnaire for executives and staff that should throw considerable light on the effectiveness of the strategic planning system of an organization. A quick glance at the questionnaire shows that it seeks to measure effectiveness for forty items. Effectiveness refers to the degree to which each item achieves the desired or required objective held for it in the mind of the evaluator. The assumption is that a comprehensive strategic planning system should achieve the purposes expressed in many of the items (parts A, B, and C) by means of a process or condition described in other items (parts D and E).

The questionnaire is divided into five parts. Part A concerns general perceptions of the value of the planning system. The assumption is made that a system is effective if the benefits appear to be greater than the costs to the top management of an organization and if top managers do not perceive that it needs basic changes to suit their purposes. These are appropriate overall measures but more detailed questions should be answered favorably before a system can be called effective.

In Part B specific questions are raised concerning results of the planning system. Good marks should be attained for every item mentioned because a poor mark in any one can result in grave problems for the organization.

Part C concerns ancillary benefits of the planning system. An effective system is one that produces such benefits as improved management, better internal coordination, and improved communications.

The items listed in parts D and E concern the processes, methods, mental attitudes, climate, and procedures of the planning system. Some of these matters are much more important in insuring or preventing effectiveness than others. Their impact on effectiveness also will vary depending upon the particular organization and the situation in which it finds itself when the appraisal is made.

	Not Effective (No)	Very Effective (Yes)

A. Overall Managerial Perceived Value

1. The chief executive officer believes the system helps him or her to discharge better his or her responsibilities.

2. Other major line managers think the system is useful to them.

3. Overall, the benefits of strategic planning are perceived to be greater than the costs by most managers.

4. Are major changes needed in our strategic planning system?

B. Does Our Strategic Planning System Produce the "Right" Substantive Answers and Results?

5. Developing basic company missions and lines of business.

6. Foreseeing future major opportunities.

7. Foreseeing future major threats.

8. Properly appraising company strengths.

9. Properly appraising company weaknesses.

10. Developing realistic current information about competitors.

11. Clarifying priorities.

12. Developing useful long-range objectives.

13. Developing useful long-range program strategies.

14. Developing creditable medium- and short-range plans to implement strategies so as to achieve goals.

EXHIBIT 19–1: How Effective Is Your Strategic Planning System?

EXHIBIT 19–1. (*Cont.*)

	Not Effective (No)				Very Effective (Yes)

15. Preventing unpleasant surprises.

16. Our major financial indicators have been better after introducing planning than before:
    Sales
    Profits
    Return on investment
    Earnings per share

17. Our company performance has been better than others in our industry not doing comprehensive managerial planning.

C. *Does Our Planning System Yield Valuable Ancillary Benefits?*

18. The system has improved the quality of management.

19. The system is a unifying, coordinating force in company operations.

20. The system facilitates communications and collaboration throughout the company.

D. *The Design of the Planning System*

21. Top management has accepted the idea that strategic planning is its major responsibility.

22. Our system fits the management style of our company.

23. The system fits the reality of our strategic decisionmaking processes.

24. The corporate planner is situated close to the top management of the company.

25. The corporate planner works well with the top management.

26. The corporate planner works well with other line managers and staff.

27. The planning committee structure is just right for us.

EXHIBIT 19–1. (*Cont.*)

<table>
<tr><td></td><td>Not
Effective
(No)</td><td>Very
Effective
(Yes)</td></tr>
</table>

E. Are the Planning Processes Effective?

28. Top management spends an appropriate amount of time on strategic planning.

29. There is too much foot-dragging about planning. It is given lip service but too many line managers really do not accept it.

30. Line managers generally spend an appropriate amount of time with other line managers and/or staff in developing strategic plans.

31. The system proceeds on the basis of an acceptable set of procedures.

32. The planning procedures are well understood in the company.

33. The work requirement to complete the plans is acceptable to our managers and staff.

34. The process is effective in inducing in-depth thinking.

35. Too much attention is paid to putting numbers in boxes. The process is too pro-ceduralized, too routine, too inflexible.

36. New ideas are generally welcomed.

37. Too many managers are not willing to face up to company weaknesses in devising plans.

38. Divisions do not get sufficient guidance from headquarters for effective planning.

39. Divisions are too much restrained by headquarters for effective planning.

40. The ability of managers to do effective strategic planning is taken into consideration in a proper manner when they are measured for overall performance.

Generally speaking, however, significant deficiencies in any one of these items can seriously reduce planning efficiency.

Implicit in many of the items in the survey, if not the entire survey, is the idea that planning effectiveness will be improved with greater sophistication of planning processes. This point is not necessarily correct. I agree with Hall, who observed that with greater sophistication in planning

> New forecasting methods will be used, new planning techniques will be employed, and new planning procedures will be followed, but the net impact of these will be to generate few, if any, new insights unless the socio-political environment within which the planning process operates encourages managers to gain these insights. . . . Pressures on time, self interest, and commitments to subordinates, peers, and supervisors typically will dominate the planning tools, systems, and procedures which are employed within the organization.[2]

Because of the different impacts of the items listed in Exhibit 18–1 people using the form may wish to weight specific items. These weights will differ from company to company and in the same company from time to time.

This questionnaire as it is presented will not yield a single grade or measure of effectiveness for the planning system. It can, however, be easily altered to do so. For example, quantitative weights could be given to different items, as a measure of their importance, and to grades given to each of the items (e.g., very effective 4 and ineffective 0). With such weighting a single grade can be derived for each completed form. Nevertheless, the purpose of the survey is not to seek a single grade for the system but rather to develop a set of observations about the individual items, and the whole system, that can be used as a base for fruitful discussion among managers and staff about ways and means to improve the planning system.

Literature Reviews

Another approach to measuring planning effectiveness is to derive from the literature a list of critical factors in effective planning systems and then to evaluate the planning system against the list. Schaffir noted that if managers wish to evaluate the effectiveness of their organizations' strategic planning programs and activities they will find important clues in each of ten areas in which planning often becomes unhinged from everyday realities.[3] He identified ten areas, which I present as questions. (Schaffir's areas roughly coincide with topics I discuss in this book; thus, only a few comments for additional clarification will be made about them.)

First, does the business plan help its author manage his own operation more effectively?

Second, does the business plan establish a mutually agreed upon commitment between the author of the plan and his boss? Schaffir noted that in some organizations planning gets started, but through an inertia of its own becomes isolated from the real world. Still, it is pursued, resulting in "a triumph of process over content!" If there is no commitment to doing effective planning there will be no effective planning. Commitment, as we have seen, will not come from rhetoric without appropriate performance and involvement of the chief executive.

Third, does the business plan contain sufficient information to lend credibility to its promise? That is, is the situation audit adequate? Are the forecasting procedures appropriate? Are strategies tested by appropriate methods? Can strategies be implemented?

Fourth, does the business plan have a strategic focus? Here Schaffir had in mind focusing on "the positioning of the enterprise's resources to capitalize on particular opportunities within a dynamic, continuously changing environment, with particular regard to competitive and other threats." Effective planning, he argued, requires that this be done upon the basis of a thorough understanding of the environment and carefully formulated strategies.

Fifth, does the planning system foster awareness of options and their likely consequences? The planning system must generate alternatives and subject them to a fair appraisal before a course of action is chosen.

Sixth, does the planning system boil up critical issues, choices, and priorities? In Schaffir's words: "A major purpose of the business plan is to keep management attention focused on those key factors, critical issues, and choices that will need to be made in the light of a particular set of priorities. Thus critical issues, choices, and priorities deserve to be summarized crisply at the very top of any business plan if they are to remain in the spotlight.''

Seventh, is the business plan linked firmly to the system for allocating and committing capital funds? Strategies are implemented generally through capital allocations. If strategic planning is done in one system and capital allocations are made in another system, and the two are not tightly meshed, the capital allocation process may not really help implement the strategic decisions.

Eighth, is the paperwork manageable?

Ninth, does the planning system and the resulting plans accommodate a plurality of managerial and planning styles? Many managers participate in the strategic planning process, and they have different styles and different needs for plans. The planning system must somehow fit these styles and needs.

Tenth, is the planning system woven into the fabric of the organization?

> At its best, planning becomes an integrating, catalytic, creative, developmental driving force in managing the enterprise. Rather than being endured as a mandated, annual burst of activity before going back to work, planning becomes a way of life for the organization. It becomes a natural part of the formal and informal processes by which management at all levels sorts its priorities, makes decisions, gets work done, and brings about change and innovation. This can only be accomplished gradually by focusing managers on tasks within an organized process they find helpful in meeting their own needs.[4]

A planning system can profitably be tested against a set of measures such as Schaffir's. Yet one can go further and develop specific questions to be raised in each of the ten areas that will help test the effectiveness of the planning system.[5]

Testing the Planning System against Listed Pitfalls

In Chapter 18 a comprehensive list of pitfalls was presented. One way to measure the effectiveness of a planning system is to rate it in connection with all or the more important pitfalls related to the company's planning system.

Measurement against Purpose

Exhibit 18–1 is based upon the assumption that the planning system being appraised is designed to achieve a number of purposes at the same time. If a planning system is designed specifically to achieve one or a few purposes the appraisal should be made in terms of the extent to which it achieves those purposes.

Maintaining a High Payoff from Formal Planning

Managers must continually supervise the planning system in order to maintain a high payoff from it. Such surveillance when periodically reinforced by systematic surveys of the type suggested here should insure that the planning system is as effective as managers expect it to be.

Managers must constantly watch for signs that the system is deteriorating. The system must fit the organization. Since the organization is constantly changing so should the system. Beyond this point, as Schaffir noted, a planning system can take on a momentum of its own—if not watched carefully that momentum tends toward deterioration rather than development.

Summary

This chapter is based on the premise that managers will profit from a periodic evaluation of the effectiveness of their formal strategic planning systems. Several approaches to measuring effectiveness of planning systems were suggested: administering a comprehensive questionnaire on the requirements for effective planning systems prescribed in the literature; testing the system against pitfalls discussed in the previous chapter; and evaluating the system against specific purposes it is supposed to achieve. These approaches are valuable more because their results can be a basis for discussion among managers and staff about how to improve the planning system than because they yield an absolute measure of effectiveness.

It was also suggested that constant surveillance of the planning system and periodic, systematic evaluation of it, as embodied in a survey form, are necessary to maintain a high payoff for the planning system.

VI Applicability of Business Planning Experience in Other Areas

20 Personal Lifetime Planning

Many of the lessons of strategic planning experience that have been discussed are applicable to planning in areas outside business. One such important area is personal planning. In this chapter ways will be presented in which experience with strategic planning in business can be applied to personal lifetime planning.*

Before discussing how to do personal lifetime planning it may be noted that two Emory University psychologists, Bonnie Strickland and Steve Nowicki, made an intensive study of public school students in the Atlanta metropolitan area and concluded that "life's losers" tend to believe that luck is the compelling factor in what happens to one and that they can do nothing about it. On the other hand, those most likely to succeed in life believe they can exert some measure of control over their own destiny.[1] This chapter is designed more for the latter than the former.

Piecemeal versus Comprehensive Personal Planning

It is not difficult to take one aspect of one's life and make a decision that will bring about a change. For instance, if I am

* This chapter is essentially the same as my article "Invent Your Own Future," which appeared in the *California Management Review*, Fall 1976.

uneducated and wish to acquire knowledge I can do so. But such piecemeal decisions, although they may improve one's life, do not constitute the best method for comprehensively addressing the question: What do I want my life to be and how can I go about achieving my design? Or, how can I invent my own future?

When such questions are first asked by an individual the problem boggles the mind. Where do I start? What elements of my personality, circumstances, and future prospects should I consider? What can I say about them? I can, of course, dream; but how do I make my dreams come true?

There is a way to approach such questions with the probability that a person can indeed make decisions that will help bring about a desired future. Although there is no certainty that this will happen, structured planning, discussed in this chapter, promises the possibility that one can influence one's own future.

Getting Started

The key to personal life planning is to know how to begin. Here, business planning is suggestive. In long-range business planning a typical starting point is some fundamental optimizing and integrating objective, such as profit or return on investment. There are no comparable objectives for individuals, but business planning does suggest one possibility—maximization of self-satisfaction over a lifetime. It is not easy to define what this means, and the definition will change over time. But if this objective is accepted, and I believe it is the central purpose of each individual, it can serve as the starting point for life planning.

With this objective it is now possible to proceed with personal life planning, as shown in Exhibit 20–1, which model will be described in the remainder of this chapter.

Starting Other Personal Long-Range Plans

Exhibit 20–1 can be used for other personal long-range plans. In place of maximizing personal self-satisfaction over a lifetime, which is now in the top box of Exhibit 20–1, other objectives can be inserted: "Have my own successful company in ten years"; or, "Be the executive vice-president of my company in ten years"; or, "Become a successful lawyer." The model is just as appropriate for career objectives as for personal lifetime plans.[2]

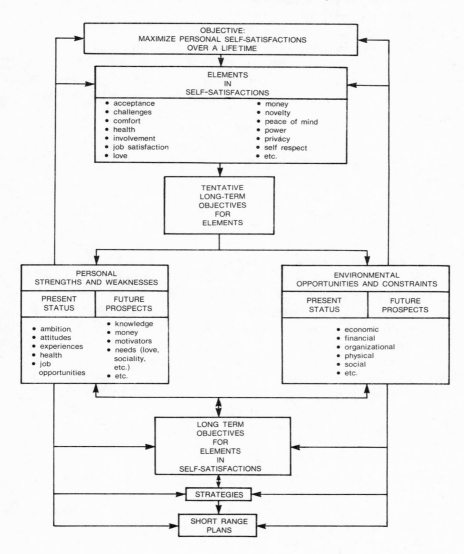

EXHIBIT 20–1:   A Conceptual Model of Personal Life Planning.

Elements in Maximizing Lifetime Satisfactions

The next step in the process is to identify the major elements that must be considered in determining how one can improve personal self-satisfaction over a lifetime. A number of these elements are shown in the model. Because this is such a crucial step in planning it is important to be aware of the wide range of elements that should be considered. A person cannot consider all of these elements in planning. One can and should deal only with the most important ones.

SETTING TENTATIVE LONG-RANGE OBJECTIVES

With some reference to the factors indentified in the boxes labeled "personal strengths and weaknesses" and "environmental opportunities and constraints," tentative objectives should be set for the elements identified as being most relevant to achieving a person's self-satisfactions. I emphasize tentative; no effort should be made at this point to formulate objectives in detail. These goals should, however, be reasonable targets in light of what an individual knows about himself and his prospects.

A suitable initial target is to set objectives for a five-year time span. This is the time horizon most typically used by business firms around the world. It is true that for separate projects, such as developing an airplane, the planning period may extend to ten or more years. So, too, for an individual. A particular program, such as becoming a medical doctor, may look beyond five years.

THE SITUATION AUDIT

These tentative objectives then must be appraised against a situation audit of personal strengths and weaknesses and environmental opportunities and constraints. The respective boxes in the chart identify the types of factors that should be considered. For personal strengths and weaknesses as well as environmental opportunities and constraints, the evaluation should be in terms of both present conditions with respect to each factor and future prospects. The first appraisal should be made as honestly and objectively as possible. The second involves forecasting the future. This entire effort should be thoughtful and searching but should not involve an exhaustive research effort.

FIRMING UP LONG-RANGE OBJECTIVES

On the basis of this appraisal it now is possible to develop firmer long-term objectives for those elements that the individual has identified as being important in his future self-satisfactions. In preparing these objectives, for five years ahead or whatever time period is chosen, the planner should not try to set detailed aims for all elements or all parts of any element. The reason is that to attempt to do so brings up an extraordinary number of complex questions that are so difficult to disentangle that the planning process becomes completely unmanageable. Also, the more detailed the objectives the more likely one is to find inconsistencies among them.

Quantitative objectives can be set for some elements, for example, money. Other objectives may be stated in general qualitative terms, such as to "improve health," "seek work with greater challenge," or "engage in church programs to widen friendships."

FORMULATING STRATEGIES

Once objectives are set the process then moves to the identification and evaluation of strategies to achieve them. For instance, if the objective is to improve health, several strategies may be identified, such as "reduce weight by dieting," "undertake an an exercise program under the guidance of an expert," or "stop smoking." Each of these will of course involve substrategies. But here again, too much detail may be fatal to the project.

In individual as in corporate planning, the planner very likely will find it useful to move back and forth between objectives and strategies, all the while referring to the strengths, weaknesses, opportunities, and constraints that were identified in the situation audit. For instance, a long-term objective for personal net worth may have been set. In thinking of strategies to achieve this goal the person doing the planning may identify a new feasible course of action that will yield a much greater potential income. The net worth objective can then be raised. Or, if it appears that no strategy can be devised that has a chance of meeting the net worth objective, it must be lowered. This process is called iteration.

Larger business firms generally develop medium-range plans in which various functional elements are interrelated. This is done to display on paper the way strategies are to be implemented so that objectives will be achieved. This plotting of objectives, called the critical path, is a method to insure the credibility of strategies. The process is difficult and probably should not be attempted by the individual, at least in the first planning effort. Yet strategies certainly should be evaluated in terms of their credibility. Credibility of course will depend heavily upon one's personal strengths and weaknesses and future prospects.

ACTION PLANS

The next step is to formulate specific plans for the next six months or year to implement strategies to achieve longer range objectives. Here one's plans should get very specific, such as "make an appointment for next week with my family doctor to get a thorough physical checkup before undertaking an exercise program"; "enroll in university to improve my ability as a marketing manager"; or "speak to the vice-president of personnel about finding a job in my company that will better utilize my capabilities." Long-range planning in business is considered to be a futile exercise if the process does not result in making better current decisions. So it is with personal planning. It may be interesting to speculate about what might be, but nothing much will happen unless specific decisions are made to take action in the immediate future.

Four Fundamental Requirements for Personal Planning

Four fundamental principles must be followed if this planning is to be useful. First, the plan must be written. The type of planning sketched here cannot be done while driving the freeways. The process is far too complicated to be worked out solely in one's mind.

Second, every effort should be made to avoid too much detail. The type of planning described here cannot be done if it is too comprehensive in scope and too deep in detail. The complexity of such planning easily can become unmanageable. Especially in making the first plan, what is done should be of a scope that the planner can comfortably handle in a reasonably short period of time. I have in mind for the first effort spending no more than, say, eight hours spread over several weeks, to assure that the planning does not get too complex and involve too much detail. The entire plan should not cover more than two written pages.

Third, the plans should be feasible. This means that the objectives, strategies, and detailed plans should be realistic and possible, as contrasted with pie-in-the-sky aims and impossible strategies to achieve them. This does not mean, of course, that the long-range objectives cannot be imaginative and hard to achieve.

Fourth, the plan should be reviewed and redone once a year, or at least every second year. Corporations have found that the planning process is not effective when plans are made and cast in bronze, so to speak. Environments are changing constantly and plans should be adjusted periodically in that light. Most corporations have found that redoing long-range plans once a year is the best policy.

Summary

This conceptual model of individual lifetime planning can be made operational in the ways described here. It should be observed, however, that there is no one way to develop a life plan. Businesses discovered long ago that there is no one way to do business planning. The process can start at any point indicated in Exhibit 20–1. For instance, one may begin by asking: What strategies am I now employing, implicitly or explicitly? The next obvious question is: Are they appropriate in light of my strengths, weaknesses, opportunities, and future prospects? One may start with objectives and then rework them by testing them against other steps noted in the chart. If all steps are not included, however, something vital in the process is lost. Many people have told me that going through this process has brought significant changes in their lives—for the better. It has that potential for everyone if done with care and with an overall policy to make sure that the personal benefits derived from the process are greater than the costs of time and effort involved in doing the planning.

21 What the Private Sector Can Teach the Not-for-Profit Sector

There are increasingly frequent calls for agencies in the not-for-profit sector (NFPS)—from hospitals to the federal government—to expand policy horizons beyond the short term. The purpose is to identify major problems ahead so as to be able to make better current decisions to deal with them; to understand better the future implications of current legislative proposals and actions; and to improve coordination among organizational activities and plans. Planning is perceived as being the most structured and professionalized mode of policymaking and implementation, which should be a key component of policy science.[1] In response to such pressures and needs some progress has been made in improving long-range planning in the NFPS, but the progress has been slow and spotty.

The purpose of this chapter is to show that many lessons learned about strategic planning in the private sector do have applicability in the NFPS. Experience in strategic planning in the private sector is often ignored in the NFPS, perhaps through ignorance of the business experience with planning, which is not surprising in light of the infrequent references to this experience in the literature on planning for the NFPS. This lack reflects a judgment that conditions are so different in the NFPS that business planning experience is inapplicable. The position taken here is that business strategic planning experience is applicable to the NFPS although there are more dissimilarities than similarities between the two areas that will influence the success of planning. As a result, great care must be taken to apply appropriate business planning experience to particular types of planning problems in the NFPS.[2]

What Is the NFPS

Broadly, the NFPS can be divided into two groups: governments, on the one hand, and all other organizations not operating for profit, on the other. Organizations in this sector cover a wide spectrum from those that operate much like private businesses to the huge bureaucracies in the governmental world—from small hospitals, shipbuilding yards, government owned railroads, and publicly owned and operated public utilities to the Department of Defense, the Department of Health, Education, and Welfare, and the State of New York. In between are other types of organizations such as savings and loan associations, trade associations, farm cooperatives, trade unions, churches, and museums. Some of these organizations closely parallel private organizations in structure and operations. The differences among them, however, are probably greater than the differences between very small and very large corporations in the private sector.

On Comparing the Two Sectors

Before one can determine the applicability of business planning experience to the NFPS it is necessary to decide which similarities and dissimilarities between the two sectors will make possible or hinder the transfer of experience. In the following sections some fundamental comparisons will be made. Care should be exercised in using these comparisons as a basis for accepting or rejecting particular lessons of private planning experience because of the great diversity of planning systems and the types of organizations in both sectors. While individual generalizations may be accepted their applicability to particular organizations may not.

Dissimilarities Between the Private Sector and the NFPS

POLITICS DOMINATE THE NFPS

An astute observer of the government commented that "everything having to do with the government and everything the government does is political, for politics is the art and science of government."[3] This means, of course, that all really important decisions are made on the political anvil. This is a fundamental difference between business and government. This political dominance of decisionmaking exists throughout the NFPS, although it varies among organizations. It is true that the higher up a decision is made in business organizations (especially large companies) the more political considerations are involved. However, the great majority of business decisions are dominated by economic factors.

PLURALISM AND NFPS DECISIONMAKING

Ours is a pluralistic society, which means that individuals and groups can and do legitimately exert power in the decisionmaking processes in their own self-interest. Governments, and other organizations in the NFPS, respond to interest groups. Managers in larger business firms believe that they must respond to the demands of various interests focused on their enterprises but there is no legal compulsion to do so. In a public organization these demands are heard, and the way in which they are weighed on the political scale decides public policy.

Roy Ash, when director of the Office of Management and Budget, summarized the impact of pluralism on decisionmaking; "Just imagine yourself as chief executive officer where your board of directors is made up of your employees, customers, suppliers and competitors. How would you like to run that business and try to be effective?" Managers even in large companies can ignore certain interests that some individuals and groups have in their affairs but organizations in the NFPS, especially governments, cannot do so.

In any planning in the NFPS almost anyone can participate if they or their groups choose to do so. Furthermore, their interests must be considered and those with the most political power ordinarily will have the most to say about decisions. If an individual or a group dislikes a decision, it is relatively easy to block action, at least for a while. One important result of pluralism is that the decisionmaking process in the NFPS is often considerably more fragmented and open than in the private sector.

MISSIONS, PURPOSES, AND OBJECTIVES

Business organizations with strategic planning systems usually have stated missions, purposes, and long-range objectives. A comparable set of aims does not exist among most organizations in the NFPS, especially governments. When aims are set for governments, for example, more often than not they are expressed in broad terms. As we have seen, planning is usually easier when objectives are specific.

For a typical private business there are comparatively few objectives established for strategic planning. In the typical government organization there are many. For an agency like the Department of Health, Education, and Welfare there are hundreds. This feature, too, complicates planning.

EVALUATING ALTERNATIVES AND DECISIONS IN THE PLANNING PROCESS

In business the fundamental criteria for determining the rationality of decisions usually are specific economic measures such as return on investment, market share, profits, sales, and margin. In the NFPS there are no such measures. The criteria for decisionmaking are much different and less concrete. Three criteria frequently used will illustrate the point, namely, the public interest, political efficiency, and cost-benefit analysis.

The public interest is the ultimate test of "good" public policy. But what is the public interest? At a high level of abstraction it refers to those phenomena of high concern to society generally about which there is a rough consensus, such as world peace, prosperity, full employment, and rising quality of life. For effective planning, of course, such vague measures must be made more specific. When this is done in the NFPS disagreements immediately arise. Every day we witness sharp disagreements among the president, congressional leaders, and leaders of pressure groups about whether a proposed measure is in the public interest. The public interest is a useful conceptual criterion for decisionmaking but not an operational one.

Another fundamental test of public policy is political efficiency, or that which has the consent of the governed. No agency in the government can exist for long without the support of public opinion. Unfortunately, it is not easy to determine when a proposed measure enjoys or will continue to have sufficient public support to give it legitimacy.

Cost-benefit analysis is being used more and more in public policy decisionmaking. Basically, this process calculates the costs associated with a program and the prospective benefits, in concrete as well as qualitative terms, and then matches the two. This method of evaluation is more applicable to specific programs than to broad strategies although it can be used in reaching conclusions about major undertakings from a military action to full employment policy. There is no one single way to make a cost-benefit analysis and equally objective researchers may come to different conclusions about the same problem.

There are other major types of tests of plans in the NFPS but these make the point that evaluation tools for choosing among alternative plans in the NFPS are not as precise as in the private sector.

IMPLEMENTATION OF PLANS

The implementation of plans in the NFPS is a much more difficult process than in the private sector for many reasons. For example, the chain of command in the NFPS is not as clear as in private industry. Common implementing mechanisms used in business are either not available or not as efficient. In mind are budgets tied to plans, cost controls, coordinating policies, and so on.

OTHER DIFFERENCES

Also distinguishing the private and public sectors are the time horizons of politicians versus those of managers, the motivations of managers, the way in which critical issues get on the policy agenda, and the constraints in the separation of powers. These differences, together with those discussed previously, underscore the point that there are fundamental dissimilarities between the NFPS and the business world that influence strategic planning. In sum, they add up to the conclusion that planning in the NFPS is a much more complex process than in the private sector.

Similarities between the Private Sector and the NFPS

Receptivity in the NFPS to strategic planning lessons learned in the private sector is enhanced by operational similarities between the two areas. Again, however, similarities vary with organizations in the NFPS. Generally speaking, receptivity is greater where organizational functioning is most similar to that in the private sector, such as a publicly owned electric power plant. At the other extreme, receptivity is less in governments. With this point in mind a few generalizations can be made about similarities of relevance to strategic planning in the two sectors.

PRESSURES ON MANAGERS TO MAKE STRATEGIC PLANNING A PART OF THEIR JOB

In the NFPS there seems to be a growing acceptance of the idea that strategic planning is an integral part of good management. Certainly, President Johnson had this notion in mind when he issued an executive order in 1965 requiring departments and agencies of the federal government to install a programming-planning-budgeting system (PPBS). This system, which had parallels with strategic planning as I have been describing it, was later abandoned in the federal government. Still, the need for strategic planning is recognized in Washington, and state and local governments are increasingly turning to PPB systems.

This is not necessarily to argue that management in the NFPS is the same as that in the private sector. There are those who assert that managerial functions are universal.[4] On the other hand, there are those who argue that the contrasts between management in the public and private sectors are so great that it is inappropriate to compare the two.[5] In between is the position that acknowledges important distinctions but regards management in the private sector and in the public sector as more similar than dissimilar.[6] The latter is a position with which I agree.

Managers everywhere are faced with increasingly turbulent environments and spend more and more time seeking to adapt their organizations to changing environmental forces. In this setting managers are concerned about future environmental impacts on their organizations; as a consequence, they spend more time looking ahead to identify critical issues.[7] There is more awareness today than ever before of the need for the federal government to look into the future to identify problems so that they can be dealt with before they become critical. We have built our government mechanisms to insure equity and due process rather than to foresee future problems that should be dealt with today. But, as a result of such current problems as shortages of energy there is more government interest in futures explorations.

Current economic problems also have stimulated demands for better plans to coordinate our economic activities. Deteriorating economic conditions have been periodically used to justify national aggregate economic plans, which will be discussed later.

In sum, managers in the NFPS are responding to environmental changes in a fashion similar to their counterparts' in private industry. A central consequence is greater pressure for both to engage in strategic planning.

ATTITUDES OF POLITICIANS TOWARD LONG-RANGE PLANNING

It is generally believed that politicians have little sympathy for long-range planning. Actually, attitudes of politicians will vary depending upon the level of government served and the nature of planning before them. Hill and Coomer surveyed over 100 mayors and city councilmen in the Houston area and found some positive relationships between the attitudes of politicians and long-range public planning. When asked whether they were concerned about long-range public planning the great majority answered affirmatively. When asked whether planning for the future was a necessary role of government, 95 percent agreed. On the other hand, when asked in what specific areas planning would be required in their own cities the responses were very conservative. They responded negatively when there was any suggestion to alter current institutional forms better to attain long-range goals.[8]

Broadly speaking, my observation is that managers in organizations in the NFPS generally are less enthusiastic about long-range public planning than are managers in the private sector about planning for their organizations. However, the increasing complexities of life are bringing changes in the attitudes of officials in the NFPS to planning. There is growing acceptance of the need for more planning though resistance continues to be strong.

COMPLEXITY OF PLANNING AND SYSTEMS DESIGN

The larger the business organization, other things being equal, the more complex are planning problems and systems design. This generalization also applies to the NFPS. Planning problems and systems design are much more complex in a huge government department than in a large business type NFPS organization such as the Tennessee Valley Authority.

In the NFPS, as in the private sector, each systems design differs from all others. Although fundamental elements of planning should be found in all systems, the details will vary from organization to organization.

Strategic Planning in the NFPS

I do not mean to leave the impression that there is no strategic planning in the NFPS comparable to that in the private sector. However, there is not enough strategic planning in the public sector and the application of lessons of experience from the private sector should stimulate more effective strategic planning in the NFPS.

To illustrate, a number of agencies of the federal government have had strategic plans for many years. The Department of Defense comes to mind as a dominant case. But other agencies also have had strategic plans for a variety of programs, such as the

National Park Service, the Federal Aviation Administration, the Federal Emergency Preparedness Agency, and the Food and Drug Administration.[9] Public Law 92-603, supported by HEW, now requires that hospitals prepare an overall long-range plan and budget for operations and capital expenditures. Few hospitals have developed an effective plan in conformance with this law but the thrust is for them to do so.

As noted previously, an increasing number of state and local agencies have developed PPB systems.[10] State and local governments for many years have had long-range plans for such areas as water supply, land use, and health care.

The business prototype of strategic planning has been applied successfully to a church,[11] to a town,[12] to higher education,[13] to hospitals,[14] and to libraries.[15] These examples make the point that there is strategic planning in the NFPS. However, everyone will agree that it is spotty and not nearly as extensive and coordinated as it should be.

Programming-Planning-Budgeting Systems

Since PPBS has been mentioned as being for the NFPS what strategic planning is for the private sector more should be said about this system. Actually, it is not identical to the strategic planning systems discussed in this book but there are more similarities than dissimilarities between the two.

Program budgeting was probably introduced for the first time in the federal government by the Army Corps of Engineers in the 1920s, but the modern version of the system was first introduced into the federal government in the Department of Defense by Secretary of Defense McNamara in 1961.[16] President Johnson, with his usual enthusiasm for a good thing, mandated in 1965 that PPB systems be used widely in government. If lessons of experience in introducing complex planning systems in the private sector had been applied at that time, PPBS still might be widely used in the federal government. But those lessons were ignored; the system failed and was abandoned by President Nixon. Nevertheless, as noted before, PPBS is growing in usage in state and local governments and many not-for-profit nongovernmental organizations.

PROGRAM BUDGETING DEFINED[17]

Program budgeting is a formal system for making decisions about an organization's resource allocations to meet its goals. It takes as given the basic policies of the organization and establishes specific goals to be met in persuing policies. Programs are then identified to achieve the goals. The alternatives that are open in achieving goals, and the issues involved in choosing from among them, are then identified and examined. Many analytical tools are used in choosing from among alternatives but cost-benefit is central. The cost-benefit analysis seeks to determine what benefits accrue from a given expenditure as compared to what costs are involved. With this information managers are in a position to determine which resource allocation will yield the highest benefit in relation to cost.[18]

Program budgeting is an extremely powerful planning tool for governmental organizations. To appreciate it one must realize that up to very recent years the budgets of federal and most other government agencies were submitted line by line. To oversimplify, the agency budget is specified in terms of pencils, typewriters, clerical personnel, and so on. The PPBS says that an agency has programs such as (for a municipal government) schools, hospitals, water treatment, and police. Once these programs are established, expenditures attached to them should be aggregated for each of them. In this way, total costs for schools, for hospitals, and so on, can be calculated, putting administrators in a better position to determine where additional expenditures will yield the greatest benefit to the community.

SIMILARITIES OF PPBS WITH BUSINESS
STRATEGIC PLANNING

Program budgeting systems differ much[19] but in theory the PPB system has characteristics comparable to those of the strategic planning system described in this book. Both are concerned with making better current decisions in light of future environmental forces; both involve participation of people; both are recycled about once a year; both are directed at achieving stated objectives; both are conceived as being managerial learning processes; both run into comparable problems in application (e.g., demanding too much time of managers, delegating too much planning responsibility to staff, generating paperwork, or complicating communications between managers and staff experts); and both must operate in an atmosphere charged with political considerations.

DISSIMILARITIES BETWEEN PPBS AND BUSINESS STRATEGIC PLANNING

Major theoretical and practical differences distinguish program budgeting and formal strategic planning. For example, program budgeting rarely becomes involved in the formulation of an organization's basic missions, creed, or philosophy, whereas in a business planning system this is of dominant concern to top management. Objectives for PPB systems are often dictated by legislative authority, which is less the case in business planning. The time horizon of business planning is usually longer than that of PPB systems. Program budgeting focuses essentially on programs, whereas formal planning in business deals with wider issues of strategy, policy, and plan implementation. Program budgeting is generally done with a top-down approach; business planning, broadly speaking, is a much more enveloping, complex, and richer process from the point of view of an organization and the people in it than program budgeting in a NFP organization.

MAJOR PITFALLS IN PPBS

DeWoolfson took the major pitfalls to be avoided in business strategic planning, as described in Chapter 18, and modified them for PPB systems.[20] His survey of practitioners showed that the ten most important pitfalls to be avoided, if there is to be an effective PPB system, were as follows, in declining order of importance:

1. Failing to apply sufficient resources to the effort.
2. Becoming so engrossed in current problems that insufficient time is spent on long-range planning, and the process thus becomes discredited.
3. Failing to select meaningful criteria of program effectiveness.

4. Attempting too comprehensive an initial implementation effort.
5. Failing to provide sufficient training for decisionmakers.
6. Permitting concern over techniques to submerge the actual purposes of PPB.
7. Failing to insure sufficient interaction between decision-maker and analyst.
8. Failing to create a climate in the agency that is congenial and not resistant to planning.
9. Failing to develop a meaningful program structure.
10. Failing to assume the necessary involvement in the PPB process of major operating personnel.

Although these ten traps are not identical with those identified by business managers and staff as being most destructive of business planning, there is some overlap (see Chapter 18). All would be avoided, however, if the lessons of experience with business planning were followed.

National Aggregate Economic Planning

The Humphrey-Javits bill was simultaneously introduced in the fall of 1975 in the U.S. Senate and House of Representatives, Ninety-fourth Congress, first session, as an amendment to the Employment Act of 1946. This bill provided for the development of a balanced economic growth plan in the United States.

In the preamble to the bill its authors pointed out that the country was in an economic depression, that there were severe economic problems, and these problems were largely the result of a previous "failure to develop a long-term national economic policy." The fundamental imbalances in the economy that existed in 1975, asserted the authors, could be prevented in the future by national planning.

From time to time prior to 1975 many reputable observers suggested that the United States formulate a comprehensive economic plan but not since the depression of the 1930s was a bill presented before Congress that had as much support as the Humphrey-Javits bill. Nevertheless, the bill did not get out of committee and is now without sponsors. I believe, however, that the fundamental ideas in it will surely be advocated again.

Like so much legislation the Humphrey-Javits bill failed to provide details on implementation. Yet, from hearings on the bill and literature prepared by its proponents it is possible to sketch what likely would have developed had the bill passed.

The bill required that the president submit to the Congress for its approval, not later than April 1, 1977, a long-term balanced economic growth plan. On a time horizon of probably five years the plan would specify economic objectives for the nation, the resources required to achieve the objectives, and legislative and administrative actions needed to achieve the objectives; a report prepared by a proposed economic planning board (in the executive branch, reporting to the president) would set forth additional information including actual results compared with plans.

The plan was to provide detailed objectives in all dominant economic areas—prices, energy, agriculture, raw materials, education, and so on. Detailed objectives and/or resource requirements would be developed for the principal industrial areas of the economy. In sum, the initiators had in mind a comprehensive plan covering all major economic functions and areas of the economy.

MAJOR LESSONS FROM BUSINESS EXPERIENCE
APPLICABLE TO NATIONAL AGGREGATE
ECONOMIC PLANNING

The Humphrey-Javits bill probably would not have been effective had it passed. The reason is that a number of lessons from business experience, applicable to the public sector, were ignored and would have doomed the effort. Four relevant lessons are as follows:[21]

First, for effective planning there must be a strong commitment by the president, the cabinet, and the congressional leaders to the notion that long-range planning is necessary and that the type of plan proposed in the bill makes sense. This clearly was not the case.

Second, experience has taught us that organizations that create a planning system for the first time should make haste slowly. Eating dinner in one gulp is likely to produce indigestion. The Humphrey-Javits bill sought to do too much.

The business community learned long ago that it is extremely difficult and ultimately futile to organize all activities of a large corporation into one monolithic plan. Most large corporations today are decentralized and strategic planning, as noted previously, takes place in each of the strategic business units. Even in large centralized companies one does not find a comprehensive, integrated plan covering all aspects of the business. The United States is simply too large and too complex to be covered by one plan.

Third, before a long-range planning system is introduced into an organization top management must have a clear understanding of the purposes of the system—who is going to do what, when, and how and how is the system to be implemented. There was no such clarification of purpose and method with respect to the Humphrey-Javits bill.

Fourth, great care should be taken to insure that concern over techniques does not divert planners and managers from the fundamental purposes of planning. If this is not done, the manipulation of numbers becomes more important than their meaning. Formal procedures and rituals drive out the creativity, innovation, and imagination needed for effective planning. Although this course is not inevitable, it has been followed by government PPB systems in the past.

SHOULD THERE BE STRATEGIC PLANNING IN THE FEDERAL GOVERNMENT?

Elsewhere I commented as follows on this question:

We as a nation must be more skilled in identifying major problems that will appear in the future and in taking prompt action to deal with them. With the type of complex, turbulent, and surprise-filled socioeconomic-political system that is evolving, it would be disastrous for us to pursue our old policies of waiting until crises arrive and then trying to solve them by throwing money at them. We must engage in better long-range planning.[22]

I do not, however, advocate the type of national economic planning envisioned in the Humphrey-Javits bill. I reject the idea of a comprehensive economic plan for the United States such as that suggested therein.[23]

Many reasons underlie this position but the dominant one is the possibility that someday the plan may be taken seriously by the government and implemented with mandatory regulations. The Humphrey-Javits bill was described by its proponents as being only indicative, not mandatory. If it were to remain solely indicative—the development of a statistical picture of the economy—there might be a useful learning experience associated with the effort. The core question, however, is this: Might an indicative plan become mandatory? A mandatory national economic plan prepared and implemented by the government would obviously impede individual decisionmaking in the market. That result would doom the free enterprise system. This potential alone is enough to question the advisability of a national aggregate economic plan.

Some proponents of national aggregate economic planning justify it on the ground that corporations have found such an approach valuable and so should the government. On the surface this is an appealing argument, but it is flawed. Government should do many of the things done in corporate long-range planning—develop credible aims, anticipate changes in the environment to identify opportunities and threats, develop strategies to achieve aims, make better current decisions in light of their futurity, and so on. There is a crucial difference between business and government, however. Government has the power to make sure that its plans are fulfilled; business does not. Government is sovereign. Business is not. Thus, if the government were to decide that not enough automobiles were being produced and consumed it could, if it chose, make sure that enough would be produced and consumed.

WHAT SHOULD BE DONE?

If we should not create an aggregate, integrated, long-range planning system for the United States, what should we do? I suggest that we should follow business experience and limit our efforts to five areas of action, as follows.

First, we should establish certain national objectives. The first set of objectives might be prepared by a presidential commission but the function should be lodged in a permanent organization, preferably located in the executive office of the president. The targets should cover more than economics because our system has a multiplicity of objectives that are interrelated. Such a set of aims, together with an estimate of priorities, would serve as a foundation for planning throughout government and in the private sector.

Second, as in business, there should be a situation audit that would involve collecting and analyzing all data relevant to planning and to the identification of significant environmental trends and threats. As in business planning great care must be taken to limit the extent of data collection and the depth of data analysis.

Third, the central strategic issues should be identified from the analyses in the situation audit. Again, since there will be a great many strategic issues demanding attention, and since not all of them can be dealt with at the same time, only a few programs should be chosen in any one year for which detailed plans will be prepared. Areas such as energy, transportation, housing, and productivity might be chosen for detailed planning. Areas of concentration will change from year to year, and periodically all program plans should be reviewed and modified in light of the changing environment. Plans developed at one time should not be expected to be applicable for many years to come without change. There should be a periodic review of the plans. One year might be too short for government; perhaps a two-year cycle would be better.

Fourth, despite the fact that the government collects masses of information many gaps must be filled if we are to have better planning. For instance, during the 1974 energy crisis the government was embarrassed by the paucity of information it had available about the energy industry. Since data collection is such a heavy burden on industry today, any additions to the data stockpile should be offset by curtailing the collection of data no longer needed in the time or the detail now prescribed. Here again, we should proceed with caution because data accumulation is expensive.

Finally, planning consciousness is needed to insure widespread participation in a national planning effort. Not only must there be participation in the process by leaders and staff in the Congress and the executive branch, but there must be citizen participation as well.

An important reason for widespread participation in planning is that we must not allow national planning to be performed exclusively by an elitist group in a government agency. Only by the leavening influence of many participants, officials and laymen, will the dangers inherent in national government planning be avoided.

The planning suggested in this chapter would place the government in a policymaking role with detailed plans, to the extent appropriate in light of traditional roles, implemented by individuals throughout the nation. The free market mechanism probably should be relied upon even more than in the recent past. In this way the United States would avoid becoming a planned society. Rather, it would be a planning society.

Overarching Lessons of Private Strategic Planning Experience Applicable to Planning in the NFPS

Throughout this book the outstanding lessons of experience with formal strategic planning in the business world have been presented. In this chapter a number of those lessons applicable to planning in the NFPS were noted. In concluding this chapter it is fitting to present a few of the outstanding lessons that have applicability to the NFPS. They are reviewed in no particular order of importance.

First, the primary benefit of the planning process is the process itself and not a plan. Planning is more a way of thinking than a set of procedures. Improvement in the planning thought processes in the NFPS would be of great value. This does not mean that individual plans are unimportant but rather that the process is more important than specific plans.

Second, too much should not be attempted at once.

Third, planning systems must be custom-made to suit the organization, the subject matter addressed, and personal styles and interests of administrators.

Fourth, planners do not plan. Planning is a line responsibility. One of the problems with planning in the NFPS, in my judgment, is that too much planning is done by planners without the acceptance of line management responsibility. Top managers must get involved.

Fifth, the climate in an organization must be congenial to planning. If it is not, planning will not be effective.

Sixth, there are different preferred approaches to completing the many stages of the planning process. There is no one way to do strategic planning.

Seventh, the basic objective of planning is to develop appropriate strategies to adapt an organization to its environment and then make current decisions to implement the strategies.

Eighth, there must be a strong commitment to plan by the top officers of the organization.

Ninth, excessive expectations of what planning can accomplish should be avoided.

Tenth, managers and planning staffs must be experienced in planning. The absence of skilled staff in federal agencies was one reason for the failure of the PPB system that President Johnson ordered.

Eleventh, every effort should be made to develop a few clear-cut goals and to reduce confusion among them.

Twelfth, every effort should be made to keep the planning process as simple as possible.

Summary

The theme of this chapter was that the NFPS can benefit greatly from the experience of the private sector with strategic planning. However, significant differences between the two sectors suggest that the public sector use caution in applying the lessons learned by business. This is not to imply that no strategic planning is done in the NFPS. Yet the planning that is done is spotty and not nearly as widespread as it should be.

Program budgeting, a planning system used in the NFPS, has some features comparable to those of business strategic planning. When the system was tried throughout the federal government it failed, a result that might not have occurred had the government known and applied the lessons on strategic planning learned in the private sector.

There have been many calls for some sort of national economic plan for the United States, the latest of which was embodied in the Humphrey-Javits bill presented to Congress in 1975. Lessons of experience with strategic planning, together with other considerations, lead to the conclusion that such a proposal should be rejected. Nevertheless, the federal government should do more than it is doing today to identify possible future problems so that they can be dealt with before they become too serious. Here again, experience in the private sector points to appropriate actions, a few of which were suggested in this chapter.

VII Concluding Observations

22 The Current State of the Art and Future Trends

It was almost a quarter of a century ago that Ernest Breech, when chairman of the board of the Ford Motor Company, articulated a powerful new idea that quickly was accepted among a growing number of managers. He said that a company could "*make* trends, not . . . follow them." He went on to say that "with a well-staffed management team in which an aggressive risk-taking spirit is backed up by cool-headed analytical planning, there will be no problem too tough to be solved."[1] That is, a manager of a company can to a great degree determine where he wants to go in the future and do the things necessary to insure that these aims are achieved.

A number of forces at the time reinforced Breech's idea. Companies were growing larger and becoming more complex to manage; competition was becoming more intense; the threats as well as the opportunities in the evolving environment seemingly were getting more difficult to foresee; product research and development lead times and costs were growing while product life cycles were shortening; and managers were recognizing what benefits formal planning in government had achieved in World War II.

Since that time the use of formal strategic planning, called long-range planning then, has spread widely in the business world. This book has sought to summarize the basic lessons of that experience for practical application in business and in the not-for-

339

340 CONCLUDING OBSERVATIONS

profit sector. In this concluding chapter a few overall observations about that experience and a few likely future trends in the process will be presented.

The Current State of the Art of Formal Strategic Planning

A body of knowledge about strategic planning has accumulated since World War II to help managers introduce such systems in their organizations and/or to improve the effectiveness of the systems they have. There is no doubt in my mind that we now know from past experience those principles and practices required for successful planning. We know what must be avoided if strategic planning is to be effective.

We know there is no single way of doing strategic planning. Planning systems must be designed to fit the unique characteristics of each company. Accordingly, managers must take the lessons of experience and apply them in a systems design to fit the particular characteristics of their company and its management.

The elements of a successful planning system in a large company have been identified in this book. They will differ from those in a small company, especially when introducing formal planning into the company. These, too, have been set forth in this book.

In sum, the state of the art of formal strategic planning is indeed sufficient to provide managers with the knowledge required to design and implement an effective system for their organization. However, the state of the art is not such that managers can pick systems off the shelf. Each system must be designed for each company.

There are gaps in the current state of the art. As noted earlier, precisely what systems design is appropriate to a particular organization at a particular time is not spelled out in the planning literature. The system must be tailor-made for each organization. In time we shall know much more about the relationships between planning design features and various managerial styles, organizational characteristics, and other forces operating in a company.

The state of the art is also deficient about ways and means to detect and avoid antiplanning biases. As pointed out in this book biases against planning often run deep and they can have a major adverse impact on planning. On the other hand, we know that people can be motivated to do strategic planning with enthusiasm.

There are also gaps in our knowledge about ways and means to improve information gathering and data analysis for strategic planning. Despite great strides in perfecting forecasting methods, for example, much remains to be learned about probing the future. Or, to take another example, we have learned much about using computer based analytical models in planning but much remains to be learned about matching our technical knowledge with the thought processes and decision problems of managers.

We have learned much about the different ways in which managers collect and use information in decisionmaking. We know a good bit about managerial intuition and judgment and their relationships to formal planning, but much remains to be known about this subject.

Our knowledge about the importance of and ways to develop basic company missions and purposes and concrete operating plans has been developed significantly. Here too, however, we need better frameworks to help managers make these strategic decisions.

Our knowledge about how to implement plans has improved immensely in recent years. Yet the literature is not able to prescribe precisely what controls and motivations are most appropriate in particular circumstances. Control systems must be tailor-made to fit each situation. Experience with planning has provided guidelines for managers in developing implementing systems but there are gaps in our knowledge about the process.

In sum, I believe that our knowledge of formal strategic planning is sufficient to permit every manager to develop and implement a system appropriate to his circumstances, a system that will produce significantly greater benefits than costs. At the same time it can be said that there are big gaps in our knowledge, which, when filled, will make it easier for managers to design and implement formal strategic planning systems for their organizations.

Evolving Trends in Formal Strategic Planning

Formal strategic planning will continue to develop and the gaps in our knowledge about it will narrow. Beyond such additions to knowledge, what significant trends may be expected? The following projections are suggested, not in any particular order of importance.

First, the varieties of strategic planning systems in use will become even greater than today. It has been said repeatedly that planning systems must fit the unique characteristics of the organization for which they are designed. Since each organization differs from all others the systems will not be identical. Nevertheless, planning systems must follow the basic patterns and preferred practices presented in this book. Formal strategic planning is not a fad. It is today and will be tomorrow inextricably interwoven into the management process and, except in rare cases, will be essential for effective management. The processes, structures, practices, and lessons of experience presented in this book will continue to be basic guides to the design and implementation of formal strategic planning systems for both large and small companies. The varieties of systems, however, will continue to grow as managers take the guides and design systems most suitable for their organizations.

Second, planning systems will be more flexible and less proceduralized, especially in larger companies. (Planning systems today in smaller companies tend to be less formal, as has been noted.) Managers will become increasingly aware that too much procedure drives out the type of creativity, innovation, and imagination needed for superior strategic planning.

Third, the use of computer based and advanced analytical tools will expand. In mind, for example, are simulation models, risk analyses, and scenarios. However, older analytical methods—such as managerial intuition and judgment, creativity, accounting data, and simple flow diagrams—will be increasingly recognized as indispensable to successful planning.

Fourth, the emphasis on strategy will continue. This is not to say that strategic planning will pay less attention to operational planning. Rather, emphasis on the formulation and implementation of strategies will grow. The reason is that environments are likely to become more turbulent and complex, making it even more essential that a company pursue those strategies that will best adapt the organization to changed circumstances.

Fifth, the participation of people in the planning process will become greater and more effective. Managers will recognize more than today that planning permits people to participate in a meaningful way in the operation of their organizations, which will increase worker satisfaction. Managers will be more concerned with this aspect of work, because satisfaction in one's job means better performance.

Sixth, almost a decade ago I wrote an article about the rise of the corporate planner in the organization.[2] That trend will continue and more and more corporate planners will get closer to the chief executive officer. The reason is simple. Since the corporate planner is helping the chief executive officer to do his job it is natural that the two will develop close working relationships.

Seventh, fewer and fewer companies will fall into the pitfalls that lead to ineffective planning. To put this another way, satisfaction with planning systems will grow. It should be kept in mind when considering expressions of dissatisfaction with strategic planning that the planning system often gets blamed for other shortcomings in an organization, such as poor management. As our knowledge grows about what is needed for successful planning there should be a parallel growth in satisfaction with strategic planning.

Eighth, more companies aside from the larger ones will develop some form of formal strategic planning. As noted previously it is rare to find a large company anywhere in the world that does not have some sort of formal strategic planning system. More and more smaller companies will discover the value of developing formal strategic planning systems to fit their circumstances.

Ninth, there will be more integration of business strategic planning systems and government planning. In mind is a meshing of plans to deal with social problems such as transportation, city rebuilding, energy development, worker retraining, and raising productivity. Envisioned is a loose relationship in which government sets policy and provides incentives and industry implements the policy.

Tenth, and finally, there will be more of a transfer of the basic lessons of experience learned in the business sector to organizations in the not-for-profit sector. The transfer, however, will not be easy and the improvement in planning in the not-for-profit sector will not be rapid. Nevertheless, there will be improvement because many of these lessons have high applicability to planning in the public sector.

The Spirit of Planning

The insightful Spanish Jesuit Baltasar Gracián three and one-half centuries ago captured the spirit of modern strategic planning in words that fittingly set the tone of this book, as follows:

> Think in anticipation, today for tomorrow, and indeed, for many days. The greatest providence is to have forethought for what comes. What is provided for does not happen by chance, nor is the man who is prepared ever beset by emergencies. One must not, therefore, postpone consideration till the need arises. Consideration should go beforehand. You can, after careful reflection, act to prevent the most calamitous events. The pillow is a silent Sibyl, for to sleep over questions before they reach a climax is far better than lying awake over them afterward. Some act and think later— and they think more of excuses than consequences. Others think neither before nor after. The whole of life should be spent thinking about how to find the right course of action to follow. Thought and forethought give counsel both on living and on achieving success.[3]

Notes

Chapter 1

1. Henry C. Egerton and James K. Brown, *Planning and the Chief Executive* (New York: Conference Board, 1972), p. 1.
2. Whenever he or she is used to refer to a person either he or she is meant. By this convention I hope to avoid the awkwardness of saying each time he or she, his or her, or he/she.
3. Quoted in A. D. Chandler, Jr., *Strategy and Structure: Chapters in the History of the American Industrial Enterprise.* (Cambridge: M.I.T. Press, 1962), p. 235.
4. *Efficiently,* as used here, refers to the skills of managers in combining resources at lowest cost in terms of time, energy, or money. *Effectiveness* refers to the ability of managers to develop processes to achieve desired end results.
5. Peter F. Drucker, *Management: Tasks, Responsibilities, Practices* (New York: Harper & Row, 1974), p. 611.
6. Ibid., p. 612.
7. Marvin Bower, *The Will to Manage: Corporate Success through Programmed Management* (New York: McGraw-Hill, 1966), pp. 17–18.
8. Ibid.
9. I use synonymously the intuition, judgment, and innovation. Actually, there are differences among such mental processes as intuition, judgment, hunch, instinct, invention, innovation, and entrepreneurship. See George A. Steiner, *Top Management Planning* (New York: Macmillan, 1969), pp. 353–355; also Chapter 7 of this volume.
10. Alfred Sloan, Jr., *Adventures of the White Collar Man* (New York: Doubleday, Doran & Co., Inc., 1941), p. 104.

11. Quoted in Eugene Raudsepp, "Can You Trust Your Hunches?" *Management Review*, April 1960. This article gives other comparable quotations.

12. Henry Mintzberg, "Planning on the Left Side and Managing on the Right," *Harvard Business Review*, July–August 1976.

Chapter 2

1. Henri Fayol, one of the first to present a broad conception of business planning, said planning "means both to assess the future and make provision for it." See Henri Fayol, *General and Industrial Management*, trans. Constance Storrs (London: Pitman, 1949; first published in French in 1916), p. 43.

   Billy E. Goetz defined planning as "fundamentally choosing." See Billy E. Goetz, *Management Planning and Control* (New York: McGraw-Hill, 1949), p. 2.

   John Friedmann argued that "planning is defined as the guidance of change within a social system." He also noted: "Planning may be simply regarded as reason acting on a network of ongoing activities through the intervention of certain decision structures and processes." See John Friedmann, "A Conceptual Model for the Analysis of Planning Behavior," *Administrative Science Quarterly*, September 1967, pp. 225, 227.

   George R. Terry defined planning as "intellectual in nature: it is mental work. Reflective thinking is required; imagination and foresight are extremely helpful." See George R. Terry, *Principles of Management*, 3d ed. (Homewood: Irwin, 1960), p. 123.

   According to Harold Koontz and Cyril O'Donnell: "Planning is deciding in advance what to do, how to do it, when to do it, and who is to do it. Planning bridges the gap from where we are to where we want to go. It makes it possible for things to occur which would not otherwise happen. Although the exact future can seldom be predicted and factors beyond control may interfere with the best-laid plans, without planning events are left to chance. Planning is an intellectual process, the conscious determination of courses of action, the basing of decisions on purpose, facts, and considered estimates." See Harold Koontz and Cyril O'Donnell, *Principles of Management: An Analysis of Managerial Functions*, 5th ed. (New York: McGraw-Hill, 1972), p. 113.

   Russell L. Ackoff wrote that "planning is the design of a desired future and of effective ways of bringing it about." See Russell L.

Ackoff, *A Concept of Corporate Planning* (New York: Wiley-Interscience, 1970), p. 1.

In the words of Aaron Wildavsky: "Planning may be seen as the ability to control the future consequences of present actions. The more consequences one controls, the more one has succeeded in planning. Planning is a form of causality. Its purpose is to make the future different from what it would have been without this intervention. Planning therefore necessitates a causal theory connecting the planned actions with the desired future results. Planning also requires the ability to act on this theory; it requires power. To change the future, one must be able to get people to act differently than they otherwise would. The requirements of successful planning from causal theory to political power, grow more onerous as its scope increases and the demands for simultaneous action multiply at a geometric rate." See Aaron Wildavsky, "Does Planning Work?" *Public Interest,* Summer 1971, p. 101.

The preceding are generic definitions of planning. There are other definitions focusing more directly on the long-range planning process. For instance, according to David Hussey, "When a manager talks of corporate planning he is referring to a comprehensive business process which involves many types of planning activity. . . . Corporate planning includes the setting of objectives, organizing ·the work, people, and system to enable those objectives to be attained, motivating through the planning process and through the plans, measuring performance and so controlling progress of the plan, and developing people through better decision-making, clearer objectives, more involvement, and awareness of progress." See David Hussey, *Corporate Planning: Theory and Practice* (New York: Pergamon, 1974), p. 6.

Peter Drucker, in a well-known quotation, described long-range planning as "the continuous process of making present entrepreneurial (risk taking) decisions systematically and with the best possible knowledge of their futurity, organizing systematically the efforts needed to carry out these decisions, and measuring the results of these decisions against the expectations through organized, systematic feed-back." See Peter Drucker, "Long Range Planning," *Management Science,* April 1959, p. 240. (Italics omitted.)

2. Ackoff, *A Concept of Corporate Planning,* p. 1.
3. Peter Lorange and Richard F. Vancil, *Strategic Planning Systems* (Englewood Cliffs: Prentice-Hall, 1977); Hussey, *Corporate Planning;* D. A. Ringbakk, "The Corporate Planning Life Cycle: An International Point of View," *Long Range Planning,* September 1972; Robert N. Anthony, *Planning and Control Systems: A Framework for Analysis* (Boston: Graduate School of Business, Har-

vard University, 1965); Robert F. Stewart, "A Framework for Busi-
ness Planning," Report No. 162, Long Range Planning Service
(Menlo Park: Stanford Research Institute, February 1963); Frank
Gilmore and R. G. Brandenberg, "Anatomy of Corporate Planning,"
Harvard Business Review, November–December 1962.

4. Leading writers in this field are in general agreement with these
concepts of strategy. See, for example, Kenneth R. Andrews, *The
Concept of Corporate Strategy* (Homewood: Dow Jones–Irwin,
1971); Lorange and Vancil, *Strategic Planning Systems;* William E.
Rothschild, *Putting It All Together* (New York: AMACOM, 1976).
There is not, however, universal agreement on nomenclature. Some
discussion of differences in definition is therefore in order.

The word *strategy* entered the management literature to mean that
which one did to counteract what a competitor did or was likely to do.
This terminology was the same as that used by the military and was,
of course, copied from that usage. Today the concept is much
broader. The academic world leans toward the original Greek meaning of the word—*strategos,* a general. Strategy literally meant the art
of the general. Or, in today's meaning, strategy is that which top
management of an enterprise does that is of great importance to an
enterprise. This is a very broad concept that includes purposes,
missions, planning objectives, program strategies, and key methods
to implement the strategies.

There is no consensus about this. Some writers still define business strategies in the older narrow military sense, noted above. Some
speak of strategies in terms of basic directional decisions, that is,
purposes and missions. Some speak of important actions to achieve
these decisions as strategies. Some speak of strategies as being the
answer to this question: What should the organization be doing?
Some speak of strategies as being the answer to this question: What
are the ends we seek and how are we going to achieve them?

In a sense, strategy is the more common term today for what used
to be called policy. Although there are distinctions that can be drawn
between policy and strategy, the two are considered synonymous in
this book and the word strategy will be used.

In every business there is a pyramid of policies. At the top of the
pyramid are broad policies concerned with company mission, purpose, thrust, and ways of doing business. These are identified as
master strategies in Exhibit 2–1. At this level, I speak of policies and
strategies as being synonymous. At the next level in Exhibit 2–1 are
program strategies. Here, again, program strategies and program
policies are indistinguishable. As one moves lower in the pyramid,
policies phase into procedures, standard operating plans, and rules.
They differ at this level from strategies and tactics.

Conceptually, policies are distinguishable from missions, purposes, long-range objectives, and program strategies. Policies, as distinguished from these elements of planning, are generally defined as guides to action or channels to thinking. More specifically, they are guides to carrying out an action. They establish the universe in which action is to be taken. For instance, a manager may say, "It is our policy to do business in Europe." The manager also could say, "Our mission is to produce electric motors for worldwide commercial markets, including Europe." Or, "Our purpose is to penetrate the European market." Or, "Our strategy is to get into the European market." Or, "Our objective is to penetrate the European market." When each of the planning elements—mission, purpose, objective, policy, program strategy—is considered individually it is possible to define each as being a separate element. But in practice they shade into one another at the top levels of corporate decisionmaking.

Generally speaking, in most companies, the word strategy is not used as broadly as here. The word refers only to what is identified here as program strategies. Mission statements are labeled as such and so are company purposes and long-range planning objectives. Everything else that is in the nature of guidance to action, at the top levels, is called policy. In larger companies these policies are recorded in policy manuals. (I have never heard of a strategy manual in a company.) Policies cover a wide range of activities in a company: staff functions, growth, planning, managerial authority, conflicts of interest, marketing, production, finance, facilities, and so on.

In this book our focus is on strategic management and at this level policy and strategy are difficult to separate. Therefore, when the word strategy is used it can also mean policy. For a fuller discussion of this semantic issue see George A. Steiner and John B. Miner, *Management Policy and Strategy: Text, Readings, and Cases* (New York: Macmillan, 1977), chap. 2; George A. Steiner, *Top Management Planning* (New York: Macmillan, 1969); chap. 10; Bertram M. Gross, *The Managing of Organizations* (New York: Free Press, 1964), esp. chap. 19.

5. For more detailed distinctions between strategy and tactics see Steiner, *Top Management Planning,* pp. 37–41.

6. W. W. Simmons, *1974–75 Exploratory Planning Briefs* (New York: AMACOM, 1975, and *Exploratory Planning: Brief and Practices* (Oxford, Oh.: Planning Executives Institute, 1977).

7. Henry L. Tosi, John R. Rizzo, and Stephen J. Carroll, "Setting Goals in Management by Objective," *California Management Review,* Summer 1970, p. 70.

8. Anthony P. Raia, *Management by Objective* (Glenview: Scott, Foresman, 1974).

9. Bernard Taylor, "Strategies for Planning," *Long Range Planning,* August 1975.

Chapter 3

1. Robert C. Gunness, "The Payoff from Planning," *Managerial Planning,* September–October 1971, p. 4.
2. Heidrick and Struggles, Inc., *Profile of a Chief Executive Officer* (New York: Heidrick and Struggles, Inc., 1977), p. 4.
3. Piet Hein, "The Road to Wisdom," *Life,* October 14, 1966.
4. The first comprehensive and documented study was Stanley S. Thune and Robert J. House, "Where Long-Range Planning Pays Off," *Business Horizons,* August 1970. H. Igor Ansoff et al., in their study "Does Planning Pay?" *Long Range Planning,* December 1970, concluded that those companies that merged with others on the basis of long-range plans did better than those that did not plan. However, a study by Robert M. Fulmer and Leslie W. Rue, *The Practice and Profitability of Long-Range Planning* (Oxford, Oh.: Planning Executives Institute, 1973), raised some doubts about the benefits of formal planning in service industries. The latest study I have seen is a doctoral dissertation that examined the experience of ninety companies in the United States in different industries and concluded that on the basis of financial measures those companies that had long-range planning systems did better than those that did not. The results are summarized in Delmar Karger, "Long Range Planning and Organizational Performance," *Long Range Planning,* December, 1975.
5. Charles B. Saunders and Francis D. Tuggle, "Why Planners Don't," *Long Range Planning,* June 1977. See also a rebuttal by D. E. Hussey entitled "Who Says Planners Don't," *Long Range Planning,* October 1977.

Chapter 4

1. For further analysis of these comments see Theodore Cohn and Roy A. Lindberg, *Survival and Growth: Management Strategies for the Small Firm* (New York: AMACOM, 1974); Peter Lorange and Richard F. Vancil, "How to Design a Strategic Planning System," *Harvard Business Review,* September–October 1976.
2. For a discussion of how different forces affect the planning design see

Dan Schendel, "Designing Strategic Planning Systems," *Academy of Management Review*, October 1978. For an older but still relevant treatment see Preston P. Le Breton and Dale A. Henning, *Planning Theory* (Englewood Cliffs: Prentice-Hall, 1966).

3. For a survey of what is included in planning manuals see G. T. Caldwell, *Corporate Planning in Canada: An Overview* (Ottawa: Conference Board in Canada, 1975).

4. Rochelle O'Connor, *Corporate Guides to Long-Range Planning* (New York: Conference Board, 1976).

5. Ibid., pp. 5–6.

6. Ibid., p. 11.

7. For approaches to strategic planning in small companies see George A. Steiner, "Approaches to Long-Range Planning for Small Businesses," *California Management Review*, Fall 1967; Cohn and Lindberg, *Survival and Growth*. For approaches to planning in the larger firm see Peter Lorange and Richard F. Vancil, *Strategic Planning Systems* (Englewood Cliffs: Prentice-Hall, 1977); George A. Steiner, *Managerial Long-Range Planning* (New York: McGraw-Hill, 1963).

8. Francis J. Aguilar, "Norton Company (C)," Case #9-114-019 (Boston: President and Fellows of Harvard College, distributed by Intercollegiate Case Clearing House, 1970).

9. Ernest Dale, *Long Range Planning* (London: British Institute of Management, 1967), p. 1.

10. Robert W. Ackerman, "Role of the Corporate Planning Executive," in Lorange and Vancil, *Strategic Planning Systems*, pp. 151–159; Alfred Friedrich and A. van't Land, "Organization of the Planning Department in a Divisionalized Concern," *Long Range Planning*, April 1974; Gerald G. Garbacz, "Planner-Line Conflict: Asset or Liability?" *Managerial Planning*, May–June 1973; Merritt L. Kastens, "Who Does the Planning?" *Managerial Planning*, January–February 1972; Milton Leontiades, "What Kind of a Corporate Planner Do You Need? *Long Range Planning*, April 1977; Peter Lorange, "The Planner's Dual Role: A Survey of U.S. Companies," *Long Range Planning*, March 1973; Donald R. Schoen, "Responsibilities of Corporate Planning: A Checklist," *Management Review*, March 1977; George A. Steiner, "Rise of the Corporate Planner," *Harvard Business Review*, September–October 1970; Richard F. Vancil, "—So You're Going to Have a Planning Department!" *Harvard Business Review*, May–June 1967.

11. For a few job descriptions of the corporate planner see the works cited in note 10 above and Caldwell, *Corporate Planning in Canada*.

12. Steiner, "Rise of the Corporate Planner."
13. Lorange, "The Planner's Dual Role."
14. E. Kirby Warren, *Long-Range Planning: The Executive Viewpoint* (Englewood Cliffs: Prentice-Hall, 1966), p. 43.

Chapter 5

1. William F. May, "Planning from the Chief Executive's Point of View" (speech before the National Society for Corporate Planning, Harvard Club, New York City, February 20, 1969).
2. Myles L. Mace, "The President and Corporate Planning," *Harvard Business Review,* January–February 1965.
3. S. C. Beise, "Planning for Industrial Growth: An Executive View" (remarks before Conference on Planning for Industrial Growth, sponsored by the Stanford Research Institute, Milan, Italy, 1963).
4. Louis B. Lundborg, *A Creative Environment: Imperative for Growth* (Los Angeles: Graduate School of Business Administration, University of Southern California, November 1966), p. 2.
5. Raymond Radosevich, "Designing Innovating Systems," *Long Range Planning,* April 1977.
6. David I. Cleland and William R. King, "Developing a Planning Culture for More Effective Strategic Planning," *Long Range Planning,* June 1974, p. 70.
7. Robert W. Haigh, "A Cure for Presidential Insomnia or the Right Answers to Five Essential Questions" (speech before the National Society for Corporate Planning, Harvard Club, New York City, January 15, 1970).
8. R. Ronald Daniel, "Team at the Top," *Harvard Business Review,* March–April, 1965, pp. 19–20.
9. Paul F. Cornelsen, "Is the Profit Squeeze Jeopardizing the Planning Executive's Future?" *Managerial Planning,* January–February 1973, pp. 13–14.
10. Henry C. Egerton and James K. Brown, *Planning and the Chief Executive* (New York: Conference Board, 1972), p. 7.
11. William L. Hennefrund, *The Chief Executive Office and Its Responsibilities* (New York: AMACOM, 1975), p. 307. See also Robert D. Hulme and John C. Maydew, "A View of the Top," *Business Horizons,* October 1972.
12. Louis Kraar, "General Electric's Very Personal Merger," *Fortune,* August 1977.
13. Egerton and Brown, *Planning and the Chief Executive.*

Chapter 6

1. Walter Reichman and Marguerite Levy, "Psychological Restraints on Effective Planning," *Management Review*, October 1975.
2. Harry Levinson, *Psychological Man* (Cambridge: Levinson Institute, 1976), p. 55.
3. Reichman and Levy, "Psychological Restraints on Effective Planning," p. 39.
4. Robert W. Haigh, "A Cure for Presidential Insomnia or the Right Answers to Five Essential Questions" (speech before the National Society for Corporate Planning, Harvard Club, New York City, January 15, 1970).
5. John W. Gardner, "How to Prevent Organizational Dry Rot," *Harper's,* October 1965.
6. Ralph M. Besse, "Company Planning Must Be Planned!" *Dun's Review and Modern Industry,* April 1957, pp. 62–63.
7. Russell D. Clark, "Group-Induced Shift toward Risk: A Critical Appraisal," *Psychological Bulletin,* August 1971.
8. Andrew H. Van de Ven and Andre L. Delbecq, "Nominal versus Interacting Group Processes for Committee Decision-Making Effectiveness," *Academy of Management Journal,* June 1971.
9. Janis coined groupthink as a quick and easy way to refer to a mode of thinking that people engage in when they are deeply involved in a cohesive in-group, when the members' strivings for unanimity override their motivation to realistically appraise alternative courses of action. ". . . Groupthink refers to a deterioration of mental efficiency, reality testing, and moral judgment that results from in-group pressures." From Irving L. Janis, *Victims of Groupthink* (Boston: Houghton Mifflin, 1972), p. 9.
10. Ibid., pp. 209–218.

Chapter 7

1. Henry Mintzberg, "Strategy-Making in Three Modes," *California Management Review*, Winter 1973, and *The Nature of Managerial Work* (New York: Harper & Row, 1973).
2. Quoted in C. J. Hitch, *Decision-Making for Defense* (Berkeley: University of California Press, 1967), p. 7.
3. C. E. Lindblom, "The Science of 'Muddling Through,'" *Public Ad-*

ministration Review, Spring 1959; C. E. Lindblom and David Bray-brooke, *A Strategy of Decision* (New York: Free Press, 1963); C. E. Lindblom, *The Policy-Making Process* (Englewood Cliffs: Prentice-Hall, 1968).

4. H. Igor Ansoff, *Corporate Strategy* (New York: McGraw-Hill, 1965).

5. James L. McKenney and Peter G. W. Keen, "How Managers' Minds Work," *Harvard Business Review,* May–June 1974, p. 80.

6. Ibid., p. 84.

7. In an analysis of thought processes on planning, a study made at the U. S. Bureau of the Census showed that different personality types took the same data and developed from them distinctly different plans. See Ian I. Mitroff, Vincent P. Barabba, and Ralph H. Kilmann, "The Application of Behavioral and Philosophical Technologies to Strategic Planning: A Case Study of a Large Federal Agency," *Management Science,* September 1977.

8. Op. cit., p. 86.

9. Robert Ornstein, *The Psychology of Consciousness* (San Francisco: Freeman, 1975).

10. Henry Mintzberg, "Planning on the Left Side and Managing on the Right," *Harvard Business Review,* July–August 1976.

11. Harlan D. Mills, *Mathematics and the Managerial Imagination* (Princeton: Mathematica, 1959), p. 1.

12. Bruce D. Henderson, "Business Thinking" (manuscript, Boston Consulting Group, undated).

13. George A. Steiner, *Top Management Planning* (New York: Macmillan, 1969) p. 353.

14. As I discuss in ibid., pp. 353–354, intuition may be distinguished from hunch, judgment, and insight in the following way: "A hunch is a strong, intuitive impression that something will or can happen. It is a common sense form of predictability. . . . Considered judgment differs from intuitive judgment in that the logic behind the opinion or conclusion is made explicit. An insight is a faculty for seeing into the inner character of a phenomenon, or apprehending the true nature of a thing, or discerning the underlying truth, by a penetrating mental vision, discernment, or intuitive understanding."

15. For a good analysis of how values are distinguished from other related concepts, see Milton Rokeach, *The Nature of Human Values* (New York: Free Press, 1973), especially pp. 17–22.

16. The values held by individuals and how they influence decisionmaking is a very large subject which can be treated here only lightly. For excellent detailed general treatments of values, see Rokeach, *The Nature of Human Values;* Gerald F. Cavanagh, *American Business*

Values in Transition (Englewood Cliffs, N.J.: Prentice-Hall, 1976); and Kurt Baier and Nicholas Rescher, *Values and the Future* (New York: Free Press, 1969).

17. There have been many studies made about the relationship of personal values to managerial decisionmaking—for example, E. Frank Harrison, *The Managerial Decision-Making Process* (Boston: Houghton Mifflin, 1975); Robert Hay and Ed Gray, "Social Responsibilities of Business Managers," *Academy of Management Journal,* March 1974; John Senger, "Managers' Perceptions of Subordinates' Competence as a Function of Personal Value Orientations," *Academy of Management Journal,* December 1971; George W. England, "Personal Value Systems of American Managers," *Academy of Management Journal,* March 1967; and William D. Guth and Renato Tagiuri, "Personal Values and Corporate Strategy," *Harvard Business Review,* September–October 1965.

Chapter 8

1. Philip Kotler, William Gregor, and William Rodgers, "The Marketing Audit Comes of Age," *Sloan Management Review*, Winter 1977.

2. Francis Joseph Aguilar, *Scanning and Business Environment* (New York: Macmillan, 1967), pp. 69–70.

3. Howard H. Stevenson, "Defining Corporate Strengths and Weaknesses," *Sloan Management Review,* Spring 1976.

4. For the list see George A. Steiner, *Business and Society,* 2d ed. (New York: Random House, 1977), pp. 95–98.

5. Ian Wilson, "What One Company Is Doing about Today's Demands on Business," in George A. Steiner, ed., *Changing Business-Society Interrelationships* (Los Angeles: Graduate School of Management, UCLA, 1975).

6. Robert E. Estes in George A. Steiner, ed., *Selected Major Issues in Business' Role in Modern Society* (Los Angeles: Graduate School of Management, UCLA, 1973), p. 30.

7. Ian Wilson, "Socio-Political Forecasting: A New Dimension to Strategic Planning," *Michigan Business Review,* July 1974.

8. Dale Tarnowieski, *The Changing Success Ethic* (New York: AMACOM, 1973).

9. *Work in America,* report of a Special Task Force to the Secretary of Health, Education, and Welfare (Cambridge: MIT Press, 1973).

10. Peter F. Drucker, *Management: Tasks, Responsibilities, Practices* (New York: Harper & Row, 1974), p. 79.

11. Wayne I. Boucher, ed., *The Study of the Future: An Agenda for Research* (Washington, D.C.: U.S. Government Printing Office, July 1977); François E. de Carbonnel and Roy G. Dorrance, "Information Sources for Planning Decisions," *California Management Review,* Summer 1973; John C. Chambers, Satinder K. Mullick, and Donald D. Smith, "How to Choose the Right Forecasting Technique," *Harvard Business Review,* July–August 1971; M. F. Elliott-Jones, *Economic Forecasting and Corporate Planning* (New York: Conference Board, 1973); Alan R. Fusfeld and Richard N. Foster, "The Delphi Technique: Survey and Comment," *Business Horizons,* June 1971; William K. Hall, "Forecasting Techniques for Use in the Corporate Planning Process," *Managerial Planning,* November–December 1972; Hurwood, David L., Elliott S. Grossman and Earl L. Balley. *Sales Forecasting.* New York: The Conference Board, 1978. Don Kennington, "Long Range Planning for Public Libraries: A Delphi Study," *Long Range Planning,* April 1977; Don LeBell and O. J. Krasner, "Selecting Environmental Forecasting Techniques from Business Planning Requirements," *Academy of Management Review,* July 1977; T. P. Merritt, "Forecasting the Future Business Environment: The State of the Art," *Long Range Planning,* June 1974; Graham T. T. Molitor, "The Hatching of Public Opinion," *Planning Review,* July 1977; Steven C. Wheelwright and Spyros Makridakis, *Forecasting Methods for Management,* 2d ed. (New York: Wiley, 1977).
12. Howard H. Stevenson, "Defining Corporate Strengths and Weaknesses."

Chapter 9

1. Drucker, *Management: Tasks, Responsibilities, Practices* (New York: Harper & Row, 1974), p. 75.
2. For one of the first and still one of the best detailed networks of aims see Charles H. Granger, "The Hierarchy of Objectives," *Harvard Business Review,* May–June 1964.
3. Stewart Thompson, *Management Creeds and Philosophies* (New York: American Management Association, 1958).
4. Thomas J. Watson, Jr., *A Business and Its Beliefs* (New York: McGraw-Hill, 1963), p. 3.
5. Vincent Learson, statement at annual meeting of IBM stockholders, Dallas, April 14, 1972.
6. D. H. Baldwin Company, *1974 Annual Report* (Cincinnati, Ohio, 1975).

7. Sir Geoffrey Vickers, *The Art of Judgment* (New York: Basic Books, 1965), p. 71.
8. James Brian Quinn, "Strategic Goals: Process and Politics," *Sloan Management Review,* Fall 1977, p. 22.
9. Ibid., p. 36.
10. J. Douglas McConnell, "Strategic Planning: One Workable Approach," *Long Range Planning,* December 1971.
11. *Business Week,* February 24, 1975, p. 75.

Chapter 10

1. Gary P. Latham and Gary A. Yukl, "A Review of Research on the Application of Goal Setting in Organizations," *Journal of the Academy of Management,* December 1975.
2. George A. Steiner, *Pitfalls in Comprehensive Long-Range Planning* (Oxford, Oh.: Planning Executives Institute, 1972).
3. Peter F. Drucker, *The Practice of Management* (New York: Harper, 1954).
4. John W. Dobbie, "Formal Approaches to Setting Long-Range Goals," *Long Range Planning,* June 1974.

Chapter 11

1. For other distinctions see George A. Steiner, *Top Management Planning* (New York: Macmillan, 1969), pp. 37–39.
2. Richard F. Vancil, "Strategy Formulation in Complex Organizations," *Sloan Management Review*, Winter 1976.
3. For a comprehensive list of strategies for each stage of the product life cycle see David J. Luck and Arthur E. Prell, *Market Strategy* (Englewood Cliffs: Prentice-Hall, 1968).
4. William H. Newman, "Shaping the Master Strategy of Your Firm," *California Management Review,* Spring 1967.
5. Sterling G. Slappey, *Pioneers of American Business* (New York: Grosset & Dunlap, 1973).
6. George A. Steiner, *Strategic Factors in Business Success* (New York: Financial Executives Research Foundation, 1969).
7. Steiner, *Strategic Factors in Business Success*; William D. Guth, "The Growth and Profitability of the Firm: A Managerial Explanation," *Journal of Business Policy,* Spring 1972.

8. Theodore Cohn and Roy A. Lindberg, *Survival and Growth: Management Strategies for the Small Firm* (New York: AMACOM, 1974), p. 5.

9. Bradley T. Gale, "Market Share and the Rate of Return," *Review of Economics and Statistics,* November 1972; Robert D. Buzzell, Bradley T. Gale, and Ralph G. M. Sultan, "Market Share: A Key to Profitability," *Harvard Business Review,* January–February 1973; Sidney Schoeffler, Robert D. Buzzell, and Donald F. Meany, "Impact of Strategic Planning on Profit Performance," *Harvard Business Review,* March–April 1974.

10. Boston Consulting Group Staff, *Perspectives on Experience* (Boston: Boston Consulting Group, 1972).

11. Richard P. Rumelt, *Strategy, Structure, and Economic Performance* (Boston: Division of Research, Harvard Business School, 1974).

12. For additional references see George A. Steiner and John Miner, *Management Policy and Strategy* (New York: Macmillan, 1977), pp. 202–203.

13. H. Igor Ansoff, *Corporate Strategy* (New York: McGraw-Hill, 1965).

14. Louis V. Gertsner, "Can Strategic Planning Pay Off?" *Business Horizons,* December 1972, p. 9.

15. *TFX Contract Investigation,* Hearings Before the Permanent Subcommittee on Investigations of the Committee on Government Operations, U.S. Senate, 88th Congress, 1963, p. 387.

16. For a fuller discussion of these matters see E. Frank Harrison, *The Managerial Decision-Making Process* (Boston: Houghton Mifflin, 1975.

Chapter 12

1. For a detailed discussion of major medium-range functional plans and their integration see Robert J. Mockler, *Business Planning and Policy Formulation* (New York: Appleton-Century-Crofts, 1972).

2. For a detailed discussion of contents of marketing plans see David S. Hopkins, *The Short-Term Marketing Plan* (New York: Conference Board, 1972); and G. T. Caldwell, *The Corporate Marketing Function: An Overview* (Ottawa: Conference Board in Canada, 1976).

3. Hopkins, *Short-Term Marketing Plan,* p. 7.

4. Ibid., p. 16.

5. David Hussey, *Corporate Planning: Theory and Practice* (New York: Pergamon, 1974), p. 197.

6. Arnold Corbin, "Using a Team Approach to Market-Oriented Planning," *Management Review,* June 1977.

Chapter 13

1. John K. Shank, "Linkage between Planning and Budgeting Systems," in Francis J. Aguilar, Robert A. Howell, and Richard F. Vancil, eds., "Formal Planning Systems, 1970" (Boston: Graduate School of Business Administration, Harvard University, 1970; mimeographed), p. 110.
2. Peter F. Drucker, *The Practice of Management* (New York: Harper, 1954), p. 126.
3. Heinz Weihrich, "MBO in Four Management Systems," *MSU Business Topics,* Autumn 1976, discusses how MBO will differ in organizations with varying management styles.
4. Dale D. McConkey, *MBO for Nonprofit Organizations* (New York: AMACOM, 1975); Anthony P. Raia, *Managing by Objectives* (Glenview: Scott, Foresman, 1974); Stephen J. Carroll, Jr., and Henry L. Tosi, Jr., *Management by Objective: Applications and Research* (New York: Macmillan, 1973); John W. Humble, *Management by Objectives in Action* (New York: McGraw-Hill, 1970); and George S. Odiorne, *Management by Objectives: A System of Managerial Leadership* (New York: Pitman, 1965).
5. Logan M. Cheek, *Zero-Base Budgeting Comes of Age* (New York: AMACOM, 1977); Walter D. Hill, *Implementing Zero-Base Budgeting: The Real World* (Oxford, Oh.: Planning Executives Institute, 1977); Peter A. Pyhrr, *Zero-Base Budgeting: A Practical Management Tool for Evaluating Expenses* (New York: Wiley, 1973); and L. Allan Austin, *Zero-Base Budgeting: Organizational Impact and Effects* (New York: AMACOM, 1977).
6. Peter A. Pyhrr, "ZBB," *Across the Board*, November 1977, p. 35.

Chapter 14

1. This and the following discussion benefited from Rochelle O'Connor, *Planning under Uncertainty: Multiple Scenarios and Contingency Planning* (New York: Conference Board, 1978).
2. Ibid., p. 17.

3. Christine A. Ralph MacNulty, "Scenario Development for Corporate Planning," *Futures,* April 1977.

4. Herman Kahn and Anthony J. Wiener, *The Year 2000: A Framework for Speculation on the Next Thirty-Three Years* (New York: Macmillan, 1967).

5. Ibid., p. 6.

6. O'Connor, *Planning under Uncertainty*; also see W. W. Simmons, *Exploratory Planning: Brief of Practices* (Oxford, Oh.: Planning Executives Institute, 1977); this pamphlet contains resumes of what is being done in specific companies, government agencies, service agencies, and institutions, and it discusses techniques for futures research. See Rene D. Zentner, "Scenarios in Forecasting," *Chemical and Engineering News,* October 6, 1975, for a history of the development of scenarios at Shell Oil Company.

7. Robert E. Linneman and John D. Kennell, "Shirt-Sleeve Approach to Long-Range Plans," *Harvard Business Review,* March–April 1977.

8. John McHale and Magda C. McHale, "An Assessment of Futures Studies Worldwide," *Futures,* April 1976.

9. For a discussion of the development of the futures movement, and a definition of futures research, see Wayne I. Boucher, ed., *The Study of the Future: An Agenda for Research* (Washington, D.C.: U.S. Government Printing Office, 1977). For another study of the movement, together with examples of business and government practices, see Edward Cornish, ed., *The Study of the Future: An Introduction to the Art and Science of Understanding and Shaping Tomorrow's World* (Washington, D.C.: World Future Society, 1977).

10. Duane S. Elgin, David C. MacMichael, and Peter Schwartz, *Alternative Futures for Environmental Policy Planning, 1975–2000* (Washington, D.C.: U.S. Government Printing Office, 1975).

11. Aside from the literature cited earlier in the chapter a few other sources are Andrew A. Spekke, ed., *The Next 25 Years: Crisis and Opportunity* (Washington, D.C.: World Future Society, 1975); Herman Kahn et al., *The Next 200 Years: A Scenario for America and the World* (New York: Morrow, 1976); Kenneth D. Wilson, *Prospects for Growth: Changing Expectations for the Future* (New York: Praeger, 1977); Staff of the White House Conference on the Industrial World Ahead, *A Look at Business in 1990* (Washington, D.C.: U.S. Government Printing Office, 1972). Two magazines that deal exclusively with futures explorations are *The Futurist* and *Futures*.

12. Simmons, *Exploratory Planning.*

13. O'Connor, *Planning under Uncertainty.*

14. Simmons, *Exploratory Planning.*

15. See, for example, Boucher, *The Study of the Future*, which has an extensive bibliography; Cornish *The Study of the Future*, especially chap. 8; Harold A. Linstone and W. H. Clive Simmonds, eds., *Futures Research: New Directions* (Reading: Addison-Wesley/W. A. Benjamin, 1978).
16. Harold A. Linstone and Murray Turoff, *The Delphi Method: Techniques and Application* (Reading: Addison-Wesley, 1975).

Chapter 15

1. Thomas H. Naylor and M. James Mansfield, Jr., "Corporate Planning Models: A Survey," *Planning Review*, May 1976.
2. Stanley J. PoKempner, *Management Science in Business* (New York: Conference Board, 1977).
3. Thad B. Green, Walter B. Newsom, and S. Roland Jones, "A Survey of the Application of Quantitative Techniques to Production/Operations Management in Large Corporations," *Academy of Management Journal*, December 1977.
4. William K. Hall, "Strategic Planning Models: Are Top Managers Really Finding Them Useful?" *Journal of Business Policy*, Winter 1973; Thomas H. Naylor, "The State of the Art of Planning Models," *Planning Review*, November 1976, and "The Politics of Corporate Model Building," ibid., January 1975; C. Jackson Grayson, Jr., "Management Science and Business Practice," *Harvard Business Review*, July–August 1973; R. V. Brown, "Do Managers Find Decision Theory Useful?" *Harvard Business Review*, May–June 1970; Clay Sprowls and George A. Steiner, "Why Computerized Planning Models Fail," in Hans D. Plötzeneder, ed., *Computergestützte Unternehmensplanung/Computer Assisted Corporate Planning (Stuttgart:* Science Research Associates, 1977).
5. Irving L. Janis and Leon Mann, *Decision Making: A Psychological Analysis of Conflict, Choice, and Commitment* (New York: Free Press, 1977), p. 15.
6. George S. Odiorne, *Management Decisions by Objectives* (Englewood Cliffs: Prentice-Hall, 1969), p. 124.
7. Ibid., p. 11.
8. C. W. Churchman and A. H. Schainblatt, "Commentary on the Researcher and the Manager," *Management Science*, October 1965, and "The Researcher and the Manager: A Dialectic of Implementa-

tional," ibid., February 1965; Grayson, "Management Science and Business Practice"; Herbert Halbrecht, E. S. Savas, Gerald Hoffman, Herbert F. Ayres, Michael Radnor, and Franz Edelman, "Through a Glass Darkly," *Interfaces*, August 1972; Hall, "Strategic Planning Models"; John S. Hammond III, "Do's and Don'ts of Computer Models for Planning," *Harvard Business Review*, March–April 1974; David B. Hertz, "Mobilizing Management Science Resources," *Management Science*, January 1965; Peter G. W. Keen, "'Interactive' Computer Systems for Managers: A Modest Proposal," *Sloan Management Review*, Fall 1976; Irwin Nathan, "Managing an O.R. Operation for a Bottom Line Return," *Columbia Journal of World Business*, Fall 1977; James E. Rosenzweig, "Managers and Management Scientists," *Business Horizons*, Fall 1967; Theodore O. Yntema and Daniel N. Braunstein, "Corporate Viewpoints: Interviews with Top Managers," *Interfaces*, February 1972.

9. Harold J. Leavitt, "Beyond the Analytic Manager: Part I," *California Management Review*, Spring 1975; "Beyond the Analytic Manager: Part II," *California Management Review*, Summer 1975.

10. Many books and articles describe these and other new quantitative techniques, some of which have been mentioned before. Illustrations are Harvey M. Wagner, *Principles of Operations Research: With Applications to Managerial Decisions*, 2d ed. (Englewood Cliffs: Prentice-Hall, 1975); Martin K. Starr and Irving Stone, *The Practice of Management Science* (Englewood Cliffs: Prentice-Hall, 1976); James B. Boulden and Ephraim R. McLean, "An Executive's Guide to Computer-Based Planning," *California Management Review*, Fall 1974; Vincent R. LoCascio, "Financial Planning Models," *Financial Executive*, March 1972; James B. Boulden and Elwood S. Buffa, "Corporate Models: On-line, Real-Time Systems," *Harvard Business Review*, July–August 1970; George A. Steiner, *Top Management Planning* (New York: Macmillan, 1969); David B. Hertz, *New Power for Management Computer Systems and Management Science* (New York: McGraw-Hill, 1969).

11. References to this sort of information were given in Chapter 8.

12. Alfred R. Oxenfeldt, "Effective Decision Making for the Business Executive," *Management Review*, February 1978.

13. Peter F. Drucker, *The Practice of Management* (New York: Harper, 1954), p. 351.

14. John D. C. Little, "Models and Managers: The Concept of a Decision Calculus," *Management Science*, April 1979, p. B-466.

15. Violet Bonham Carter, *Winston Churchill: An Intimate Portrait* (New York: Harcourt, 1965), p. 36.

Chapter 16

1. William Trafers Jerome III, *Executive Control: The Catalyst* (New York: Wiley, 1961), pp. 32–33.
2. William H. Newman, *Constructive Control: Design and Use of Control Systems* (Englewood Cliffs: Prentice-Hall, 1975).
3. C. J. Slaybaugh, "Pareto's Law and Modern Management," *Price Waterhouse Review*, Winter 1966.
4. For an analysis of how controls differ among high-, middle-, and low-level managers see Leonard Sayles, "The Many Dimensions of Control," *Organizational Dynamics*, Summer 1972.
5. John Humble and Kit Grindley, *The Effective Computer* (New York: McGraw-Hill, 1973); Ephraim R. McLean and John V. Soden, *Strategic Planning for MIS* (New York: Wiley, 1977).
6. Harold Koontz and Robert W. Bradspies, "Managing through Feedforward Control: A Future-Directed View," *Business Horizons*, June 1972.
7. Newman, *Constructive Control*.
8. Robert J. Mockler, *The Management Control Process* (New York: Appleton-Century-Crofts, 1972).
9. Peter F. Drucker, *Management: Tasks, Responsibilities, Practices* (Harper & Row, 1974), p. 499 (italics omitted).

Chapter 17

1. There are controls that produce automatic responses in machines or physical systems without the need of human action, but I do not include them in the concept of managerial control used here.
2. See, for example, Cortlandt Cammann and David A. Nadler, "Fit Control Systems to Your Managerial Style," *Harvard Business Review*, January–February 1976; John Campbell, M. D. Dunnette, Edward E. Lawler III, and I. E. Weick, *Managerial Behavior, Performance, and Effectiveness* (New York: McGraw-Hill, 1970); Edward E. Lawler III and John Grant Rhode, *Information and Control in Organizations* (Pacific Palisades: Goodyear, 1976); Harry Levinson, *Psychological Man* (Cambridge: Leninson Institute, 1976); and L. W. Porter, Edward E. Lawler, and J. R. Hackman, *Behavior in Organizations* (New York: McGraw-Hill, 1975).

3. Richard A. Johnson, Fremont E. Kast, and James E. Rosenzweig, *The Theory and Management of Systems* (New York: McGraw-Hill, 1963), p. 281.

4. F. J. Roethlisberger, *Management and Morale* (Cambridge: Harvard University Press, 1941), pp. 61–62.

5. Rensis Likert and Jane Gibson Likert, *New Ways of Managing Conflict* (New York: McGraw-Hill, 1976).

6. Levinson, *Psychological Man*, p. 105.

7. D. Gerald Searfoss and Robert M. Monczka, "Perceived Participation in the Budget Process and Motivation to Achieve the Budget," *Academy of Management Journal*, December 1973.

8. Lawler and Rhode, *Information and Control in Organizations*.

9. S. J. Carroll and H. Tosi, *Management by Objectives: Applications and Research* (New York: Macmillan, 1973).

10. For a few case histories of distorted behavior used to meet control standards see Frank J. Jasinski, "Use and Misuse of Efficiency Controls," *Harvard Business Review*, July–August 1956; Chris Argyris, *The Impact of Budgets on People* (New York: Controllership Institute, 1952); these contain old but still valuable insights.

11. William H. Newman, *Constructive Control: Design and Use of Control Systems* (Englewood Cliffs, Prentice-Hall, 1975), p. 41.

Chapter 18

1. George A. Steiner, *Pitfalls in Comprehensive Long Range Planning* (Oxford, Oh.: Planning Executives Institute, 1972).

2. Ibid, p. 6.

3. The fifty pitfalls were aggregated into categories by Nils Hoegh Krohn while a visiting scholar at UCLA in November 1973: Authority pitfalls (1, 9, 10, 12, 18, 25, 26, 27, 29, 30, 38, 45, 50) Leadership pitfalls (2, 3, 5, 11, 13, 17, 21, 23, 24, 26, 49) Knowledge and information pitfalls (1, 4, 5, 6, 7, 10, 11, 15, 16, 28, 32, 33, 37, 39, 41, 43) Feedback and control pitfalls (8, 19, 32, 36, 37, 41, 42, 44, 47) Shortcomings in setting objectives (14, 15, 20, 22, 25, 28, 31, 34, 35, 38, 40, 43, 44, 46, 48, 49)

4. E. Kirby Warren, *Long-Range Planning: The Executive Viewpoint* (Englewood Cliffs: Prentice-Hall, 1966), pp. 51–60.

5. Edward R. Bagley, "How to Avoid Glitches in Planning." *Management Review*, March 1972; Xavier Gilbert and Peter Lorange, "Five Pillars for Your Planning," in Peter Lorange and Richard F. Vancil, eds.,

Strategic Planning Systems (Englewood Cliffs: Prentice-Hall, 1977), reprinted from *European Business*, Autumn 1974; Harold W. Henry, "Formal Planning in Major U.S. Corporations," *Long Range Planning*, October 1977; Patrick H. Irwin, "Why Aren't Companies Doing a Better Job of Planning?" *Management Review*, November 1971; E. Kirby Warren, *Long-Range Planning*; Malcolm W. Pennington, "Why Has Planning Failed and What Can You Do about It?" *Planning Review*, November 1975; Kjell A. Ringbakk, "Why Planning Failed," *European Business*, Spring 1971; Paul J. Stonich, "Formal Planning Pitfalls and How to Avoid Them," *Management Review*, June and July 1975.

6. Ringbakk, "Why Planning Failed," pp. 18–24.
7. George A. Steiner and Hans Schollhammer, "Pitfalls in Multi-National Long-Range Planning," *Long Range Planning*, April 1975.

Chapter 19

1. Robert I. Laxer and Walter S. Wikstrom, *Appraising Managerial Performance: Current Practices and Future Directions* (New York: Conference Board, 1977).
2. William K. Hall, "The Impact of Managerial Behavior on Planning Effectiveness," *Managerial Planning*, September–October 1977, p. 23.
3. Walter B. Schaffir, *Strategic Business Planning: Some Questions for the Chief Executive* (New York: Presidents' Association, Chief Executive Officers' Division, American Management Associations, 1976).
4. Ibid., pp. 39–40.
5. For other short lists of what is required for effective planning see J. C. Camillus, "Evaluating the Benefits of Formal Planning Systems," *Long Range Planning*, June 1975; Edward J. Green, "Decisions—Commitments—Results," *Managerial Planning*, May–June 1972; George A. Steiner, "How to Improve Your Long Range Planning," *Managerial Planning*, September–October 1974.

Chapter 20

1. *Los Angeles Times*, December 9, 1970.
2. William E. Reif and John W. Newstrom, "The Practice of Business Career Development by Objective," *Business Horizons*, October 1974.

Chapter 21

1. Yehezkel Dror, *Ventures in Policy Sciences* (New York: American Elsevier 1971).
2. For the applicability of business planning to types of planning problems in the NFPS see Horst W. J. Rittel and Melvin M. Webber, "Dilemmas in a General Theory of Planning," *Policy Sciences*, Fall 1973; Dennis A. Rondinelli, "A Public Planning and Political Strategy," *Long Range Planning*, April 1976.
3. Paul H. Appleby, *Policy and Administration* (University, Ala.: University of Alabama Press, 1949), p. 153.
4. Harold Koontz and Cyril O'Donnell, *Management: A Systems and Contingency Analysis of Managerial Functions* (New York: McGraw-Hill, 1976).
5. Joseph L. Bower, "Effective Public Management," *Harvard Business Review*, March–April 1977.
6. Michael A. Murray, "Comparing Public and Private Management: An Exploratory Essay," *Public Administration Review*, July–August 1975.
7. R. J. East, "Comparison of Strategic Planning in Large Corporations and Government," *Long Range Planning*, June 1972.
8. Kim Quaile Hill and James C. Coomer, "Local Politicians and Their Attitudes to Planning," *Long Range Planning*, December 1977.
9. Gerald L. Barkdoll, "Making Planning Relevant to Public Agency Management," *Long Range Planning*, February 1976.
10. David Novick, *Current Practice in Program Budgeting* (New York: Crane, Russak, 1973).
11. David E. Hussey, "Corporate Planning for a Church," *Long Range Planning*, April 1974.
12. Roger E. Paine, "Corporate Planning for a Town: A Case Study," *Long Range Planning*, October 1975.
13. Charles W. McKay and Guy D. Cutting, "A Model for Long Range Planning in Higher Education," *Long Range Planning*, October 1974.
14. Joseph P. Peters, *Concept, Commitment, Action: A Manual for Planning Programs and Resources by Health Care Institutions in New York City* (New York: United Hospital Fund of New York and the Health and Hospital Planning Council of Southern New York, 1974).
15. Jo Ann Bell and R. B. Keusch, "Comprehensive Planning for Libraries," *Long Range Planning*, October 1976.

16. David Novick, "The Origin and History of Program Budgeting," *California Management Review*, Fall 1968.
17. Adapted from George A. Steiner and John B. Miner, *Management Policy and Strategy: Text, Readings, and Cases* (New York: Macmillan, 1977), pp. 177–178.
18. David Novick, ed., *Program Budgeting* (Cambridge: Harvard University Press, 1965).
19. Novick, *Current Practice in Program Budgeting*.
20. Bruce H. DeWoolfson, "Pitfalls in Planning-Programming-Budgeting Systems" (Ph.D. diss., University of California, Irvine, 1974).
21. Adapted from George A. Steiner, "Proposal for a National Policy Assessment and Action Program," *Planning Review*, September 1975.
22. Ibid., p. 4.
23. For arguments for and against national aggregate economic planning see Tom Alexander, "The Deceptive Allure of National Planning," *Fortune*, March 1977; Thornton Bradshaw, "My Case for National Planning," *Fortune*, February 1977; discussion among John Kenneth Galbraith, Henry Wallich, Melville J. Ulmer, and Murray L. Weidenbaum, "The Case for and against National Economic Planning," *Challenge*, March–April 1976; Wassily Leontief, "National Economic Planning: Methods and Problems," *Challenge*, July–August 1976; Henry Hazlitt, "Planning Disaster," *Challenge*, July–August 1975; Bruce Scott, "How Practical Is National Planning?" *Harvard Business Review*, March–April 1978; Rexford Guy Tugwell, "The Humphrey-Javits Planning Bill: A Critique," *Center Report*, December 1975; Murray L. Weidenbaum and Linda Rockwood, "Corporate Planning versus Government Planning," *Public Interest*, Winter 1977.

Chapter 22

1. Ernest R. Breech, "Planning the Basic Strategy of a Large Business," in Edward C. Bursk and Dan H. Fenn, Jr., eds., *Planning the Future Strategy of Your Business* (New York: McGraw-Hill, 1956), p. 17.
2. George A. Steiner, "Rise of the Corporate Planner," *Harvard Business Review*, September–October 1970.
3. Baltasar Jerónimo Gracián y Morales, *The Science of Success and the Art of Prudence*, trans. Lawrence C. Lockley (Santa Clara: University of Santa Clara Press, 1967), p. 45.

Index

Index